How to Become a Highly Effective Leader

Ten Skills a Leader Must Possess

Tri Junarso

iUniverse, Inc.
New York   Bloomington

How to Become a Highly Effective Leader
Ten Skills a Leader Must Possess

iUniverse books may be ordered through booksellers or by contacting:

iUniverse
1663 Liberty Drive
Bloomington, IN 47403
www.iuniverse.com
1-800-Authors (1-800-288-4677)

ISBN: 978-1-4401-1791-6 (pbk)
ISBN: 978-1-4401-1793-0 (cloth)
ISBN: 978-1-4401-1792-3 (ebk)

Printed in the United States of America

iUniverse rev. date: 3/16/2009

FOREWORD

An effective manager possesses the skills to motivate, evaluate, problem solve, resolve conflict and more importantly produce extraordinary results. These are achieved through his/her position. When you are step ahead against others, you are a leader.

Leadership is not a role or a position. Therefore, becoming a highly effective leader needs not only knowledge, skill, attitude, but leadership values. It means he/she should:

a. Be knowledgeable: Understand the goals and objectives of the organization and making sure carried out; understand his/her responsibilities, duties and expectations; able to adopt his or her leadership style to the situation at hand, and possess management capability, set of best practices, methods and systems to match with organization needs

b. Possess excellent skills: Demonstrate abilities maximize the potentiality of others to meet the organization's vision, mission, and goals; i.e. build image, communication skill, supervise others, organizational skill, survival skill, resolve conflict, allocate time, decision making, and enforce organization's values

c. Display great attitude: An important key to high productivity and effective leadership is to have and maintain a positive attitude.

d. Create value: Effective leadership is the foundation for creating value within the organization. The leader must first recognize people's value. Both leader and followers will, then, have congruent value systems, respect and share the common value and beliefs, and promote ethical behavior, which is highest standard of personal and professional ethics in leadership.

    The leader emphasizes well-functioning of the organization's values.

If a manager is able to influence people to achieve the goals of the organization, without using his or her formal authority to do so, then the manager is demonstrating effective leadership. The manager is a leader for the organization he/she leads.

Becoming highly effective leaders, automatically you show the ability of doing the best practices of highly effective people, which include be proactive, begin with the end of mind, put first things first, think win-win, seek first to understand then to be understood, synergize, and sharpen the saw.

This book's title, How To Become A Highly Effective Leader, will effectively guide The Readers to becoming, not only an ordinary leader, more than this, Highly Effective Leader. Welcome to Leader's World!

ACKNOWLEDGEMENT

Actually I don't have any obsession to be an author. On other hand, I believe that I have the power to be whoever I wish. Therefore, no one will stop me from becoming who I want to be. This book is the 4th book I have written. My books seem to be having links one to other and create a meaning, i.e.:

1. The Best: Comprehensive Approach To Corporate Governance is best practices for performing corporation. The book offers the biggest challenge before the corporations, is how to replace greed as a driver of corporate agenda, which may call for a progressive shift in the corporate culture.

    The success of a corporation is now not devoted to shareholders only, but all the stakeholders.

2. The Successful: 7th Principle of Success is set of rules, attitudes and behaviors that you will use to guide what you do and how you do it, to make your life happy and successful.

    The book's title guide you acting as a reminder of what you stand for; the approach to life you wish to take and the values which you aim to live your life by; ensure you develop a strong personal identity and live in a way which is right for you

3. The Great: Leadership Greatness describes the extraordinary qualities of your leadership, in which you may bring out greatness throughout the organization. As a great *leader, you have to act with sense of greatness.*

4. The High: How To Become A Highly Effective Leader leads you to display high level of competency, which includes skills,

behaviors, attitudes, and knowledge to produce extraordinary results.

I understand there will be errors, misspellings, or omissions. For the time being, it is the best I could do. If you find any error, please do not hesitate to let me know so that I can improve this book performance in future.

I would also like to thank the many people who have supported, and helped with this book, especially my family, my wife, and my colleagues.

Author

Contents

INTRODUCTION

Effective leadership demonstrates the ability to draw others into the active pursuit of the strategic goals of the organization.

Leadership unleashes energy, sets the vision so we do the right thing.

Management controls, arranges, does things right which involves planning, organizing, staffing, directing, and controlling, and it is job oriented to the extent that people are viewed merely as instruments to accomplish jobs.

If a manager is able to influence people to achieve the goals of the organization, without using his or her formal authority to do so, then the manager is demonstrating leadership.

Bossing people around doesn't mean becoming an effective manager. An effective leader wants to lead, not boss.

Complex organizations need management, while uncertain organizations need leadership.

Effective means get the things right. Effectiveness is a measure of quality.

Effectiveness shows that one's capabilities directly impact his/her ability to do the job; that is a capacity to produce a desired result

Leaders possess the capacity to recognize all that they perceive. Capacity describes ability to achieve objectives, solve problems and perform in which one functions.

Competence is a measure of the ability to perform a task; effectiveness is a measure of the success achieved in the performance of a task.

Competency means possessing the requisite capacities and knowledge base to undertake one's agreed upon functions. A highly effective leadership displays high level of competency, which includes skills, behaviors, attitudes, and knowledge.

If you can't manage yourself, you can't lead others. The clearer you are, about who you are, and what you stand for, the more credibility you will have as a leader of others.

Emotional competence is a learned capability based on emotional intelligence that results in outstanding performance at the organization.

Leaders need to develop and demonstrate physical competence, such as sport skills, physical fitness, and physical appearance. So that he/she gains social acceptance and support from the followers.

The requirement for spiritual influence is competence which doesn't imply that you have to be better than everyone else; but about doing your best.

Leaders who possess psychological competence will demonstrate their ability to successfully reach developmental tasks expected for their function.

Leaders bring together diverse groups of people with very different histories, values, perspectives and cultures. The leader possesses social competence, how he/she deal with relationships.

A leader should be able to share his/her ethical concerns to the organization. Knowing what is right is absolutely critical to the leader, followers and organization ethics. Yet, ethics only happens when good beliefs lead to good behaviors.

Leadership requires an understanding of one's own beliefs and assumptions and an ability to recognize other team members' cultural values and behaviors.

A highly effective leader knows how to use the skills, knowledge, and energy of team members to accomplish the task and mission.

An important key to high productivity and effective leadership is to have and maintain a positive attitude. It may not solve all your problems, but it will annoy enough people to make it worth the effort.

Attitude determines our altitude. Attitude is to leadership as oxygen is to life form. It is the mindset of your disposition and the catalyst for your character. Effective leadership is based in behavior, not in job title/position.

A leader must exhibit and promote behaviors that build esteem and must work to rid the organization of behaviors that destroy esteem.

The basis of effective leadership is honorable character and selfless service to your organization. Leaders motivate followers during good times and bad.

Knowledge is an essential part of our individual and organizational ability to innovate, compete and succeed. An effective leader should be technically and tactically proficient.

Leaders should not fall neatly into a compartment on an organization chart. They show high pinnacles of the command and control organization; be intensely focused on the promotion of knowledge management practices and solutions; and in confidence decide what kind of leadership.

An effective leader will find himself/herself switching instinctively between styles according to the people and work they are dealing with.

Leadership style differs from person to person according to the tasks, team and individual capabilities.

Leading others is not simply a matter of style, or following some how-to guides or recipes. Ineffectiveness of leaders seldom results from a lack of know-how or how-to. It is typically due to inadequate managerial skills.

Leadership is the ability to motivate a group of people toward a common goal. The skills of a leader will ensure that the work of the organization is what it needs to be.

Many leaders assume image building is superficial and therefore unimportant or only for celebrities, but actually image is an asset that can and must be managed. Your effectiveness as a leader is tied directly to your image.

Image may not necessarily be everything, but it is a critical factor in leadership's overall effectiveness.

Character is the core foundation on which individual leadership is based. Character refers to self-concepts and individual differences in goals and values, which influence choices, intentions, the meaning and salience of what is experienced in life. A person of character is characterized by attributes which include trustworthiness, respect, responsibility, fairness, caring, and citizenship. Effective leaders are people of sound character.

Personality plays a key role, principally in making it harder or easier for a particular individual to learn the key leader behaviors. A highly effective leader has strong personality.

Communications are shaping organization's culture. Therefore, communication skills are essential for the success of individuals and to the accomplishment of organizational goals. Faulty communication causes the most problems. The effective leaders have the ability to make their intentions known in a clear and unambiguous manner. To be an effective leader, you must be an effective communicator.

Effective communication helps to ensure smoother interpersonal interactions, more productive organizations, more positive employee relations, more authentic outcome, clarity of vision, and effective leadership.

A substantial portion of communication is nonverbal. Senses, eyes, ears and feelings and words and symbols are used to create meanings.

Verbal communication skill requires ability the use of words, vocabulary, numbers and symbols and is organized in sentences using language.

The purpose of writing a communication plan is to effectively use communications as a tool to help solve a problem or exploit an opportunity. The key to truly effective writing is being absolutely clear about what we want to say, what we want people to do, think or feel as a result of reading our writing.

Leaders should continually improve their verbal skills. They can't inspire and energize people by using only written communication.

Simplifying the communication not only streamline it, but make it more effective and productive, and leading to greater results. Leaders make complex communication as simple as possible. Simplicity is an important element of communication.

A leader must build not only individual commitment but also organizational capability. Organizational capability refers to the processes, practices, and activities that create value for the organization. The leader needs ability to translate organizational direction into roadmaps, vision into action, and purpose into process.

A leader is a team builder. To become a great leader, you must develop a great team. Leaders are great at directing, coordinating, and controlling. Leadership is ability to direct others, but more important is to have those people, who are directed, accept it. The strengths of members and the organization are in the strength of the leader.

Leadership of survival is one's ability to manage risk and the development of resource protection. Leaders should strive to see that the organization is relatively free of aberrations, or disruptions that make organization continuity impossible.

An effective leader should demonstrate management skills, particularly survival skill. Survival skills are skills that may help one to survive in difficult situations.

Effective leaders engage not only in collaboration and but also conflict resolution. Conflict generally results from poor communications, disruptions in routines, unclear goals or expectations, the quest for power, ego massage, differences in value systems, or hidden agendas.

Effective conflict resolution skills have become crucial for today's leaders. Conflict can reduce productivity, lower morale, create continued problems and conflicts, and cause team members to become frustrated and aggravated with the planning process. When it is managed appropriately, conflict is actually good.

A highly effective leader generates higher productivity, lower costs, and more opportunities than ineffective leaders. The leaders create results, attain goal, and realize vision and other objectives more quickly and at a higher level of quality than ineffective leaders.

Sufficient time is the key to making changes that stick. One of the worst aspects of modern working life is the constant pressure to hurry. Not only does it create needless stress and tension, it goes a long way to making people seem dumber and more resistant to change than they are.

Time management is important to any leader. The process of developing your time management strategy is to be flexible in your planning. Allow for the unexpected.

Leaders must be capable to translate organizational performance review findings into priorities.

A key skill in becoming a successful leader is the skill of decision making. Good decisions are highly leveraged with low cost/high benefit. A decision-tends to be more effective when the framework for leadership is clear. Quality decision demonstrates the knowledge and skills of effective leadership.

When decision failures occur, we should not focus on the issues involved, and they to identify the wrong judgments and flawed assumptions that they made. Decisions delegated without adequate strategic context may answer the wrong question, be too risk averse, prioritize the wrong factor, or else simply float back up to the top. Careful decision-making requires a sense of right and wrong rooted in character.

During The United States crisis in 2008, White and Sharon Otterman wrote on International Herald Tribune: "Even as the investment bank Lehman Brothers pleaded for a federal bailout to save it from bankruptcy protection, it approved millions of dollars in bonuses for its departing executives".

*People know, the financial crisis began with a portrayal of Lehman Brothers as a company run by irresponsible leaders who continued to reward executives and spend billions on stock buybacks and other capital-depleting programs, even as internal documents warned of the impending crisis. (*Ben White and Sharon Otterman, *2008)*

Effective leaders are capable, contributing, and caring. They care. They are compassionate. Care means showing concern for others through words and action. Discover greatest satisfactions that come from kindness to others.

Leader has to recognize that some violations against value and ethical behavior so severely threaten the well-being of people and the organization that these violations should carry with them harsh consequences.

A highly effective leader is creating value through leadership. Leaders must have a rock-solid value system which is congruent with their followers' values. Leadership in value means respect and share common value and beliefs, and promoting ethical behavior. The leader must first recognize people's value. Leaders and followers have congruent value systems.

1st

HIGHLY EFFECTIVE LEADERSHIP

What distinguishes a leader and a member? When you are step ahead against others, you are a leader. Leadership is not a role or a position. You can lead others from any role. Leadership is occasional initiatives that influence others. If you have the desire and willpower, you can become a leader.

Effective leadership demonstrates the ability to draw others into the active pursuit of the strategic goals of the organization. This ability energizes faculty to take the organization to greater heights of achievement.

Leader And Manager

Leadership unleashes energy, sets the vision so we do the right thing. Leaders developed through a never ending process of self-study, education, training, and experience. But on other hand, the skills of a manager facilitate the work of an organization because they ensure that what is done is in accord with the organization's rules and regulations.

Management controls, arranges, does things right. Manager needs to make the best use of all resources to achieve an existing direction.

Managers are people who do things right and leaders are people who do the right thing.

Management involves planning, organizing, staffing, directing, and controlling, and it is job oriented to the extent that people are viewed merely as instruments to accomplish jobs. Managerial motivators are money, prestige, promotions, and other material rewards. Leadership involves natural and learned abilities, personal skills, and characteristics that inspire responsible subordinate actions through interpersonal relationships.

Management is the activity that allocates and uses resources to achieve organizational goals. Managers are more interested in efficiency, current issues and doing things right. On the other hand, leadership is the art of influencing people to accomplish an organization's purpose. Leaders are more concerned with effectiveness, foresight and innovation while doing the right things.

Management is about arranging and telling. Leadership is about nurturing and enhancing. Both are vital to success, but organizations must recognize the difference between the two. The differences between leader and manager briefly include but not limited to:

Leader	Manager
Seek influence	Seek control
Attract followers	Pull, prod, push followers
Emphasize what is invisible	Emphasize what is visible
Focus on becoming	Focus on doing
Concerned about the spiritual	Concerned about the physical
Show originality	Copy other
Mission oriented	Goal oriented
Focus on the whole	Focus on the parts
Provide meaning	Provide form & structure
Play with the boundaries	Stay within the boundaries

Promote instability	Preserve stability
Do the right things	Do things right
Values-led	Needs-driven
Long-term perspective	Short-term perspective
Create what does not yet exist	Administer what already exists
Steward resources	Administer resources
Train for self development	Train for skill development
Influence through love & caring	Influence through power & authority
Seek to serve followers	Expect followers to serve
Where we are going	How we are going to get there
Deal with the interpersonal aspects of a manager's job	Plan, organize, and control.
Seize opportunities	Avert threats
Interpersonal influence directed toward the achievement of goals.	Given formal authority to direct the activity of others in fulfilling organization goals.
Establish direction - develop a vision of the future and determine the strategies for producing the desired change.	Establish the steps needed to achieve specific results, create a timeline for completing those steps, and obtain the resources necessary for goal accomplishment.
Align people - communicate the vision to those whose cooperation is needed and form coalitions to support the change.	Establish the structure needed to implement the plan and then organize and staff - acquire and assign the needed personnel.

Motivate and inspire - energize people to overcome barriers to change.	Control and problem solve - monitor results and take action to correct deviations from the plan.
Amplify strengths	Reduce weaknesses
Deal with change, inspiration, motivation, and influence.	Deal more with carrying out the organization's goals and maintaining equilibrium.
Not possess the formal power to reward or sanction performance	Have to rely on formal authority to get employees to accomplish goals.
Produce change - disrupt the status quo and encourage creativity and innovation.	Produce order - establish stability, predictability, and consistency.
Deal with getting people to do what needs to be done	Task and process oriented
Cope with change	Cope with complexity
Execute the win with passion	Set up the win with perfection for her team
Harness the power inherent in human motivation.	Rely on authority to make things happen
Leading people	Managing work
Have followers	Have subordinates
Facilitate decision	Make decision
Power comes from personal charisma	Power comes from formal authority
Appeal to heart	Appeal to head
His/her energy is passion	His/her energy is control
Proactive	Reactive
Persuade by selling	Persuade by telling
Leadership style: transformational	Leadership style: transactional
Excitement for work	Money for work

Preference - striving	Preference - action
Want achievement	Want results
Take risk	Minimize risk
Break rules	Make rules
Use conflict	Avoid conflict
Show new direction	Use existing direction
Seek truth	Establish truth
His/her concern - What is right	His/her concern - Being right
Give credit	Take credit
Take blame	Blame others
Create future	Maintain present
Plan from imagination	Plan from memory
Motivate people	Manage things
Process driven	Product driven
Value anchored	Technically anchored
Opportunity driven	Crisis driven

One key difference is that a manager's authority derives from the organization while a leader's authority comes from the followers.

People do as a manager says because the organization has given the manager the authority to speak and act on behalf of the organization. If employees wish to remain in the organization, they must respect the manager's authority. Employees may not respect the manager, but they do respect the authority the manager has been given.

Followers follow the direction of leaders by choice. The leader remains in the lead role only as long as followers choose to follow. Followers can revoke a leader's authority by withdrawing their consent to follow. A consideration of authority leads to a discussion of power.

Managers tend to use power derived from their position and their control of rewards and punishments. Positional or legitimate power derives from the manager's position in the organization. This pertains to the above discussion on authority.

Reward power derives from the manager's ability to award benefits people are seeking. Coercive power issues from the manager's ability to impose negative consequences. The power exercised by leaders tends to emerge from what the leader knows or who the leader is.

Expert power is based on expertise, special skills, or particular knowledge possessed by the leader and perceived as valuable by followers. Referent power arises from desirable resources or traits the leader possesses.

Although your position as a manager, supervisor, lead, etc. gives you the authority to accomplish certain tasks and objectives in the organization, this power does not make you a leader; it simply makes you the boss. Leadership differs in that it makes the followers want to achieve high goals, rather than simply bossing people around.

Leadership is an interactive conversation that pulls people toward becoming comfortable with the language of personal responsibility and commitment. Leadership is not just for people at the top. Everyone can learn to lead by discovering the power that lies within each one of us to make a difference and practicing the law of reciprocity.

Managers need to be leaders; their workers need vision and guidance. Leaders also need to be good managers of the resources entrusted to them.

A leader is the person who is able to take the line forward in an orderly fashion by setting the example for others; provides the vision for how the line fits into the larger scheme of things, and engages the line-followers in a respectful manner.

A manager is the person that designs the construct of a line, sets the expectations for the line to form, thinks through how the line might be best composed and prioritized, and ensures that the queue is executed per spec. Good managers do not necessarily make good leaders and good leaders do not necessarily make good managers. Each has a distinct role.

Leadership qualities are far less tangible and measurable whilst most management processes can be measured. When you understand your role as guide and steward based on your own most deeply held truths you can move from manager to leader.

Leader And Boss

A boss creates fear, a leader confidence. A boss fixes blame, a leader corrects mistakes. A boss knows all, a leader asks questions. A boss makes work drudgery, a leader makes it interesting. A boss is interested in himself/herself; a leader is interested in the group. In management, "boss" has so many negative connotations. Bossing people around doesn't mean becoming an effective manager.

An effective leader wants to lead, not boss. The hallmark of an effective leader is his/her ability to set the tone of the organization.

Most people leave their jobs because they don't like their boss, as relationship with the boss. When the relationship is bad, everything else is becoming bad. When the relationship is good, even other less-than-satisfactory conditions are both more tolerable and more likely to be worked out.

Leadership is a process of getting things done through people. Leader is getting things done by working through people. The leader uses the process of leadership to reach certain goals. He/she is the person in which the others look to get the job done; and expect him/her to take the responsibility of getting the job done. A boss pushes and orders other people around. What boss cares about is getting the job done, and sap the energy of the individuals in his/her groups. Bosses consider themselves better than everyone else and they don't care who knows it.

A boss is superior who constantly berates his/her people, creates division within the group instead of harmony, and condescends to talk to the individuals in their group, but never listens to anyone input. The boss can be a supervisor, executive or a manager. A boss may significantly decreases production and increases cost. He/she can make organization an unpleasant place to work.

Leadership And Management

Complex organizations need management, while uncertain organizations need leadership. Management is about making sure that clear goals are established and then carried out, despite organizational size, number of offices, sub-specialization, and other forms of complexity.

Management focused on the short-term (usually one-year increments), and depends on analytical, rational, data-based, cognitive strategies to be effective.

Leadership, on the other hand, is focused on a longer time horizon (five years or more); is much more people-focused, inspirational, emotional, non-linear and visceral. To lead, you must gain buy-in and commitment.

The difference between managers and leaders is the way they motivate the people who work or follow them, and this sets the tone for most other aspects of what they do. Managers have a position of authority vested in them by the company, and their subordinates work for them and largely do as they are told.

Management style is transactional, in that the manager tells the subordinate what to do, and the subordinate does this not because they are a blind robot, but because they have been promised a reward (at minimum their salary) for doing so.

Leaders do not have subordinates - at least not when they are leading. Many organizational leaders do have subordinates, but only because they are also managers. But when they want to lead, they have to give up formal authoritarian control, because to lead is to have followers, and following is always a voluntary activity.

Leaders with a stronger charisma find it easier to attract people to their cause. As a part of their persuasion they typically promise transactional benefits, such that their followers will not just receive extrinsic rewards but will somehow become better people.

Effective leaders must possess management capability, set of best practices, methods and systems to match with organization needs, i.e. communication management, crisis management, risk management, etc. Management science is objective, sees things as they are; and shows us how to do this. We will be fully aware of the consequences of what we are doing.

In management, things are clearly defined, i.e. authority and responsibility; and how authority is balanced between top and bottom, participation in decision- making.

A successful management is shown into organization effectiveness and results. Governance needs good management and administration Leadership is not a substitute for management. A modern organization can exist with woefully deficient leadership, but cannot exist without applied management skills.

Leadership is an option. Leaders also perform their leadership functions outside of and beyond their realm of technical expertise. Management may require efficiency, profitability, depends on minimal inputs for maximum returns. Leader can both lead and manage.

Leadership and management are like sales and marketing - they serve different organizational purposes or functions. The larger the organization the more difficult it is to achieve the necessary degree of co-operation and that larger organizations are usually much less effective than smaller ones as people are working against each other instead of co-operating.

The effectiveness of the organization is determined by the way work is organized and by the way people work with or against each other. The way, in which people co-operate with each other, with the leadership and with the community, indeed the extent of their commitment to their organization, depend on management.

Management is about making sure that clear goals are established and then carried out, despite organizational size, number of offices, sub-specialization, and other forms of complexity. It is focused on the short-term (usually one-year increments), and depends on analytical, rational, data-based, cognitive strategies to be effective.

Leadership and management are not the same. To be a leader, one needs an exclusive set of human relations and interpersonal skills. This essence is being able to influence.

Effectiveness

It begins with the full range of competencies that a leader brings to the role - his or her motives, values, traits, self-image, technical skills, and behaviors, and knowledge.

Effective means get the things right. Effectiveness is a measure of quality. When you hire for effectiveness you are saying that the only way to meet the business's competitive needs is to find a person who is a demonstrably correct fit for a detailed and rational specification.

Since quality is often a qualitative term, the real measure of effectiveness is satisfaction. Effectiveness shows that one's capabilities directly impact his/her ability to do the job. In brief, effectiveness is a capacity to produce a desired result

Managers must know how to lead as well as manage. A person becomes an effective manager because he/she tends to be very good at the hard stuff. They are concerned with measurable outcomes – sometime obsessed with process at all costs. They appear to be driven by the need to prove their effectiveness in some tangible way.

Leadership effectiveness is indicated by how effectively a leader communicates and translates the vision and strategy of the organization to the members. Effective leaders know that there is no one best way to manage people.

If a manager is able to influence people to achieve the goals of the organization, without using his or her formal authority to do so, then the manager is demonstrating leadership.

Highly Effective Leadership

Developing highly effective leaders at all levels within the organization is critical to the success of the organization itself. An effective leader is a person with a passion for a cause that is larger than they are; someone with a dream and a vision.

The most important quality of leadership is extraordinary performance, with the goal of achieving extraordinary results. These results then serve as an inspiration to others to perform at equally exceptional levels. A highly effective leadership demonstrates following characteristics:

a. Follower: Without followership, a leader at any level will fail to produce effective organizations. A highly effective leader makes sure followers can better achieve their potentials. They feel they are working from their own initiative.

   The leader recognizes and fulfills his/her responsibilities in developing specific follower attributes or competencies within the organization.

b. Organization: Able to establish, reinforce and re-align the organization culture and promote collaborative and participatory environment in working toward common goals. The culture supports the effectiveness of organization that is built upon trust and ethical behaviors, learning and growth, healthy communication and interpersonal relationship, etc.

c. Leader: Bring the exceptional performance. The leader becomes an inspiration for the followers, spark the kind of energy and enthusiasm that make productivity and performance soar.

d. Peer: Recognize that the leader harmoniously builds a highly effective and collaborative team, leads by using an equal partnership, and respect amongst the leader's peer.

e. Community: The leader cares deeply about the community, respects individual authenticity and interpersonal harmony within the community, empowers individuals, and helps people develop talents and attitudes that will enable them to become social change agents, solves the community problems and fosters conflict resolution

Highly effective leadership is not merely the ability or static capacity of a leader; it should display the dynamic nature of the relationship between leader and followers which influence each other in the pursuit of goals, understanding the dynamics of the local community, how to find and engage influential, identifying and overcoming barriers, building participation and support in the community, build trust with others, and be a role model for the leader's peer.

Capacity

An effective leader shows his/her capacity. Leaders possess the capacity to recognize all that they perceive. Capacity describes ability to achieve objectives, solve problems and perform in which one functions. Capacity relates to soundness of mind and to an understanding and perception of one's actions.

Capacity is personal competence, which is influenced by values, i.e. cultural, knowledge, etc. Capacity can be recognized from one's ability to make a decision and count consequences of each option (i.e. risks, burdens, and benefits). Leaders need to take the time and effort to show followers what they're good at and why followers should be confident in the leader's ability.

Capacity is also the ability to distinguish right and wrong; and to understand the outcome at the time of the act. Everyone has the capacity for leadership.

Competency

Competency is power to perform. Leader's competency implies his/her well qualified skill and knowledge. Competency bears capacity and ability. Ability and capacity mean about the same thing but are grammatically different: ability is to do something; capacity is for doing something; ability is qualitative while capacity is quantitative.

Capacity refers to a general ability to comprehend an issue or perform a task; capability implies a reference to one of a set of such abilities.

Competency is a requirement for an individual to properly perform a specific task. It encompasses a combination of knowledge, skills and behavior utilized to improve performance. A person possesses a competence enabling the person to perform effective action within organization. Competency refers to an individual's demonstrated knowledge, skills, or abilities (performed to a specific standard).

Competencies are observable, behavioral acts that require a combination execution. They are demonstrated in a job context and, as such, are influenced by an organization's culture and work environment.

Competence is a measure of the ability to perform a task; effectiveness is a measure of the success achieved in the performance of a task. Competencies should be consistent with the organization's strategic objectives; so that you are able to successfully perform the task.

Leaders are responsible for their own decision; realize that their actions will have consequences.

2nd

LEADERSHIP COMPETENCY

A highly effective leadership displays high level of competency, which includes skills, behaviors, attitudes, and knowledge. Leaders are not going to master every competency. However, they will need to be aware of all of them, know their own shortcomings, focus on developing competencies in themselves.

A leader should be able to recognize these qualities in others so they can select people who compensate for their weaknesses.

An effective leader may possess at least 7 (seven) kinds of competency, which include:

a. Emotional competency - Skills, based on emotions, such as those related to empathy, adaptability, self-control, emotional self-awareness, ability to develop others, and so forth, contribute significantly to leader effectiveness.

b. Physical competency - Whether a leader knows how physically capable they are; such as physically active, involvement in physical activity, sport skills, physical fitness, and physical appearance.

c. Spiritual competency – Ability to build relationships based on individuals' spiritual gifts and interests; be concerned for where people are in their spiritual journeys; treat each person with grace; help members grow spiritually; and be a model for what life purpose looks like to others.

d. Psychological competency - A leader should possess mental readiness to accept and prepare for new challenges, be capable to deter and defeat threats, and intellectually prepare to train, guide and lead the members.

e. Social competency - If leadership skill is not complemented with social competency, competitiveness will become an unavoidable problem, therefore a leader should have a high level of social competency on top of his/her leadership skills. To act in a social competent manner means the leader must be emotionally intelligent.

Unfortunately, many leaders showed they thought that for their work what they needed was their head and not their heart. They said that they could not take hard decisions without emotional distance. Emotional intelligence is the capacity to use the power and consciousness of emotions as to efficiently sense and use information, membership and influence.

f. Ethical competency – Be responsible on their acts - be aware of the responsibilities that accompany their works, establish ethical standards that members are expected to adhere to in the performance of their duties, inspire and motivate people to strengthen their faith.

Leaders recognize the authority of leadership comes from trust/ faith, and act with integrity and competence, respecting the dignity, rights and responsibilities of others and embracing a commitment to the organization and members.

g. Cultural competency – Ability to work effectively across cultures, be a leader in diversity and inclusion, and actively participate in paving the way for a more engaged and inclusive multicultural activities.

Culture encompasses all the learned beliefs, traditions, language, values, customs, rituals, manners of interacting, forms of communication, expectations for behaviors, roles and relationships commonly shared among members of organization.

Competency (competence) alone can't make a leader. An incompetent leader has almost unlimited opportunities to be ineffective. Being competent doesn't mean that a leader knows how to do everything, but rather that they know what to do and how to get it done. Even the most brilliant leader who tries to go it on their own is setting themselves up for failure. A good leader will know where their strengths and weaknesses lie and thus know what kind of expertise they will need to surround themselves with.

Competence engenders confidence in a leader. We have placed too much emphasis on professional competence and not enough on character. And it has gotten us into trouble.

Emotional Competency

Intelligence and technical ability may get you in the door, but emotional competence is what will get you to the top. Emotional intelligence is the ability to access, manage and make use of your feelings. This ability can be more important to your success than your intelligence or technical skill.

Emotional Intelligence refers to your capacity to recognize your own feelings and those of others, for motivating yourself, and for managing emotions well in yourself and in your relationship. It describes abilities distinct from, but complementary to, academic intelligence, the purely cognitive capabilities measured by IQ.

Many people who are book smart but lack emotional intelligence end up working for people who have lower IQs than they but who excel in emotional intelligence skills. The ability to manage feelings and handle stress is another aspect of emotional intelligence that has been found to be important for success. Emotional intelligence has as much to do with knowing when and how to express emotion as it works by controlling it.

The emotional competencies are linked to and based on emotional intelligence. A certain level of emotional intelligence is necessary to learn the emotional competencies. It is the ability to recognize accurately what another person is feeling enables one to develop a specific competency such as influence.

Similarly, people who are better able to regulate their emotions will find it easier to develop a competency such as initiative or achievement drives. Ultimately it is these social and emotional competencies that we need to identify and measure if we want to be able to predict performance.

Emotionally competent means one must be aware of his or her emotions and how they play a role in contacts with others. Recognizing one's feeling and ensuring they do not negatively impact others is an important part of managing emotions in such a manner that they contribute to the situation.

Competence consists of those attributes that a person exhibits in managing himself or herself in the conduct of business, and especially how one controls his or her actions. It includes:

a. Self-awareness: The ability to read and understand our own emotions and recognize their impact on work performance and relationships. Know yourself and seek self-improvement. Real leadership means leading yourself. Only when somebody is aware of their strengths and weaknesses can they maximize their potential.

    Know your feelings and use them to make career choices you can live with. Be aware of situations that may cause stress and be prepared to seek help in handling and diffusing them. Self-awareness needs emotional self-awareness, accurate self-assessment, and self-confidence.

    Leadership is applicable to all facets of your life: a competency that you can learn to expand your perspective; set the context of a goal, understand the dynamics of human behavior and take the initiative to get to where you want to be. Through discovering who you are and your life's work, you develop the self-awareness and confidence required to lead.

Leading is not so much about what a leader does as it is about who the leader is. Leading is an act of self-expression. This expression may not be conscious.

However, the leader's actions still emerge from within whether the actions are initiated consciously or unconsciously. The leader's effectiveness can be improved through increased self-awareness.

Since we are complex beings, our awareness needs to be multifaceted. Our actions emerge from a myriad of interrelated factors. These include, but are by no means limited to, our values, goals, roles, thoughts, feelings, prejudices, intentions, moods, assumptions, attitudes, circumstances, environment; the list goes on. It is unlikely that we can be aware of all the underlying factors influencing our actions.

However, the more aspects of our inner and outer environments we can be aware of, the better our ability to make conscious choices regarding our behaviors. Such awareness requires cultivating the skill of mindfulness.

As we become more mindful of more aspects of ourselves, we attain increased self-control. As a result we can better lead ourselves and thereby become better leaders of others. This quality is an understanding of yourself as a leader. The more you are aware of your own values, needs, and biases, the less likely you will be to project your feelings onto your followers.

b. Self-management: The ability to keep disruptive emotions and impulses under control. It includes trustworthiness that display integrity; adaptability that adjusting to changing situations; initiative that is readiness to seize opportunities.

Good leaders know their own values, strengths, and limitations and are able to control their emotions and behaviors. They must seek personal development by being willing to seek help when needed or admit when they have made a mistake and by engaging in continuous learning. They should be able to manage and adapt to stressful or dynamic situation.

If you can't manage yourself, you can't lead others. The clearer you are, about who you are, and what you stand for, the more credibility you will have as a leader of others. This includes your values, beliefs, purpose, goals, plans, being a continuous learner, and having confidence and a positive mental attitude. Self-management may need:

a. Self-coaching which helps you acquire useful leadership skills; clarify your values and guiding principles and actively build your reputation; guide you to become the master of yourself so you will be ready, willing and able to lead others.

   Self leadership happens through self-learning and self-coaching. As you build your capability to lead, people become attracted to you and this opens the door for trusting you. When they trust you, people will be open to listening to what you have to say.

b. Self-knowledge which provides personal integrity to engage in powerful action oriented relationships. The crux of leadership development that works is self-directed learning, intentionally developing or strengthening an aspect of who you are or who you want to be, or both.

c. Self-development. - Development of your capabilities or potentialities Personal improvement provides your key to a great fulfillment in life and your basis for achieving your desires. It is the bedrock of success and the gateway to a rewarding and fulfilling life.

   To attain personal improvement whether physically, mentally, spiritually, or socially, you must equip yourself with the skill or knowledge to bring about what you wish to achieve in order to enhance your lifestyle. No personal improvement, no success.

If you do not intend to improve yourself, do not expect any great measure of success in life. The way you think or act, the choices you make, all affect you personally.

Whatever you do to bring pleasure to your life involves you, and any measure of success begins with your personal improvement. Development equips leaders with skills to manage their external environment - skills such as effective communication, team building, decision-making, negotiation and conflict management.

Self-management is matter of using awareness of your emotions to manage your response to different situations and people; learn to keep anger and anxiety under control, and mobilize positive personal and organizational support; self-monitoring and goal setting. It's an endless effort in:

a. Focus on success - The most important of the elements of success; which creates change and brings success, is the ability to sustain the focus in our daily lives; never quit pursuing your dream because the journey to success has proven valuable inwardly and outwardly. Be thankful that all of the struggles, disappointments, victories, and major accomplishments have done more than strengthen you and enrich your life.

    Don't make the mistake of thinking you cannot be content, excited, optimistic, or proud until you have achieved your desired level of success. Train your mind to focus on success; start to be focus on your probability of success, instead of failure. Learn to love the challenge and expect success, but allow yourself the freedom to fail.

b. Self-control - The ability to make decisions about how and when we express our feelings, and which of our impulses to act on. This is a life-long process which is critical to the healthy development of people. Validate feelings, not behavior, as different behaviors and actions lead to different consequences.

Response can have a powerful influence on behavior; the more emotional your response, the more likely the behavior will continue, because an intense reaction, positive or negative, is gratifying and reason to repeat the behavior.

c. Conscientiousness - The quality of being conscientious; a scrupulous regard to the dictates of conscience; how to self help knowledge base to answer questions on control, management and understanding self, helping one deal, learn, know and master self.

Conscientiousness is related to emotional intelligence and impulse control; which has elements include self-discipline, carefulness, thoroughness, organization, deliberation (the tendency to think carefully before acting), and need for achievement. Individuals who are low on self-discipline (conscientiousness) are unable to motivate themselves to perform a task that they would like to accomplish.

Our emotional competence shows how much of that potential we have translated into on-the-job capabilities. Emotional competence is a learned capability based on emotional intelligence that results in outstanding performance at the organization. It involves empathy (the ability to read others feelings) and social skills (which allows handling feelings of others).

Competence lays the foundations for interactions with others, both in a business and social environment. Those possessing competence are often referred to as having presence. Effective leaders are good at reading the emotional states of others and being conscious of how their emotion expression affects communication.

Emotions of leaders highly influence the amount of attention that they receive from followers. Charisma is a quality of a person that has three main characteristics:

a. Have a strong sense of feeling, in touch with their feelings

b. Have the ability to express their emotions convincingly

 c. Have the potential for senders of emotion

Emotionally competent leader will express emotion appropriate to the situation and their needs and they will not seek to suppress emotions in others.

Physical Competency

Leaders need to develop and demonstrate physical competence, such as sport skills, physical fitness, and physical appearance. So that he/she gains social acceptance and support from the followers. It involves:

 a. Provide essential information for understanding the mechanisms by which the leaders come to evaluate their self-competencies in physical activity

 b. Create an environment that will enhance his/her perceived competence - Using information to understand and enhance performance; application of concepts from disciplines such as learning and development

 c. Help other help themselves by providing them with self regulation skills (e.g. goal setting) that enhance their own perceptions about enjoyment, self-esteem, and motivation

 d. Physical activity behavior - Promote personal and group success in activity settings, i.e. safe practices, etiquette, cooperation and teamwork, ethical behavior, and social interaction.

Physical competence is about whether a leader knows how physically capable he/she is. It can be recognized by:

 a. Commitment - Desire and resolve to continue participation in physical activity; have comprehensive perspective on the meaning of a healthy lifestyle

 b. Enjoyment - Positive affective response to physical activity that reflects feelings of pleasure, liking, and fun. Enjoyment of physical activity has sometimes been treated synonymously with motivation.

c. Personal investments pertain to the time, effort, energy - Provide awareness of opportunity both in organization and community

d. Involvement opportunities - Participation in physical activity which gains positive interactions and enhance physical conditioning or appearance

When a leader meets the standard of competence, he/she will be able to show creative physical activities both individual and within a team; analyze and develop various movement concepts and applications; demonstrate knowledge of rules, safety and strategies during physical activity; assess individual fitness levels; set goals for fitness improvement; and demonstrate cooperativeness within the group of physical activity.

Spiritual Competency

Leaders are 'living symbols' of a particular set of values that the followers subscribe to, enabling an almost spiritual feeling of being part of something greater than oneself. Be spiritual describes ones have faith in something beyond themselves, and the ones who are able to use their faith to overcome adversity are the ones that see meaning in their lives.

Having faith does not necessarily mean you are part of a religious group. Spiritual competence means:

a. Able to judging the rights and the wrongs of their daily lot; and promote morality - Valuing principles such as decency, compassion, honesty, and fair play.

b. Serving - Devoting time and energy to institutions, communities, and the world.

c. Have sense of connection - Join their individual selves to the selfhood of humanity; look at their own existential beliefs and identify their own definition of quality of life; aware of our own spiritual beliefs; observe and study the heritage and beliefs of others.

Individuals vary within other religions as much as they vary within our own. Demonstrating our sincere desire to understand the needs of others will go a long way toward improved communication and a better matching of appropriate care.

The requirement for spiritual influence is competence. This competence doesn't imply that you have to be better than everyone else; or about doing your best.

Psychological Competency

Leaders who possess psychological competence will demonstrate their ability to successfully reach developmental tasks expected for their function.

Psychological competency is set of knowledge, abilities, attitudes, and personality traits, which includes attention, concentration, reality orientation, memory, reasoning, judgment, emotional state, and especially knowledge and appreciation of the nature and purposes of the decisions that are the subject of the competency action (e.g. manage finances) and the ability to carry them out (mathematical ability or knowledge of banking rules, investing, etc.).

Psychological competence demonstrates personality of the individual, e.g. behavior, thought and emotion. It evolves:

a. Behavioral display - Mental attitude appropriateness, which includes

i. Decisional ability - The capacity to make independent decisions, ability to exercise judgment and interpret experiences, i.e. cope with anxiety, depression, disturbances, etc. both in the environment and in relation to others

ii. Reasoning ability – How to deal with the source of the problem effectively

b. Intelligibility - Intellectual functioning or IQ, able to differentiate between relevant and irrelevant information, able to apply knowledge to develop a solution

This competence engages a person/leader to social skills, i.e. attribution, interpretation, and prediction in daily activities, especially in social interaction, and communication

Social Competency

Leaders should have competencies that include how to read and understand the environment, build alliances, recognize the importance of social responsibility, manage complexity, use information technology, and encourage creativity. Increasingly, leaders are using a proactive stance in taking their organizations into uncharted territory.

Social competence describes a condition of possessing the social, emotional, and intellectual skills and behaviors needed to succeed as a member of society.

Social competence refers to the social, emotional, and skills and behaviors that individuals need for successful social adaptation. Understand different roles, learn to take other perspective, and develop an understanding of the social rules and conventions of their culture.

Social competence focuses in social behavior, with an emphasis on how people think towards each other and how they relate to each other.

Leaders bring together diverse groups of people with very different histories, values, perspectives and cultures. Social competencies are about how we deal with relationships. It is the second part of emotional intelligence. Social competence includes:

a. Social awareness - Knowing how one is perceived by others in that environment Based on perceptions of the social environment, a leader must also alter his/her behaviors as needed to more effectively relate to others, a process that has been termed interpersonal adaptability. Social awareness promotes empathy - Sensing other's emotions, understanding their perspective and taking active interest in their concerns. Empathy displays capacity of sensing emotions of others, understanding their perspective and taking an interest in their concern.

Organizational awareness-ability to read currents of organizational life, build decision networks and navigate situations, understand the perspectives of other people including their motivations, their emotions, and the meaning of what they do and say.

Empathy describes the ability to imagine oneself in anther's place and understand the other's feelings, desires, ideas, and actions; by a kind of introjections, feel himself/herself involved in what he/she observes or contemplates.

Empathy is the understanding of others and how they feel in different circumstances so that we may deal with them in the proper context. Sensing others' feelings by being attentive to emotional cues and listening can contribute to early resolution of issues.

b. Organizational awareness: Recognize the currents, decision networks, and environment at the organizational level

c. Service: Recognizing and meeting follower needs

d. Relationship management: The capacity for visionary leadership, influence, developing others, communication, change catalyst, conflict management, building bonds, teamwork and collaboration.

It means using awareness of one's own emotions and the emotions of others to manage relationships to a successful outcome. This skill involves showing sensitivity to others feelings. Become aware of your own reactions in similar situations. To learn to calm down and figure out what upsets others the most; to learn and understand a fellow beings point of view. Talk calmly and clearly; listen carefully and look to address the emotions of others, as well as the situation in a positive way.

Leaders need to take the time and effort to show followers what they're good at and why followers should be confident in the leader's ability. Use care, however, never to upstage or embarrass someone else as you demonstrate competence.

Building emotional intelligence in a life is important because it creates solid relationships and trust. Respect all people for their ideas, their work, and their contributions to the community, which involve developing others, influencing, communication, conflict management, leadership, change catalyst, building bonds, and teamwork & collaboration.

Social skills are used to achieve effective leadership results, includes communication, conflict management, negotiation, team development. The influence that one exhibits through a combination of skills can have a positive effect on others, to include teams, that leads to the desire results.

Leaders know their own values, strengths, and limitations and are able to control their emotions and behaviors. They must seek personal development by being willing to seek help when needed or admit when they have made a mistake and by engaging in continuous learning. They should be able to manage and adapt to stressful or dynamic situation.

Today's organizations need leaders who understand their own social identity in order to lead others effectively. Understand your own social identity as a leader, as well as the social identity of others, and its impact on the organization.

Ethical Competency

A leader should be able to share his/her ethical concerns to the organization, which may contribute beneficence (maximum good outcomes, minimum risk/harm), promote respect to the people (protect the statutory rights and privacy of members) and advance social justice.

Leadership in the broadest sense of the term encompasses behaviors that are ethical as well as those that are generally considered unethical. Leadership is the creation and fulfillment of worthwhile opportunities by honorable means

Ethical behavior enhances the well-being of everyone because it comes from, reinforces, motives and emotions such as love, joy, generosity and compassion. Ethical behaviors should be in line with following principles:

    a. Respect for the dignity: People do not want strong leader who will dominate us, telling them what to do and how to behave; but they want a leader who has dignity. When they offer each other respect, dignity dwells among them. When they disrespect one another, the opportunities for dignified living plummet. To be a leader with dignity, you should:

    i. Value statement, not engage in degrading comments about others; strive to use respectful language; abstain from all forms of harassment or abuse.

    ii. Avoid disrespecting rights of others: Create an atmosphere of understanding and mutual respect

    iii. Practice non discriminative acts: Advance equality and value diversity

    iv. Work and act in a spirit of fairness to others: Leaders must act with integrity, fairness, and in an ethical manner

b. Be responsible - Engage only in those activities in which he/she has competence, accept responsibility for the consequences of their actions, avoid doing harm to others, and minimize risk

c. Show integrity – Free of conflict of interest, keep trust of others, not misuse the authority, accuracy and honesty; straightforwardness and openness; the maximization of objectivity and minimization of bias

Competency means possessing the requisite capacities and knowledge base to undertake one's agreed upon functions. An ethical competent leader must:

a. Practice ethical obligation at a high level of integrity, i.e. determine whether the activity is ethical – identify circumstances in which the ethical problem arose.

b. Ensure trust of others, i.e. ethical decision making and act in good faith - consider other entity potentially affected by the decision; take responsibility for consequences of action

c. Challenge violation against ethics and law, i.e. prevent future occurrences of the dilemma; consider seriously others' concerns about one's own possibly unethical actions - not to be vexatious or malicious.

d. Resolve conflict of interest and promote organization's interest is as best served, i.e. develop alternative courses of action which may conflict

Ethical cultures are the result of diligent effort--frequent, scheduled conversations between leaders and members about what the standards of the organization. As a leader, you have to set the standard yourself, constantly keeping your actions above reproach.

Leaders must act with integrity, honesty, and justice. They must work in the best interest of others, showing respect and empathy for unique individual and cultural differences.

Leaders create a culture that promotes high ethical standards along with personal, organizational, and civic responsibility.

Ethical leaders recognize and conduct themselves in concert with universal moral principles as well as specific values, laws, and ethics relevant to their group/organization. Some leaders build trust and loyalty through social events or team-building activities.

Knowing what is right is absolutely critical to the leader, followers and organization ethics. Yet, ethics only happens when good beliefs lead to good behaviors.

Cultural Competency

Cultural competency is defined as a set of behaviors; attributes and policies enabling an organization (or individual) to work effectively in cross cultural situations.

No single definition of cultural competence is yet universally accepted. Most have a common element, which requires the adjustment or recognition of one's own culture in order to understand the culture of others.
Cultural competence describes a set of congruent behaviors, knowledge, and attitudes that come together in a system, organization, or among the people that enables effective work in cross-cultural situations. It conceives in no spirit of racial animosity, fostering no ethnic antagonisms; encourage mutual cooperation and helpfulness.

Culture refers to integrated patterns of behavior that include the language, thoughts, actions, customs, beliefs, and institutions of racial, ethnic, social, or religious groups. This competence implies a leader having the capacity to function effectively as an individual or an organization within the context of the cultural beliefs, practices, and needs of the communities, includes:

    a. Demonstrate an understanding of the manner in diverse cultures and belief systems, i.e. value the importance of curiosity, empathy, and respect; ability to work on community-based values, traditions, and customs

b. Provide the necessary knowledge, skills, experience, and attitudes to effectively serve diverse communities; ensure that a system, agency, program, or individual can function effectively and appropriately in diverse cultural interaction and settings; influence on attitudes, behaviors and lifestyles within a cultural context; know what is perceived to be culturally acceptable

c. Recognize cultural biases, i.e. discrimination (sexual orientation, gender, age, race, ethnicity, class, etc), disparity (socioeconomic, environment, language, etc), stereotyping (community, religion, tradition, etc)

d. Dealing with harm as a result of cultural discord, i.e. develop strategy to eliminate racism; appraise the literature which relates to disparities; promote effective cross-cultural communication; invite community partnerships etc

Cultural competence is the ability to deliver effective outcome to people from different cultures. His/her principles, goals, initiatives and philosophy encompass all sector of the community; reflect true actions in his/her mission, and commitment to improve outcomes for people of color. Leadership requires an understanding of one's own beliefs and assumptions and an ability to recognize other team members' cultural values and behaviors. The competence should demonstrate ability of:

a. Creating equal opportunities to participate and to listen. All voices can be heard, that there is respect for diverse views (coupled with a willingness to be curious), and that listening is as important as speaking.

b. Value the community, respect its diversity, and carefully listen to what the community has to say about its needs, strengths, hopes, and desires

c. Pay close attention to factors related to diversity – provide an impetus for greater attention and focus on multiculturalism

All persons have a right to have their innate worth as human beings appreciated and that this worth is not dependent upon their culture, nationality, ethnicity, color, race, religion, sex, gender, marital status, sexual orientation, physical or mental abilities, age, socio-economic status, or any other preference or personal characteristic, condition, or status.

Leaders must be able to increase understanding and appreciation of cultural differences between groups. Leader's competence or expertise is important on a leader's effectiveness.

A highly effective leader knows how to use the skills, knowledge, and energy of team members to accomplish the task and mission. The leader must provide a clear and compelling vision to guide the team toward the goal and must model the level of commitment, perseverance, and resilience necessary for mission accomplishment.

Leaders lead others by their character, by their competence, and by their actions; therefore, effective leader development must focus on the leader's character and values, his/her competencies, and his/her decisions and actions.

3rd

LEADERSHIP ATTITUDE

An important key to high productivity and effective leadership is to have and maintain a positive attitude. Nothing else will have a greater effect on you than your attitude. People have preferences that affect the way they see, decide, interact, and control other people and activities.

Attitudes are usually defined as a disposition or tendency to respond positively or negatively towards a certain thing (idea, object, person, and situation). They encompass, or are closely related to, our opinions and beliefs and are based upon our experiences.

A positive attitude may not solve all your problems, but it will annoy enough people to make it worth the effort. Our role as leaders is not to catch people doing things wrong, but to create an environment in which people can become heroes.

Attitude is an independent measure of affect for or against the attitude object, which is a function of belief strength and evaluative aspect associated with each attribute. Attitude is a person's evaluation of an object of thought. Reasons we should focus on changing attitudes, i.e.

    a. We can't directly influence behavior and we have to find a proxy or indirect agent

b. Attitudes play a major role in determining behavior. To change other people's behavior is to change their attitudes. You don't have control over other people's actual behavior. People do have free choice and pretty much do as they please.

Behavior is driven by attitude. They'll do that by themselves because their attitude is favorable toward that behavior. Attitudes drive behavior. Factors that make attitude drive behaviors include

a. Attitude availability: Available (accessible or active. It is more likely to drive behavior. An attitude is available when you can think of it, when you know that you've got an attitude on this topic, and when that attitude is "turned on".

b. Attitude relevance: Relevant or useful or applicable or pertinent. It is more likely to drive behavior. An attitude is relevant when it applies to the situation at hand; when the attitude is relevant in the situation.

Attitudes represent our covert feelings of favorability or un-favorability toward an object, person, issue, or behavior. Attitude is a learned predisposition to response in a consistently favorable or unfavorable manner with respect to a given object.

Our learned attitudes serve as general guides to our overt behavior with respect to the attitude object, giving rise to a consistently favorable or unfavorable pattern of response.

Our attitudes shape who we are, and how we live our lives. We potentially have total control over things in life is our attitude. Whatever the situation, we have a choice in how we react, and those reactions shape our future. It's not so much what happens to us, it's how we allow it to affect us. The more we allow external circumstances to affect us, the less powerful we are within, and vice versa.

Changes in opinions can result in attitude change depending upon the presence or absence of rewards. The learning of new attitudes is no different in nature than any other verbal or motor skill, except that opinions relate to a single proposition whereas other skills involve a series of propositions.

The acceptance of a new opinion (and hence attitude formation) is dependent upon the incentives that are offered in the communication.

Attitude determines our altitude. It is the mindset of your disposition and the catalyst for your character. It could limit your comprehension, or allow you a limitless passion to overcome and succeed.

Attitude is the action of toleration, distinguished by tactful ingenuity, the tenacity to unite, and the decisiveness to encourage. These are the primary ingredients for developing, strengthening, and sustaining quality leadership. Whether by choice, appointment, election, or default, once you've accepted a leadership position, you are responsible, and therefore accountable, for the outcome.

Through your attitude, magnetism and persuasion, you must enlist others in your dreams. Attitude is more important than facts. It is more important than the past, than education, than money, than circumstances, than failures, than success, than what other people think, say or do. It is more important than appearance, gift, or skill.

The remarkable thing is we have a choice every day regarding the attitude we will embrace for that day. We cannot change our past. The only thing we can do is play on the string we have, and that is our attitude. Attitude changes that was influenced, when beliefs are unbalanced, stress is created and there is pressure to change attitudes.

A leader's attitude toward followers has a strong impact on performance.

Behavior

Effective leadership is based in behavior, not in job title/position. A leader is someone who motivating, guiding, encouraging, and serving, no matter what job title/position he or she holds. If you want to become a more effective leader, you have to master the critical behaviors.

Leadership is a product of awareness and command of the reactions and influences of a group on the individual as well as the individual on the group. Leaders become or remain successful because they are able to self manage and change their behavior.

When a leader is shown how to self-manage himself or herself and significantly up-grade his or her mind, personal and professional skill sets, feel balanced, alert, in control and powerful - can he/she only then move into a zone of optimum, sustainable best performance and fulfill his/her potential.

By choosing your behavior, you are empowering yourself and also allowing yourself greater control over your experience. Reacting may give you instant gratification of emotional release, and the consequences usually are far more detrimental than the payoff. It may be difficult, as you should catch yourself responding in an undesirable manner. But you are aware of it and the moment you become aware that you could respond differently; take the next step and change it.

Mental condition is part of a complex interplay between our body and our environment. Brain controls behavior. But the environment actually also creates the diversity of human behavior.

Leadership, like other behavior, is learned. The leader's responsibility in learning a new, effective leadership behavior is to practice that behavior until it becomes a habit. Behavior is action or reaction of an object that in relation to the environment.

Behavior describes a person's actions – which are controlled by the sum of their personality, attitudes and complexes of beliefs and feelings about specific ideas, situations, or other people.

Mandela was often afraid during his time underground, during the Rivonia trial that led to his imprisonment, during his time on Robben Island. But as a leader, he suggests, you cannot let people know. 'You must put up a front.' And that's precisely what he learned to do: pretend and, through the act of appearing fearless, inspire others._He knew that he was a model for others, and that gave him the strength to triumph over his own fear. (Richard Stengel, 2008)

Since leaders have special roles where they affect the lives of others they also have a special responsibility to develop themselves and provide a role model. If a leader of people doesn't know who they are and hasn't worked on their own growth and development, how can they best impact other people effectively, help other people grow and affect positive individual and organizational results.

However, today, it's not enough just to develop yourself. Leaders also have to understand the context and the environment of their corporate world -the hidden dynamics and forces at play in organizations that have tremendous impact on what people see and do. Behavioral traits that effective leaders demonstrate include, but not limited to:

a. Pro-activeness: Leader may forgo tasks that he or she feels passionately about in order to take care of more pressing matters.

b. Think Win/Win: Display mutual respect and trust, advance cooperative negotiation, and lead to mutually beneficial results.

c. Courage: Leaders allay fear.

d. Synergy: Demonstrate synergistic working relationship; value diversity and are open to each other's differing perspectives and contributions, building on each other's strengths and compensating for weaknesses, and apply the principles of cooperative creativity and value differences.

e. Self-Renewal: Constantly adapting to changing organizational circumstances requires that the leader not only be creative, but also encourage creativity on the part of followers. It is the leader's example of creative behavior that allows the organization to renew itself continually and flourish, regardless of the stage of organizational development involved.

There are dozens of major behaviors that effective leaders have, i.e.:

- Accepting
- Accomplishing
- Accountable
- Accurate
- Achieving
- Acting
- Active
- Advance
- Affectionate
- Alert
- Ambitious
- Appearing
- Appreciate
- Approaching
- Appropriate
- Artistic
- Aspire
- Attentive
- Attractive
- Aware
- Balancing
- Believing
- Brave
- Candid
- Capable
- Caring
- Challenging
- Changing
- Cheerful
- Coaching
- Co-dependent
- Collaborating
- Compassionate
- Competent
- Competing
- Complying
- Communicative
- Comprehensive
- Conscious
- Confident
- Conforming
- Considerate
- Consistent
- Constructive
- Contributing
- Controlling
- Cooperative
- Courageous
- Courteous
- Cautious
- Creative
- Credible
- Decisive
- Dedicative
- Deliberate
- Demonstrative
- Determined
- Developing
- Devoting
- Different
- Directing
- Discrete
- Diverse
- Dynamic
- Educate
- Effective
- Efficient
- Empathetic
- Empower
- Encourage
- Endure
- Enjoy
- Ensuring
- Enthusiastic

- Esteem
- Expansive
- Excel
- Excite
- Explorative
- Expressive
- Fair
- Faithful
- Flexible
- Focus
- Forgiving
- Friendly
- Frank
- Fulfilling
- Generous
- Gentle
- Giving
- Grateful
- Hard work
- Helping
- Honest
- Happy
- Hard working
- Helpful
- Heroic
- Humble
- Idealistic
- Impartial
- Importance
- Improving
- Inclusive
- Independent
- Initiate
- Inter-dependent
- Interest
- Involve
- Just
- Keeping
- Kind
- Learning
- Loving
- Loyal
- Maintain
- Mature
- Modest
- Motivating
- Objective
- Open
- Open minded
- Optimistic
- Patient
- Patriotic
- Peaceful
- Perfect
- Persistent
- Persevere
- Pleasant
- Practical
- Praise
- Proactive
- Professional
- Proper
- Proportional
- Punctual
- Quite
- Rational
- Realistic
- Reliable
- Reliant
- Respectful
- Responsible
- Responsive
- Sacrificing
- Satisfying

- Seeking
- Safely
- Selective
- Selling
- Sensitive
- Serious
- Sharing
- Sincere
- Smart
- Stable
- Straight forward
- Succeeding
- Sportive
- Supportive
- Sympathetic
- Systematic
- Talent
- Thoughtful
- Tolerant
- To the Point
- Tranquil
- Transparent
- Trusting
- Truthful
- Willing
- Win-win

By positively changing a leader's behavior at any one of the above levels the organization as a whole will benefit as the individual increases his or her effectiveness. Behavior is purposeful, directed towards some end. That is, it is motivated. The driving force is need.

Leadership is a means used to cause people to do what we want them to do, but there are many ways to achieve that end and most of them are not leadership. The leader must exhibit and promote behaviors that build esteem and must work to rid the organization of behaviors that destroy esteem.

A competent leader will demonstrate creativity, analytical reasoning, strategic skills, tactical skills, risk taking, integrity, drive, organizational skills, teamwork, willingness to change, enthusiasm, ambition and life balance, just to name a few.

Organization success depends on the ability of a leader to influence, motivate, and enable others to contribute toward the effectiveness and success of the organizations of which they are members.

Self-awareness, effective understanding and management of personal behaviors, social sensitivity, and relationship management skills - create a leader who is effective in a multitude of situations.

Leadership is one of the ways that affect the behavior of people in the business. Most successful managers are also successful leaders. They get people to work to accomplish the organization's goals.

A leader can be a manager, but a manager is not necessarily a leader. The leader of the work group may emerge informally as the choice of the group. If a manager is able to influence people to achieve the goals of the organization, without using his or her formal authority to do so, then the manager is demonstrating leadership. Some people assume that leadership and management are synonymous, but the terms are not interchangeable.

Management is the formal authority people are given within an organization. Leadership is informal, is not necessarily conferred by the organization. It is said that managers do things right; leaders do the right thing. While there is no single definition of leadership, there seems to be an understanding that a leader is the person who commits people to action, converts followers into leaders and converts leaders into agents of change.

Leadership is an interactive conversation that pulls people toward becoming comfortable with the language of personal responsibility and commitment.

Those who want to be leaders can develop leadership ability. Some people are born more naturally to leadership than others but in the end "leaders are made, not born!" Leadership requires we focus on our leadership skill, knowledge and attitude. Leadership skills are the abilities we have developed through training. Leadership knowledge is what we know about the practice of leadership and leadership attitude springs from who we are. It is the sum total of everything that makes us who we are, our beliefs, values, emotions, experiences.

In our leadership practice, attitude is the most important; it's our attitude that determines how effectively we can use our skills and knowledge to influence our world. It's our attitude that releases our leadership potential!

We can gain knowledge from books, mentors and observation, skills are gained from practice. It is only practice that makes permanent. A person with superior skill and knowledge cannot contribute as much as a leader with appropriate skill, knowledge and a great attitude.

The basis of effective leadership is honorable character and selfless service to your organization.

4th

LEADERSHIP KNOWLEDGE

Knowledge is the key ingredient in gaining a competitive advantage and it is a firm's main inimitable resource. Knowledge must be effectively transferred within organizations. Effective leaders set standards for others to meet, communicate high expectations, and lead by example. They must motivate followers during good times and bad. They must build high-performance teams. And, they must always be concerned for the best interests of their organization.

Since leadership involves the exercise of influence by one person over others, the quality of leadership exhibited by a leader is critical determinant of organizational success. Leadership evolves interpersonal relationship - cooperate or work together, influence - the power to affect others, and common goal. Leadership deals with change, inspiration, motivation, and influence.

Leadership traits include but not limited to care - show empathy toward others and act as good friend would; courtesy, use manners and basic good grace; respect, treat others fairly, honestly and keep their dignity in tact.

Leaders must show self-discipline, self-control of feelings, and actions; avoid all conflicts of interest between work and personal affair; sustain a culture where ethical conduct is recognized, valued, and exemplified; provide a work environment supportive of flexible work practices and adaptable; behave in ways consistent with personal values. An effective leader should possess:

a. Social characteristics include charisma, charming, tactful, popular, cooperative, and diplomatic

b. Personality traits include being self-confident, adaptable, assertive, and emotionally stable

c. Task-related characteristics include being driven to excel, accepting of responsibility, having initiative, and being results-oriented. They should demonstrate a desire to give back and to make a difference; encourage developments; serve others which take hard work and some sacrifice; have commitment and acting responsibly; and show awareness of the needs of others.

An organization has the greatest chance of being successful when all of the elements work toward achieving its goals. A leader should have leadership skill in order to influence the actions of members toward the achievement of the goals of the organization.

Knowledge means be technically and tactically proficient. Since leadership involves the exercise of influence by one person over others, the quality of leadership exhibited by a leader is a critical determinant of organizational success. Study leadership in order to influence the actions of members toward the achievement of the goals of the organization is essential.

Leadership training is worthwhile; therefore ones need to cope with leadership techniques and leadership competencies.

Knowledge is result of perception, learning and reasoning. It is result of acquiring information that may create new thing which could be used to define and solve problems. Knowledge is what is known. Your knowledge is your ability to gather and analyze information and make decisions that will benefit your life; tool to work collaboratively with and learn from other; confidence to take risks; capacity to shift your mistakes to become strength.

Knowledge creates expertise. Your knowledge should be broad, and in addition to knowing your job. Therefore, increase your knowledge by remaining alert. Listen, observe, and find out about things you don't understand. Knowledge people use their intellect to convert their ideas into products, services, or processes. Intellectuality may represent one's intelligence that reflects:

a. Perceiving - Ability to obtain information. Personal contact might be mattered and mostly required, as well as discussions and follow-up with co-workers. Follow-up refers to efforts that leaders make to solicit continuing and updated ideas for improvement from their co-workers.

b. Learning - Create knowledge from information, i.e. classify, organize, abstract, and generalize information

c. Reason - Ability to use knowledge for achieving goals. Once you have knowledge, it is your social responsibility to identify, create, represent, and distribute the knowledge for reuse, and learning across the community.

Knowledge and skills are necessary to become highly effective leaders. The leaders have a thirst for knowledge. They keep abreast of the latest developments in their field. They are informed of possible problems, their causes, and solutions, and are aware of the needs of their teammates. It is not only their knowledge that inspires confidence, but their integrity.

Leadership receives input, ensures that it is enriched and focused, and then orchestrates functional and energetic flows out to the body of the organization or enterprise. Anyone with critical knowledge that could alter organization direction can show leadership.

Managing the knowledge of a process is a requirement in any organization. You may find many people have you met who have an immense amount of knowledge, are like walking encyclopedias but aren't very wise. Many people also are very simple and don't have a wealth of knowledge or information but are very, very wise. Creating and sharing knowledge is central to effective leadership.

Knowledge is the key ingredient in gaining a competitive advantage and it is a firm's main inimitable resource. Knowledge must be effectively transferred within organizations. Knowledge leader shows wisdom to followers. Leaders who have a wealth of wisdom see context, relevance and how it impacts people/organization.

Effective leaders set standards for others to meet, communicate high expectations, and lead by example. They must motivate members during good times and bad. They must build high-performance teams. And, they must always be concerned for the best interests of their organization.

Effective leaders provide learning opportunities for people to develop the knowledge. Since leadership involves the exercise of influence by one person over others, the quality of leadership exhibited by a leader is critical determinant of organizational success.

Leadership evolves interpersonal relationship - cooperate or work together, influence - the power to affect others, and common goal. Leadership deals with change, inspiration, motivation, and influence.

The organization needs to hold leaders up as a model for other to learn from, so that they too can become highly effective knowledge leaders. An organization has the greatest chance of being successful when all of the elements work toward achieving its goals. A leader should have leadership skill in order to influence the actions of members toward the achievement of the goals of the organization.

Leadership is needed to foster the climate, the practices and the incentives for knowledge sharing. Knowledge is an essential part of our individual and organizational ability to innovate, compete and succeed. An effective leader should be technically and tactically proficient.

Knowledge gaps, bottlenecks, absence or under-utilisation of knowledge, lack of communication or collaboration, lack of access to or re-use of existing knowledge, difficulty in storing or retrieving knowledge, organisational or cultural issues may all contribute significant barriers to knowledge sharing and innovation, and leaders need to be able to identify and act on such areas to improve the organisational performance. An effective leader takes the following actions:

a. Listen to subordinates to diagnose or solve problems

b. Set goals and develops short- and long- range action plans

c. Give directions about who is to do which tasks to what standards

d. Provide feedback on task performance

e. Reward or disciplines task performance and personal characteristics

f. Develop people: The leader should people develop in-depth understanding and skill through practice and positive feedback.

Leaders should not fall neatly into a compartment on an organization chart. They show high pinnacles of the command and control organization; be intensely focused on the promotion of knowledge management practices and solutions; and in confidence decide what kind of leadership. They need to succeed the organization relevant tasks. Leaders share knowledge within the organization, which enable the members to meet organization's goals.

However, there is no one best style of leadership. The effectiveness of a particular style is dependent on the organizational situation.

This knowledge may improve intelligence, performance, competitive advantage, or higher levels of innovation. Shared knowledge should ensure that the right information is delivered to the right person just in time, in order to take the most appropriate decision.

Leadership Style

An effective leader will find himself/herself switching instinctively between styles according to the people and work they are dealing with.

Success in leadership comes when the leadership style is matched with the characteristics of the follower.

Problems with leadership come when the leadership style does not fit the follower. If you're not sure what kind of a leader you should be, consider the one person that comes to mind when you think about someone you respect as a competent leader.

It is often overlooked, but Bill Clinton assumed the presidency in one of the most difficult times in our nation's history. The former president's demonstrated complex leadership techniques, including his attention to public opinion, his ability to take quick corrective action, and his efficient damage control in the face of political and personal difficulty.

From diversity to decisiveness, from consensus to compromise, each chapter explores how Clinton employed important leadership principles and the ways in which they were--or were not—effective. (Donald T. Phillips, The Clinton Charisma, 2007)

Leadership styles need to be continually learnt not only through leadership training and books but also from observing other good leaders. Most importantly, practice because the best learning will be that which you learn from your own experience. Leading others is not simply a matter of style, or following some how-to guides or recipes.

Ineffectiveness of leaders seldom results from a lack of know-how or how-to. It is typically due to inadequate managerial skills. Leadership is even not about creating a great vision. It is about creating conditions under which all your followers can perform independently and effectively toward a common objective. There are many ways to lead; leaders have their own style. The leadership style includes:

a. Laissez-Faire Leadership: Provide little or no direction and give followers as much freedom as possible. All authority or power is given to the followers and they must determine goals, make decisions, and resolve problems on their own. This style can be effective in situations where group members are highly qualified in an area of expertise; it often leads to poorly defined roles and a lack of motivation.

b. Democratic Leadership: Keep his or her followers informed about everything that affects their work and share decision making and problem solving responsibilities.

The leaders offer guidance to group members, but they also participate in the group and allow input from other group members. They encourage group members to participate, but retain the final say over the decision-making process. Group members may feel engaged in the process and are more motivated and creative. This type builds flexibility and responsibility and can help identify new ways to do things with fresh ideas.

c. Situational Leadership. Situational leaders are able to adapt their leadership style to fit their followers and situations in which they are working. Situational leadership will make conscious choices between their use of directive behavior and supportive behavior; being autocratic or democratic.

The key for the successful situational leader is to know which of the styles to use in a particular situation with a particular person. The situational leader bases the choice of a leadership style on the competence and commitment of the person being led rather than on the leader's usual or preferred style.

The key of being a situational leader is by knowing when to use each style. The decision is primarily a function of two variables: the degree of difficultly of the task and the development level of the person doing the task.

d. Bureaucratic Leadership: Everything must be done according to procedure or policy. The leaders ensure that their team to follow procedures exactly. This is a very appropriate style for work involving serious safety risks or where large sums of money are involved.

e. Autocratic Leadership: Retain as much power and decision-making authority as possible. The leader does not consult followers, nor are they allowed to give any input. The followers are expected to obey orders without receiving any explanations.

The motivation environment is produced by creating a structured set of rewards and punishments. Leaders provide clear expectations for what needs to be done, when it should be done, and how it should be done. There is also a clear division between the leader and the followers.

This style is best applied to situations where there is little time for group decision-making or where the leader is the most knowledgeable member of the group. It can be very effective if your organization seems to be drifting aimlessly.

f. Coaching Leadership: focuses on helping others in their personal development and in their job-related activities. The coaching leader aids others to get up to speed by working closely with them to make sure they have the knowledge and tools to get their job done.

g. Pacesetting Leadership: Be affective when followers are self-motivated and highly skilled. This style sets very high performance standards for themselves and the group and exemplifies the behaviors they are seeking from other members of the group.

The leader has a strong drive to achieve, has high standards, initiative, but low on empathy and collaboration, impatient, micromanages and is numbers-driven.

h. Affiliative Leadership: Be effective in situations where morale is low or teambuilding is needed. The leader promotes harmony, is nice, empathetic, boosts moral, and solves conflicts.

i. Coercive Leadership: It's based on the concept of "command and control" which usually causes a decrease in motivation among those interacting with the leader. This style is effective during disasters or dealing with under performing members - usually as a last resort.

The leader is commanding, threatening, has tight control, monitors studiously, creates dissonance, contaminates everyone's mood, and drives away talent.

j. Charismatic Leadership: Leaders inject huge doses of enthusiasm into their team, and are very energetic in driving others forward. The leaders tend to believe more in themselves than in their team.

k. People-Oriented or Relations-Oriented Leadership: Focus on organizing, supporting and developing the people in the team. It tends to lead to good teamwork and creative collaboration.

l. Task-Oriented Leadership: Focus only on getting the job done. The leader will actively define the work and roles required, put structures in place, plan, organize and monitor.

m. Transactional Leadership: Members agree to obey their leader totally when they take a job on. The organization pays the team members, in return for their effort and compliance. On other hand, the leader has the right to "punish" team members if their work doesn't meet the pre-determined standard. The leaders ensure that routine work is done reliably.

n. Transformational Leadership: Inspire his or her team with a shared vision of the future. Transformational leaders are highly visible, and spend a lot of time communicating. They don't necessarily lead from the front, as they tend to delegate responsibility amongst their teams. The leaders look after initiatives that add value.

o. Servant Leadership: Lead by virtue of meeting the needs of his or her team. The whole team tends to be involved in decision-making. The leaders achieve power on the basis of their values and ideals.

There are many more. Leadership style differs from person to person according to the tasks, team and individual capabilities. Leader's ability to adopt his or her leadership style to the situation at hand is important to their organization's success.

The best leaders are skilled at several styles and instinctively understand when to use them. The more leadership styles that you are able to master, the better the leader you will become. Learning a new leadership style therefore takes practice and perseverance. The more often the new style or behavior is repeated, the stronger the link becomes in our brains between the situation at hand and the desired reaction.

Leadership style is the pattern of behavior used by a leader in attempting to influence group members and make decisions regarding the mission, strategy, and operations of group activities. Effective leaders capitalize on their strengths. Leadership without exposure to the right environment may not develop to full potential.

5th

LEADERSHIP SKILL

Skills are the knowledge and abilities that a person gains throughout life. The ability to learn a new skill varies with each individual. Some skills come almost naturally, while others come only by complete devotion to study and practice.

To be an effective leader you require skills and the ability. Leadership is the ability to motivate a group of people toward a common goal. The skills of a leader will ensure that the work of the organization is what it needs to be.

Leaders facilitate the identification of organizational goals. They initiate the development of a vision of what their organization is about. You have to possess these skills to become a highly effective leader, at least but not limited to:

a. Image building skill: Able to build your desired reputation and organization image

b. Communication skill: To be an effective leader requires strong communication skills and the ability to inspire, encourage, and facilitate others to accomplish their goals. Communication and leadership are inseparable.

In almost any organization, effective communication between leaders and followers is essential, not only for getting individual and organizational needs met, but also for developing significant interpersonal relationships and for assuring the adequate functioning of the people in the organization.

c. Supervisory skill: Leadership requires a high level of supervision. The leader must meet supervisory challenges.

d. Organizational skill: Ability to help organizations create and continuously improve sustainable organizational performance.

e. Survival skill: To be effective, leaders must compete for survival. The first thing you must do in order to survive at the organization is to think strategically which will bring you to the logical conclusion.

f. Conflict resolution skill: Conflicts within the organization need to be confronted assertively. These conflicts - as uncomfortable as they may be to deal with - are often the only opportunities for growth into the fourth stage of development.

The effective leader must be sensitive to conflicts as they occur and applies creative problem-solving and effective communication to bring about appropriate resolution. Sometimes an effective leader may even orchestrate productive conflict to help the organization get unstuck.

g. Time allocation skill: Priorities and time allocation need to be aligned with organization strategies. Time is a limited resource in business. The leaders need to have a clear sense of what is important, where to devote their time and resources, and how to communicate priorities to others.

h. Decision making skill: Leaders understand decisions must be effective. The leaders, who make decisions, commit to seeing them through. They develop the skill of making the best decision possible with the best information possible in the timeliest manner. They are quick to decide and quick to take responsibility for their decisions. The key skill in becoming an effective leader is the skill of decision making.

i. Caring skill: Effective leaders care about people and organization. They manage people with something we call tough empathy. The leaders empathize passionately - and realistically - with people, and they care intensely about the work people do. Leaders know disciplined approach to value creation. They have ability to define disciplines that cut costs, maintain efficiency, invest in profitable products, and get rid of the unprofitable ones. Leaders also balance power with caring.

j. Enforcement skill: Organization requires deterrent enforcement mechanisms to ensure recognition of good result and punishment for failure and indiscipline acts. Enforcement can be dangerous and stressful, but highly rewarding for those called to serve.

Enforcement activity protects the integrity of the organization. These challenges require effective, highly competent individuals to serve as leaders.

Effective leadership skill includes being certain that the thoughts and attitudes we hold are in alignment with the role we perform. Leaders must maximize the potentiality of others to meet the organization's vision, mission, and goals. They must be able to manage individual and group performance with an understanding of group dynamics and team building.

Leaders must actively listen and communicate effectively to persuade others and build consensus and trust. They should understand and be empathetic toward individual's emotions and needs and be able to resolve conflicts in a respectful manner.

Leadership takes place in many levels throughout an organization. Leaders bring out the best in the people around them, and encourage others to see the big picture rather than honing in on the details. It takes a certain natural tendency combined with learned skills to be an effective leader. Effective leadership skill includes being certain that the thoughts and attitudes we hold are in alignment with the role we perform.

6th

IMAGE BUILDING SKILL

Leadership is about working with people, and no formula can turn you into a leader unless and until you commit yourself to being a person people want to follow. Leader shows the capacity to lead others or promotes the activity of leading; which includes: lead, direct, command, rule, etc. Leaders must maximize the potential of others to meet the organization's vision, mission, and goals. They must be able to manage individual and group performance with an understanding of group dynamics and team building.

Leaders must actively listen and communicate effectively to persuade others and build consensus and trust. They should understand and be empathetic toward individual's emotions and needs and be able to resolve conflicts in a respectful manner.

Leading a team is not the same as managing them. Leaders need to develop new directions, i.e. inspiring the team to change direction. Leading means the manner and approach of providing direction, implementing plans, motivating people; and influencing people in reaching a goal, etc.

Leadership capacities should start to become apparent. He/she will decide whether he/she wants to lead or follow the pack.

The image of an organization is the perception of the organization based on what that organization says or does. Behind everything that an organization says and does are its members, so building the image or your organization will depend solely on what members you have.

You must communicate the goals and ideals of your organization to your members, as they are the organization's ambassadors to the general public. Leaders feel that it is far better to proactively manage their leadership image rather than leave it to chance.

Many leaders assume image building is superficial and therefore unimportant or only for celebrities, but actually image is an asset that can and must be managed. Your effectiveness as a leader is tied directly to your image. Image is impression of one or something; which evolves a mental conception; symbolic of an attitude and orientation; representation or description of a person or something; and set of values that corresponds to a particular personality.

Self-image is a psychic structure; part of one's sense of self, it is a construct in the mind. Self image not only gives the individual his sense of personal identity, but it determines subsequent experience of him/herself, his/her life, and his/her environment; determines his/her sense of being, and his/her inner experience.

The self-image is constituted of self-boundaries that determine the range of the individual's experience, perception, and actions. Leadership image can be enhanced by focusing on three key principles, i.e.:

a. Know what you stand for: Able to explain core beliefs and values which becomes the foundation for a leadership image, both authentic and compelling.

b. Communicate across cultures: Leaders must develop critical leadership qualities and to successfully communicate to several cultures. Leaders manage their image, with consistency and cultural sensitivity

c. Build credibility, trust, and loyalty: The cornerstone of credibility is expertise and relationships that are built on trust. Credibility is the foundation upon which image rests. Organization images depend on leaders who operate with a high degree of credibility and integrity, not leaders who focus solely on self interests and the bottom line.

Image may not necessarily be everything, but it is a critical factor in leadership overall effectiveness. You may believe that the best possible preparation for success is to have a strong and positive self-image. Improve your self-image by accepting things about yourself that are true. All these characteristics can be positive or negative depending on what meaning you choose to attribute to them. Image doesn't make the entire package, but it does reflect, visually, who people think you are.

Your appearance strongly influences other people's perception of you and it will affect how they relate to you. You may know who you are; however your image may fail to convey it. Your view of yourself is shaped by your unique thoughts and beliefs.

Image - the perception that others form of you as a result of the impression you make on them - has a significant correlation to perceptions of leadership skill and the ability to perform on the job. You can successfully manage and control other people's perception of you, simply by projecting the right visual and behavioral style. Your image can give you the competitive edge that is crucial in ensuring success.

Lee Kuan Yew of Singapore stands out, in many respects, as one of the great transformational leaders of our times. Why? Because, through a three-decade period, he shaped and drove Singapore's development, catapulting the city-state from a Third World backwater, to the front ranks of the First World. (Aditya Vikram Birla, Transformational Leadership, 2008)

People who are skilful in making good impressions generally command a higher degree of personal power, trust and credibility. You should know how to handle yourself properly in your daily interactions with other people - this can help you achieve greater interpersonal impact.

Self-image will boost your self-esteem and make you feel better, more confident and self-assured. Your image as a leader can be a huge asset - or a liability. Once you understand what others see, you can determine how well their perceptions align with the image you want to portray - and then develop skills to close the gap. Image building is matter of recognizing genuine aspects of yourself that should be coming across to other people.

Crafting your image requires you to gain a clear picture of the image people are currently perceiving, decide what image you would like to portray, and develop the skills to close the gap.

Character

Character sets the foundation for leadership. The main ingredient of good leadership is good character. Behavior is an indication of one's character. This behavior can be strong or weak, good or bad. A person with strong character shows drive, energy, determination, self-discipline, willpower, and nerve. She sees what she wants and goes after it. She attracts followers.

Character is the core foundation on which individual leadership is based. Character refers to self-concepts and individual differences in goals and values, which influence choices, intentions, the meaning and salience of what is experienced in life.

Differences in character are moderately influenced by socio-cultural learning and maturity throughout life. Principle of character recognition is defined by what you do, not what you say or believe. Every choice you make helps define the kind of person you are choosing to be.

Good character requires doing the right thing, even when it is costly or risky. You don't have to take the worst behavior of others as a standard for yourself. You can choose to be better than that. What you do matters, and one person can make a big difference. The payoff for having good character is that it makes you a better person and it makes the world a better place

Character is made, not born. It is a springboard from which all we do and say in life comes. Character is moral order seen through the medium of an individual nature. Each individual brings to bear on his or her life the formative forces of perseverance, hope, compassion and creativity.

Character is what you are. Character is formed by a variety of minute circumstances, more or less under the regulation and control of the individual; not a day passes without its discipline, whether for good or for evil. Character is undergoing constant change, for better or for worse either being elevated on the one hand or degraded on the other.

Character may bask in the limelight, surrounded by enormous popular acclaim, or he or she may labor lifelong in the shadows, hailed only by those whose lives they immediately touch.

Character equals integrity that means you always do what is right; even when no one is watching you. It means that fear and guilt are all but eliminated from your life because you have nothing to hide and nothing to hold you back from achieving success

The individual who has character is the potentially to accomplish at a far greater level; has fully absorbed and assimilated the present social environment and its conventions and ideas; has taken these a step further by personalizing, individualizing them with his own values, attitudes, and energies. A person of character shows

   a. Know the difference between right and wrong - Promote to do
       what is right - solve moral dilemmas; morality of believing that
       there are real and objective standards of behavior, that there
       are such things as virtues, and such things as vices; that certain
       things are unarguably good, and others unarguably bad

   b. Set a good example for everyone - Use wisdom and good judgment;
       and be positive; have faith in vision; excited, enthusiastic, and
       confident that his dreams can be accomplished; committed
       to excellence and continuous improvement; tolerate failure -
       learn from failure, realize not everything goes right; believe
       passionately in teamwork - discourage rivalry, interpersonal
       conflict, and competition between groups

The best sort of character, however, can not be formed without effort. It needs exercise of self watchfulness, self discipline, and self-control.

Character is not the richest in means, but in spirit; not the greatest in worldly position, but in true honor; not the most intellectual, but the most virtuous; not the most powerful and influential, but the most truthful, upright and honest; exhibits itself in conduct, guided and inspired by principle, integrity, and practical wisdom. Your characters will become symbolic if:

a. Show your quality: Great quality doesn't come easy. It takes commitment. Leaders with the necessary leadership skills, trust of their colleagues, and the right attitude, overcome most challenges and get things done.

b. Have dominant traits: Know how to embody the traits that a leader must embody to be effective, and how to perform the functions that a leader must perform to be effective.

A person of character is characterized by attributes which include trustworthiness, respect, responsibility, fairness, caring, and citizenship. A leader "walks his/her talk" and does what he/she says he/she will do; treating members of group or team fairly and consistently within the values he/she articulates. It means he/she must be sensitive to what he/she says and makes commitments to, so that there is no disconnect between what he/she says and does.

Effective leaders are people of sound character. The character and living out of a set of principles grounds us and gives us stability. Our character is basically a combination of our habits. This will be an attempt to identify and establish the habits that, when combined with strong character, will produce highly effective people.

Habits express our character and produce our effectiveness. Leaders increase effectiveness and productivity by focusing on the things most important to the organization.

Personality

Some persons believe that great leaders are born. Yes, it may be true, some people have are born with natural talents. Leaders are continually working on themselves and studying for self improvement of their natural talents. The integration of character and temperament reflects one's personality. The temperament of any person depends on

a. How he/she feels moved to action whenever something impresses him/her - Quickly and vehemently excited, or only slowly and superficially

b. How he/she reacts, when he/she is praised or rebuked or offended, when he/she feels sympathy for or aversion against somebody - act at once, quickly, in order to oppose the impression; or does he/she feel more inclined to remain calm and to wait

c. How he/she act if in a storm, or in a dark forest, or on a dark night the thought of imminent danger comes to him/her - the excitement of the soul last for a long time or only for a moment; impression continue, so that at the recollection of such impression the excitement is renewed; he/she conquer such excitement speedily and easily, so that the remembrance of it does not produce a new excitement.

A highly effective leader has strong personality. Personality plays a key role, principally in making it harder or easier for a particular individual to learn the key leader behaviors.

If you have the right personality traits without the resulting behaviors, you'll see no improvement in leadership effectiveness; but if you do the right behaviors, even if you don't have the best personality traits, you'll be a long way along the road to leadership effectiveness.

Personality is that peculiar, incalculable thing that distinct us from everyone else. Each human being is known for its personality. Our personality is what we show to others; which reflects our inner character and temperament. Our temperament is a combination of traits, as we were born with and that subconsciously affects our behavior.

Personality plays a key role, principally in making it harder or easier for a particular individual to learn the key leader behaviors. If you have the right personality traits without the resulting behaviors, you'll see no improvement in leadership effectiveness; but if you do the right behaviors, even if you don't have the best personality traits, you'll be a long way along the road to leadership effectiveness.

To be a leader, you must be able to influence others to achieve organization goals. Leadership is not about personal power. It is not about harassing persons or managing them using fear factors. It is about encouraging others towards the goal of the organization. It is helping everyone in the business to see the big picture of the organization.

You must be a leader, a respected personality but never a boss. Leader's personality is about who you are, what you know, and what you do.

The personality is not about what you make others work on. Personality embraces your moods, attitudes, opinions, motivations, and style of thinking, perceiving, speaking, and acting. An individual's personality is a combination of lifetime experiences as well as genetic characteristics.

Personality is an indelible characteristic and results in a pattern of predictable behavior. You can not be a leader and unless you have right judgment, you must be able to determine situations, weigh the decision, and actively seek out for a solution. Good decision-making is vital to the successfulness of your personality and organization.

Effective leadership is the foundation for creating value within the organization. To achieve success, you must be able to cultivate highly effective leaders throughout the organization. A leader must embody to be effective, and how to perform the functions that a leader must perform to be effective. Self-image in effective leadership includes, but not limited to:

Assertiveness

Assertiveness plays a key role. Assertive means speak or act in a manner that compels recognition; in anticipation of denial or objection. It states confidently without need for proof or regard for evidence. A leader can confidently state personal and group needs in an effective manner. Assertion is a matter of getting recognition from the others; therefore it's to be stated positively with great confidence.

Assertiveness is expressing our views, needs, wants and rights directly, without guilt or anxiety and without violating the rights of others. In a broad sense, assertiveness is expressing any emotion (except debilitating anxiety or fear) in its appropriate context.

Physically, assertiveness is giving the facial and postural actions or expressions which are appropriate to the emotion or message we wish to send or which are congruent with what we feel inside. Assertive are appropriate to the emotion or message we wish to send or which are congruent with what we feel inside.

Assertive action is the direct, appropriate behavior intended to constructively fulfill our needs such as in healthy interactions with others. Being a leader you should remember, that it is your job to make certain decisions for desired outcome. You need to assert your delegated decision in a way that people are clear as to what is expected of them.

There is a difference between being a tough and being an assertive leader. Being tough all the time is a sign of a weak leader, using his power of leadership not to get the job done, but simply because they can. He/she leaves the follower unsure of what is expected of them, and the job doesn't get done right; or being too passive, showing they are not confident of their capabilities.

The assertive style is characterized by a great deal of group involvement. When this style is used, the leader employs behaviors such as the following: diplomacy, respect for others, attention to needs of associates, flexibility, honesty, straightforwardness, empathy, patience

The assertive leader is comfortable with him/herself and this encourages others to be comfortable. The assertive leader tends to look on the positive side of things and to expect cooperation from, and pleasant interactions with others. The assertive leader will give others trust and the benefit of the doubt when it is sensible to do so.

Assertiveness uses behavior which is confident, sincere, caring, open and non-judgmental. Assertive leaders know how to really listen, without being easily threatened by whatever is said to them. They are willing to be convinced of new or different views, if they make sense.

Assertiveness is an integral part of effective communication. Assertive – standing up for oneself in such a way that does not violate the basic rights of other people. It is a direct, honest, and appropriate expression of one's feelings and opinions.

Be assertive in not necessarily aggressive - standing up for oneself in such a way that the rights of the other person are violated in the process. It is an attempt to humiliate or put down the other person. To be positively assertive, you need to communicate needs honestly and non-confrontationally. You may gain self-respect.

We can distinguish between assertive affect (emotion), assertive expression or communication (verbal and non-verbal), assertive valuing, assertive thinking and assertive action or behavior. Assertive expression is expressing oneself directly, appropriately, and effectively; without anxiety, guilt, or endangering the rights and well-being of others.

Assertive thinking or cognition is thinking which supports assertiveness and assists in its expression. Assertive emotion, desire and valuing is the honest expression of any healthy emotion, want, desire, need, opinion or value in an appropriate context in a manner helpful to the individual or group.

Assertive expression can be converted into assertive behavior or action. Assertive behavior has positive effects on us and others, achieves our goals, meets our needs, realizes our values, and advances the welfare of the individual, group or society without endangering their rights or welfare.

Assertive behavior is direct, problem solving behavior that expresses the person's true needs, wants, values and goals without endangering the welfare and rights of others. Leaders, who are perceived as under-assertive, fail to stand up for oneself, or standing up for oneself in such an ineffectual manner that one's rights are easily violated. Highly assertive tend to be viewed as less effective.

Too much or too little perceived assertiveness may be the most common weakness in would-be leaders. Assertiveness requires intelligence, self-discipline, and charisma, which will be beneficial to:

a. Increase productivity through more effective communication. People who are highly assertive can be seen as being aggressive while people who lack assertiveness are often passive and get taken advantage of. There are times when it is appropriate to be more or less assertive and we need to recognize when these times are.

b. Increase confidence handling difficult behavior in others: Leadership is the process of directing the behavior of others toward the accomplishment of some common objectives.

c. Reduce interruptions: Leaders can reduce the harm interruptions inflict. They reduce complexity to clarity.

d. Gain more time for creative and development opportunities: Effective change in the organization starts with the leader's own self-development. Creativity is more than a "soft" leadership skill which generating good ideas from others. Highly effective leadership has associated with the ability to successfully solve problems, a hallmark of creative thinking.

e. Able to manage time more effectively and enjoyed greater self-esteem

f. Improve decision making and reduction in procrastination

g. Able to manage others effectively: The strength of a leader is measured by the ability to facilitate the self-leadership of others. The most effective leadership is to help others feel they are working from their own initiative.

h. Increase work effectiveness and productivity: Productivity will be higher and problems solved more rapidly if people are encouraged to explain problems and start working through solutions. People who are working in more effective environment exhibit more productivity.

i. Feel more in control: Leaders have to take control and map their destination in a clear goal. Effective leadership demonstrates vision in actions.

Assertion seems to be obvious but it is often forgotten by those who rise to leadership positions; the only thing that makes people successful leaders, is if other people will willingly follow them. A leader should be flexible and adaptable, utilizing assertiveness appropriately depending upon the situation.

The leaders are still the ones who know when - and how - to get tough. They know how to assert their authority. Assertiveness is the backbone of leadership, if you don't stand up for your own beliefs and goals, you can't expect anyone to follow. Wishy-washy people don't make good leaders.

One of the four basic interpersonal skills that provide a foundation for leadership is assertion (the others are self-management, negotiation and empathy). Leaders need to be able to express their ideas, opinions, desires, feelings, strategies, observations, orders, and persuasive messages in an effective way.

Without assertiveness leaders must rely solely on their abilities to model effective or use body language of some type. The latter two influence styles are important, however, but cannot be the total package of a leader's communication skill.

Active

An effective leader is active, not passive. Active leaders establish and communicate their subordinates' authority, responsibilities and work parameters. Having this knowledge of what is expected of them and the encouragement to perform well, followers will gain the autonomy that most of them crave.

Powerful people impress by saying less. The more you say, the more likely you are to say something foolish. Stay with a task and don't give up; diligent with the inner strength and determination to pursue well-defined goals. Although a task may become difficult, individuals will continue to work until it is completed. It may teach self-discipline and bring satisfaction. Active is marked by

a. Initiate the action - Perform an outcome, show efforts

b. Express the thought - Posing questions, evaluate and suggest solution

c. Not quiescent - Act rather than contemplate, encourage involvement, exert influence

d. Take participation - Engage in full-time activity.

Silent is not a golden behavior anymore. Use words appropriately and positively. Always say less than necessary. When you are trying to impress people with words, the more you say, the more common you appear, and the less in control. Even if you are saying something banal, it will seem original if you make it vague, open-ended, and sphinx-like.

Active person plays a key role in helping other to learn about life, make sound decisions, and solve problems. Initiate activities and literally convince others to become active, or be responsible participants will be a positive experience.

Initiative

Often what most people lack is the courage - the courage to initiate. Initiative means moving outside your comfort zone. It means seeking out opportunities and being willing to act. Leaders encourage initiative. Leaders elicit ideas, listen to opinions, and encourage followers.

Leaders draw out the talent and performance that will enhance the reputations of their followers and accomplish the goals of the organization. They might be ambitious, persistent, and energetic, and above all, take also the initiative for change. Initiation refers to a leader's ability to start activities and organize work. Strong initiators prefer not to let the group completely structure its work or make all of the on-the-job decisions. They prefer not only to determine what must be done but also who does it and how it is to be done.

Effective leadership is not the result of doing one thing. Success is the result of the dynamics that leaders have set in motion. Effective leadership dynamics are the results of everything that a leader has done that produces forward motion. Success, therefore, doesn't come about because you did one thing but many things that play on each other.

A leader takes initiatives to do things differently; make a difference through your actions. Leadership is about learning that leads to constructive change. Leadership is to promote adaptive or useful changes. A leader must have talent or specific skills at some task at hand. He must possess initiative, tied up with a certain degree of charisma that motivates and stirs people to motion.

Problem Solver

How you face problems is one of the critical factors that helps determine how successful you will be in organization. It's also one of the key qualities of a leader. Leaders solve problems- followers go to leaders to get their problems solved. The things to do when you face with a problem are

a. Assume there is an answer out there: Worrying about the problem gets you nowhere; working towards the answer will get you everywhere. Recognize you control your attitude and thoughts about any given situation. Leaders control their attitude and focus on results.

b. Collect all the facts about the problem - Most problems are not as big as they seem at first, once everything is known. Keep asking questions. Leaders are great at asking the right questions-and listening.

c. Put things in perspective to what they really are; and ponder what actions you might personally do that could resolve the problem. Brainstorm all ideas; bounce your ideas off other everybody.

d. Be decisive, pick a solution, and implement it. Break the solution into small steps, and then focus on the most immediate steps.

Effective leaders solve problems and make decisions with a high level of competence.

Role Player

Leaders have learned to play different roles in different situations. They may take the role of teacher, coach, dictator, etc. This allows them to deal with different group members, peers or superiors in different ways.

If leaders possess certain skills, and role playing is one of those skills, then anyone who can role play can learn to be a leader. As they become more proficient and gain confidence in playing the role of leader, their personality gradually changes, and they become more comfortable in the leadership role. A role player should:

1. Facilitate: A leader is facilitator in the group. Leaders create teams and organizations where people can talk openly and honestly about the difficult issues needing to be discussed.

81

Facilitative leadership solves problems in a way that takes into account many people's interests, not just the leader's.

As a result, facilitative leadership leads people to take responsibility and ownership for their actions. Finally, it enables teams to learn from their experiences. Leaders should particularly well suite to discussion of international conflict management and resolution; i.e.:

a. Role confusion: Situation where an individual has trouble determining which role he/she should play. In the organization, when developing a system, be sure to provide enough information about each role so that the person role playing can assume a realistic persona.

    Role ambiguity or role confusion, on the other hand, occurs when members of the role set fail to communicate to the focal person, the expectation they have or information needed to perform the role. People experience role ambiguity when they do not know what is expected of them.

b. Role conflict: Situation where a member who fulfills a certain role has a conflict with fulfilling another role. Leaders focus upon the dynamics of conflict. The emphasis is upon methods of more effectively handling conflict.

    Role conflict occurs when members of the role set expect different things from the focal person, and when internalized values, ethics or personal standard collide with other expectations.

2. Challenge: A leader must project fearlessness in facing challenges. Challenge motivates the followers become newly engaged, working in problem-solving teams with leader to tackle problems. Leaders are using challenges as opportunities for growth and transformation. A few challenges are:

a. Deliver value for the organization. Leader has to deliver value. He/she can define, measure, and communicate the value delivered to the organization Without clear definition or agreement concerning what "value" actually is and the ability to set and manage expectations around it, his/her future is effectively doomed.

b. Meet organization's objectives: Once a leader sequences organization objectives within a given time frame, the next step is to create activities that will help members meet each objective.

   Leaders decide which activities are most relevant to your desired objectives. Take the time to revise existing activities and to create new ones that meet the needs of the organization.

c. Develop organization's strategy: Strategy development follows the creation and affirmation of the organization's purpose statement, environmental and data collection and analysis, and identification of critical issues.

   It entails: examining the organization's critical issues; determining how the organization's strengths and skills can be employed to address the critical issues; analyzing opportunities and strengths and looking for ways to synthesize it; exploring and choosing the best approaches for the organization.

d. Deal with change and uncertainty: Organization should continue to change. Change is inevitable. More importantly, change is necessary for the organization and people to survive.

e. Attract the members: The members are the heart of the organization; if you don't attract them, you'll never get your organization off to a good future. And if you can't keep them, the organization will fizzle out and die.

f. Create conducive environment: Working environment does have significant impact on productivity, and creativity.

3. Promote connectivity, i.e. collaboration, cross-fertilization, and coordination. Most members may not feel the need to role-play;

therefore it has no tangible effect on their day-to-day life and organization's progress.

Leader encourage member to perform actively role plays that illuminate issues and engage the stakeholders, and interact a member with other

Members should be encouraged by the leader to bear in mind that, even in the verge of potential conflict, there are always sufficient elements to revert into cooperation potential; i.e. improve the enabling environment for cooperation within the organization, facilitate cooperation and concrete solutions to the most acute problems, and explore tools that implies the opening of positive grounds for joint activities and decision-making.

A leader is the key player in the organization that is comprised of challenge and risk.

Attractive

You cannot be an effective leader without knowing your own strengths and weaknesses. Power comes from attraction. Leaders have to rely more on a combination of inducement and attraction. The ability to establish preferences tends to be associated with intangible assets such as an attractive personality, culture, etc.

Leaders, who are authentic, attract followers, they are viewed as always being themselves, and therefore followers know what to expect from them and can rely on them, come thick or thin.

Authenticity provides the leader with the currency to obtain 'buy-in' from key stakeholders, because it builds and maintains trust. Authenticity is the bedrock upon which the other facets are built. Most people would acknowledge that many leaders have the look. They tend to have that tall, lean, attractive appearance.

Leaders work hard on maintaining an image of health and robustness. They work out, jog, diet and take care of personal grooming and wardrobe. They feel that being attractive is part of their charisma and since attractiveness is influence, and influence is power, that they increase their ability to lead.

Creative

It's not enough for the leader to be creative. The people who are led must also be taught to be creative. When the leader hogs all the knowledge, then nobody knows what to do until the leader gives the word. Effective leaders don't tell people what to do; they help people decide for themselves what to do.

The leaders search for and discover opportunity, introduce positive change and make quantum leads forward in creating new product and processes. Individuals who are creative are able to bring about change and visualize future opportunities. The effective leaders are a critical resource needed to find answers to difficult problems.

Creativity means finding ways to get things done, even in the face of obstacles or doubt. Effective leader knows that creativity is important. Sometimes the best way to accomplish a goal is to do something different and leaders know when to encourage and foster that kind of creativity.

Leaders are also creative in terms of how they lead their team. The leaders expect excellence in those around them, and they make those expectations known. They invite people to speak up, and they listen and respond to those who do; not guardians of the status quo. They foster a climate in which the search for quality and better methods becomes a way of life; don't bark orders.

They use positive reinforcement to influence people toward the behavior they desire; don't isolate themselves from the people they lead. They create a sense of family by mingling with them, becoming acquainted with their problems and concerns, and looking for ways to help them; don't pretend to have all the answers and don't try to do it all themselves.

They ask for information and advice, before making decisions, and make full use of the talents and skills of those around them. The creative process is what drives you to play the game of life. Creative is a synergistic combination of your capabilities:

a. Creative thinking skills: The kind of thinking that leads to new insights, novel approaches, fresh perspectives, and whole new ways of understanding and conceiving of things.

b. Cross-functional expertise: Individuals from different backgrounds draw upon their pools of tacit to contribute.

c. Internal motivation: Motivation addresses the degree to which ones want to or are willing to complete the work necessary for them to reach their goals

The fuel for creative breakthroughs is not only passion, purpose, and power, but also confusion, conflict, and collapse. Successful organizations will be those that spread knowledge throughout all levels and encourage people at all levels to apply that knowledge in creative ways.

There are many characters that demonstrate leader's self-image, include but not limited to:

Courage

Courage is strength to lead in the difficult circumstances. Courageous leaders are strong and unlikely to quit. This kind of courage displays itself in an organization when a leader is willing to admit his/her mistake; when he/she is willing to stand up for his/her beliefs; or when he/she must challenge others. Have the perseverance to accomplish a goal, regardless of the seemingly insurmountable obstacles. Display a confident calmness when under stress.

Leadership is not always seen in the brightest or the most talented, but it is always found in the courageous.

Productive

Conclude with the win that works. Advance towards an important goal whenever possible, even if that takes you in an unpopular direction.

Effective leaders generate higher productivity, lower costs, and more opportunities; create results, attain goal, realize vision and other objectives more quickly and at a higher level of quality.

Optimism

In a related vein, be positive and upbeat. People are not likely to believe or to follow if they are not convinced that success is at hand. Don't be fool-hardy, but be confident in your own abilities and those around you. This is the tendency to take the most hopeful and cheerful view and to expect the best outcome.

Optimists see opportunities, possibilities and silver linings in every situation. They often contend that, with hard work, focus, resilience and a bit of luck, a positive outcome is possible.

People are naturally drawn to leaders who are positive, upbeat and cheerful - who have a "We can do this!" type of attitude.

Pro-activeness

Deeply understand the situation. Acting without thought can seem very Jedi, but consensus trumps a light saber every time. Leaders are proactive; instead of waiting for breaks. They identify and fine-tune their attitudes, beliefs, and actions.

Proactive people meet challenges head on and affirm that they will achieve the desires of their heart.

Confidence

Effective leaders also need to be transparent - resulting in exhibition of confidence. A leader is a person who inspires confidence in others.

Confidence and belief are essential for effective leadership. A leader can maintain a clear vision of where he wishes to go

Enthusiasm

People will only push themselves to accomplish extraordinary things for you when they share in your enthusiasms. That sharing is called critical convergence, the joining of your enthusiasms and theirs so they are as enthusiastic as you about meeting the challenges you face.

Until a critical convergence happens, you can't get great results consistently. Leaders must possess genuine enthusiasm and have a positive outlook, which helps in persuading others to take action or risks and keeps them motivated.

Self-control

Leaders must choose what they will do and not do and then accept the consequences of their choices. This includes personal discipline in behaviors and lifestyle.

Self-control implies that as a leader you have sufficient drive and initiative, as well as a clear vision and focus.

Self-control keeps a person motivated and focused on goals, and it also contributes to momentum. Leaders must be able to create climates that foster not only performance but also pride and purpose.

They must have what we refer to as emotional intelligence - a heightened sense of self-awareness, the ability to manage their emotions as well as those of others, to build rapport and relationships with a diverse group of people, to motivate others, create a believable vision, and negotiate a broad range of social and business situations.

Responsiveness

Responsiveness is the extent to which people are willing to respond to us and our questions.

Some people are highly responsive and will give lots of information about themselves, their problems and needs. Others are unwilling or unable to respond in this way and we see these people often as being negative or difficult.

A leader must be credible, having competency and displaying consistency and wholeness in words and behavior such that others have a deep confidence in his or her abilities and behavior. He or she must be inspiring, as well as courageous, able to make the tough calls and perform the tough tasks, and having a propensity for taking risks. The leader has to produce results, achieving the vision in the most efficient, holistic and measurable manner.

Leaders employ leadership skills in highly effective, more creative and powerful ways. The leaders of organization demonstrate and develop the skills needed to improve personal and professional effectiveness, increasing trust and influence in their roles; skills that spark the kind of energy and enthusiasm that make productivity and performance soar.

7th

COMMUNICATION SKILL

To be an effective leader, you must be comfortable talking to other people about their behavior or performance. You must be willing and able to make decisions. And you should enjoy helping others succeed. Communication skills are essential for the success of individuals and to the accomplishment of organizational goals.

Many of the problems that occur in an organization are the direct result of people failing to communicate. Faulty communication causes the most problems.

The effective leaders have the ability to make their intentions known in a clear and unambiguous manner. They are able to direct others concisely so as to leave no room for misinterpretation or doubt. They direct in a supportive, non-threatening way, focusing on the job to be done and their confidence in doing it.

Communication is one of the most important elements in motivation. Leader's attitude, listening, and feedback are essential for good communication. The things which can make a follower gets motivated are: challenging task, recognition, positive communication, good relation, broad range of responsibilities, being a part of organization, respect, freedom to learn, freedom for innovation and empowerment.

Motivated followers know what their duties are. They know how their tasks relate to organization's goals and objectives, what results are expected of them, and they are free to accomplish results in their own way.

Just being able to talk has little to do with effective communication. To be an effective leader, you must be an effective communicator. Communication is the means by which information flows into, through, and out of an organization.

An organization's culture is perpetuated through communication, and communication is at the heart of an organization's ability to do its work. The quality of the culture, and of the work, is dependent upon the quality of the communication. Effective communication has three critical areas which are the key to winning organizational trust and confidence, i.e.:

a.   Help members understand the organization's overall strategies. Make your expectations clear, then back up a bit and give employees room to do their job. That doesn't mean to never look back.

   Even your top performers need clear expectations; give them a target, provide resources and guidance and remove obstacles when necessary. Then let them do their job. Don't forget to check back later; and inspect what you expect isn't micromanagement. But it's a good management.

b.   Help members understand how they contribute to achieving key objectives. If leaders become actively involved and promote organizational and personal success, they can empower people to perform better.

   Effective leaders influence people not by ordering them to do something, but by causing them to want to attempt it. Not by telling others what to do, but by explaining why something is important. In pursuing excellence, the leaders focus on defining goals in simple terms so that members in all parts of the organization can believe that mutual goals are important and attainable.

c. Share information with members on both how the organization is doing and how member's own group is doing - relative to the objectives.

Communicate means to provide information and insights into the major issues, problems and opportunities facing the organization. Communication flows in 2 (two) ways, i.e.:

a. Formal - Messages move along its prescribed and regulated pathways

b. Informal - Messages are exchanged unofficially in the organization

Effective communication occurs only if the receiver understands the exact information or idea that the sender intended to transmit. Two types of organizational communication include:

a. External communication: Ensure people aware of your organization. Image is extremely important in external communication.

b. Internal communication that is essential to attracting and retaining members. You must provide the direction for the organization by consistently communicating the important message; motivate members through various forms of communication.

Simply using the words, i.e. hope, feel, appreciate, understand, disgust, in your everyday sentences can help conveying a positive communication style with others. When a leader picks up on subtle wording patterns; your members will be most persuaded not by logic, but by the emotional impact that they receive with interpersonal communication. This type of communication focuses on how you respond and how others react.

"Communication skills and the ability to work well with different types of people are very important," Bill Gates said. (Shane Schick, Bill Gates Needs To Brush Up On His People Skills, 2007)

Communication is composed of different methods: words, voice, tone and non-verbal clues. Of these, some are more effective in delivering a message than others. Interpersonal communication consists of:

a. Verbal communication, i.e. oral communication and written communication

b. Non-verbal communication, i.e. physical, visual, auditory, and chemical communication

It is crucial for members to be informed in effective way to help or and avoid meaningless meetings. Your words can explain, promise, and authorize but become a mess in the minds of others if you do not communicate effectively. Interpersonal communication will help you to:

a. Relate to others and build relationships: Interpersonal communication enhances teamwork, build strong working relationships.

b. Express ourselves and meet our needs: Communication connects to the needs and feelings of one and others. When people have their needs met, they feel good and when their needs are not met, they feel bad.

c. Share with others Followers don't need a shoulder to cry on, a buddy, a simpatico or a commiseration. Everyone wants to be liked. While you shouldn't advocate a monk-like existence, you need to keep in mind that although followers would like to have you as a friend, they'll need a leader if they want to be successful.

Just being able to talk has little to do with effective communication. To be an effective leader, you must be an effective communicator. Good communication should:

a. Answer basic questions like who, what, when, where; be relevant and not overly wordy

b. Focus on the people's interests: Effective communication interacts people, connects their own and other people's interests. Communication seeks to integrate people's culture, attitudes, knowledge, practices, perceptions, needs and interest.

c. Use specific facts and figures and active verbs

d. Use a conversational tone for readability; include examples and visual aids when needed

e. Be tactful and good natured: Tact is the ability to induce change or communicate hurtful information without offending through the use of consideration, compassion, kindness, and reason. A tactful person recognizes others they don't want to hear something.

f. Be accurate: Effective communication leads to better understanding and provides accurate messages

g. Non discriminatory: Leaders use non-discriminatory language in all forms of communication.

Unclear, inaccurate, or inconsiderate communication can waste valuable time, alienate members, and destroy trust.

Communicating with others is an essential skill. When it comes to communication, what you say and what you don't say are equally important. Keep your followers informed.

Effective communication helps to ensure smoother interpersonal interactions, more productive organizations, more positive employee relations, more authentic outcome, clarity of vision, and effective leadership.

Non Verbal Communication

There is no doubt that people have different communication styles. Some people like to start off approaches with 'small talk', establishing rapport, and just getting to know others. People see you; not your credentials, i.e. sitting while others stand, lean back in their chairs, expansive gesturing, talking more, in louder voices, and interrupt others.

A substantial portion of communication is nonverbal. Every day, we respond to thousands on nonverbal cues and behaviors including postures, facial expression, eye gaze, gestures, and tone of voice. From our handshakes to our hairstyles, nonverbal details reveal who we are and impact how we relate to other people.

From the way we dress to the way we move, our nonverbal signals can reveal a great deal about our emotions, perceptions, and intentions, although many of these behaviors are so subtle that we rarely notice them consciously. By paying closer attention to other people's nonverbal behaviors, you will improve your own ability to communicate nonverbally.

Senses, eyes, ears and feelings and words and symbols are used to create meanings. Several different types of nonverbal communication are but not limited to:

    I. Physical communication: Things that are communicated on the physical level of body language. This is the personal type of communication. It includes facial expressions, tone of voice, sense of touch, sense of smell, and body motions. It includes:

    a. Expression: Something that communicates feeling. The ways we communicate without words is essential to becoming an effective leader. Non-verbal expressions, i.e.:

    1. Facial expression: Facial expressions are all forms of non-verbal communications that individuals send to each other. Leaders are responsible for the proportion of nonverbal communication.

Consider how much information can be conveyed with a smile or a frown.

While nonverbal communication and behavior can vary dramatically between cultures, the facial expressions for happiness, sadness, anger, and fear are similar throughout the world.

2. Eye contact: Looking, staring, and blinking are important nonverbal behaviors. When people encounter others or things they like; the rate of blinking increases, and pupils dilate. Looking at another person can indicate a range of emotions, including hostility, interest, and attraction. It signals interest in others and increases the speaker's credibility.

   People who make eye contact open the flow of communication and convey interest, concern, warmth, and credibility.

3. Body posture: Posture and movement can also convey a great deal on information. Nonverbal behaviors can indicate feelings and attitudes, research suggests that body language is far more subtle and less definitive People in power appear large, strong with relaxed posture i.e. slight forward lean, body facing speaker, relaxed posture, etc

4. Head and facial movements: Communication refers to head and facial movements, i.e. affirmative head nods, calm, expressive facial movements, appropriate smiling, etc. These are movements of the ears, eyes and eyebrows, mouth, nose and head.

   Smiling is a powerful cue that transmits happiness, friendliness, warmth, and liking. So, if you smile frequently you will be perceived as more likable, friendly, warm and approachable. Smiling is often contagious and people will react favorably. They will be more comfortable around you and will want to listen more.

5. Distracting personal habits: i.e. playing with hair, fiddling with pen or pencil, chewing gum, etc.

b. Gesture - Deliberate movements and signals are an important way to communicate meaning without words. Words can be manipulated, but gestures are harder to control. Common gestures include waving, pointing, and using fingers to indicate number amounts. Other gestures are arbitrary and related to culture.

If you fail to gesture while speaking; you may be perceived as boring and stiff. A lively speaking style captures the listener's attention, makes the conversation more interesting, and facilitates understanding.

c. Body language - Body language is the oldest language. There is a discrepancy between someone's words and their physical actions. Confusion may occur regarding what is heard or the message seems to be mixed. Usually in these instances, the verbal and non-verbal messages are in conflict. Body language accounts for a large part of meaningful communication.

The way we sit, stand, gesture, or orient ourselves in a group often helps others make accurate judgments about our thoughts, feelings, and intentions. Mannerisms such as a clenched jaw, narrowed eyes, or slumped posture can be interpreted as conveying anger, distrust, or disinterest. On the other hand, steady eye contact, a tilted head, and a reassuring smile can demonstrate interest and empathy.

II. Visual communication: Form of communication with visual effect, communication through visual aid. It is the conveyance of ideas and information in forms that can be read or looked upon. i.e.:

a. Aesthetic: Type of communication that takes place through creative expressions: playing instrumental music, singing, dancing, painting and sculpturing.

b. Signs: Mechanical type of communication, which includes the use of signal flags, the 21-gun salute, horns, smoke, and sirens.

c. Symbolic: Type of communication that makes use of religious, status, or ego-building symbols.

III. Auditory communication: Use patterns of sound for symbols which enable communication with others, include non-vocal noises, i.e.: show vocal quality, i.e. pleasant intonation, appropriate loudness, moderate rate of speech, etc.

IV. Chemical communication: Use pheromones to communicate or attract others, i.e.: smell (Women use perfume to attract men), tear, spit/expectorate, sweat, etc

Members project attitudes and feelings through non-verbal communication. Some needs such as approval, growth, achievement, and recognition may be met in relation to how perceptive the leader and members are to non-verbal communicate in themselves and in others on the organization.

Non-verbal communication plays a critical role ensuring the group truly receives and understands key messages. When in doubt people will trust the non-verbal message (what they see). Therefore, we can overlook non-verbal signals. On other hand, we are educated to use words to communicate. We may not verbally call someone stupid/dumb, but we may send the mess age non-verbally without realizing it.

Non-verbal cues, when interpreted correctly, provide individual with one means to do so. If the members show a true awareness to non-verbal cues, the organization will have a better chance to succeed, and honest.

Verbal Communication

Communications are shaping organization's culture. Many of the problems that occur in a organization are the direct result of people failing to communicate. Faulty communication causes the most problems. It leads to confusion and can cause a good plan to fail. Verbal communication is a communication type which uses words (verbal) to convey message to others

Communication is the exchange and flow of information and ideas from one person to another. Verbal communication skill requires ability the use of words, vocabulary, numbers and symbols and is organized in sentences using language.

Words spoken, listened to or written affect your life as well as others. They have the power to create emotions and move people to take action. When verbal communication is delivered accurately and clearly, you activate the mind and encourage creativity.

Verbal communication includes phrasing your words clearly and positively. Your words and the explanations you give affect thoughts and determine emotions. Verbal communication that includes questions helps you challenge beliefs.

If the nonverbal cues and the spoken message are incongruous, the flow of communication is hindered. Right or wrong, the receiver of the communication tends to base the intentions of the sender on the nonverbal cues he/she receives. Verbal communication is effective if:

a. Clear and concise: When you want something specific done, say so specifically, using clear and plain language. Members may have some difficulty doing their basic jobs, but adding mind-reading to their description is just plain unfair. Do not use hints, implications, or innuendos. Say what you want, and use plain English. Directness counts.

b. Friendly and professional: Effective communication should be able to reduce communication related delays and enhance collaboration; and stay connected with people

c. Give appropriate feedback: Positive and uplifting spoken or messages motivate and inspire.

d. Actively listened: We can improve communication if we listen actively, and speak competently, not just mindlessly.

e. Show awareness of non verbal communication styles: Good communication skills require a high level of self-awareness. Understanding your personal style of communicating will go a long way toward helping you to create good and lasting impressions on others. By becoming more aware of how others perceive you, you can adapt more readily to their styles of communicating. It can make another person more comfortable with you by selecting and emphasizing certain behaviors that fit within your personality and resonate with another.

f. Understand the cultural differences: Differences in the way people communicate often cause misunderstandings. Culture is often at the root of communication challenges.

There are many ways we can continually improve our verbal communication skills. These might include joining Toastmasters, taking a public speaking course, getting personal video-based speaking feedback, personal coaching, participating in interpersonal skill training, getting training on facilitating meetings, etc. A highly effective leader does whatever they can to continually improve their ability to speak to groups and persuade others to follow their lead.

Written Communication

Written communication skill involves any type of interaction that makes use of the written word. It is one of the two main types of communication, along with oral/spoken communication.

Letters are the most personal of written communications. They can help build relationships particularly by using a friendly and sincere tone. Formal and stereotyped expressions, on the other hand, keep the relationship between writer and reader stagnant.

Effective communication will sharpen interaction and develop skills in leading others in all types and at all levels of organizations. The purpose of writing a communication plan is to effectively use communications as a tool to help solve a problem or exploit an opportunity.

The key to truly effective writing is being absolutely clear about what we want to say, what we want people to do, think or feel as a result of reading our writing. Written communication is appropriate if:

    a.   People require a record of the communication for future reference.

    b.   People refer to details of the changes.

    c.   People need to communicate something with multiple parts or steps that ensure them to understand it.

It is wise to use both written and oral communication. The more emotional the issues, the more important it is to stress oral communication first. Written communication can be used as backup. Some of the requirements to ensure effective written communication include:

    a.   Try not to use abbreviations (unless appropriately defined), steer away from the use of symbols (such as ampersands [&]); brackets are used to play down words or phrases, dashes are generally used for emphasis, great care should always be taken to spell the names of people and companies correctly; numbers should be expressed as words when the number is less than 10 or is used to start a sentence (example: Ten years ago, my brother and I...).

The number 10, or anything greater than 10, should be expressed as a figure (example: My brother has 13 Matchbox cars.), quotation marks should be placed around any directly quoted speech or text and around titles of publications.

b. Simple and easy to understand: Straight to the point and avoid unnecessary repetition, avoid too many technical terms, clichés should be avoided, keep sentences short

c. Avoid slang, offensive language and discriminatory, racist or sexist language, jargon and hard-to-understand language

d. Don't use big letters, avoid overuse of bold, italics, underline

Written communication is very common in organization activities, so it is important for leaders to develop effective written communication skills. Some of the various forms of written communication that are used include:

a. Memos: A memo (short for memorandum) is a business document sent within the organization. A memo is an informal correspondence, often sent from one to another. Memos can be used to make announcements, discuss specific issues, or fulfill many other purposes, etc.

b. Electronic Mail: Email has become ubiquitous because it's so quick and easy to write and send. Despite its convenience, email should be crafted as carefully - or even more carefully - than any other type of business writing.

   Since the contents of an email can easily be forwarded on to others, stored for the long term, or monitored by your company, never include sensitive or potentially embarrassing information in an email.

c. Letters: A letter is used to communicate with people outside the organization. Always follow the fairly strict conventions that govern letters. Writing to each individual is the way most likely to gain their attention.

The effect is very strong if the letter is signed by a senior person. Internal memos have significantly less impact than business letters.

Only use letters for highly important messages otherwise it will rapidly become devalued and the target population may be annoyed.

d. News Releases: There may be a need to publicize the changes to customers, suppliers, investors, or the general public. Any external communication should be constructed with the organization's purpose

e. Bulletins/Newsletters: General messages can be placed in the organization's regular news media. Typically this is used for general awareness and promoting a good image. It is not a good vehicle for detailed information unless they are relevant to all readers.

f. Manuals: Detailed manuals, user guides, code lists, etc, may be a necessity with most systems. Expect them to become dusty - few people bother to refer to hard-copy documentation. Where possible, make them available electronically and linked to the system.

g. Poster: Some change messages might be suitable for notices

h. Others: Brochure, Job Description, Bookmark, Booklet, Name card, Marquee, Proposals, Websites, Telegrams, Fax, Postcards, Contracts, Advertisements, Documentation, Technical report, Performance reviews, Audit programs, Instructions & Procedures, Flyer, etc.

Effective communication depends on the message being received by the receiver intact and interpreted by the receiver to have the same meaning as when transmitted. In written communication the units of code are words and symbols (e.g. figures, punctuation). Most important uses of written communications are to:

a. Confirm agreements and actions: Communication enable a good coordination, and facilitates actions. Well-crafted agreements are powerful, clarifying intentions, detailing actions in support of a goal and creating momentum toward a shared vision. It helps reducing or even eliminating doubt because each person understands what is expected.

b. Motivate people: Communication can motivate, inspire and energize people, and recognize achievements. Communications make complexity manageable.

c. Build goodwill and relations: Communication really improves relationships. Leaders offer open communication with members in an atmosphere of mutual trust and respect.

d. Keep people informed: A leader uses a number of different means of communication to keep everyone informed. He/she keeps the lines of communication open.

The importance of writing skills has become more evident; even as many organizations rely increasingly on computers and other new technologies to meet their obligations.

Oral Communication

People keep their thoughts in their heads. They may not even know how to convey their thinking they're so out of the habit of talking, discussing, and debating. Ask questions after giving or receiving instructions.

Leaders ask feedback to make sure the message gets through. Don't give orders; discuss things that are going to happen. Measure your success in terms of the job getting done and the degree to which instructions are followed. Be sure to take a moment to think before you speak and have an idea of what you want to say rather than winging it.

Leaders should continually improve their verbal skills. They can't inspire and energize people with memos, mission statements, data and analysis, charts, goals and objectives, measurements, systems, or processes. Highly interconnected and dependent upon is effect of a leader's communication skills - especially verbal communication skills.

Leaders who are learning the basic persuasion skills of clarifying and simplifying what the leader's saying, tuning into the members, and grabbing them by handling their emotions, is critical to effective leadership.

To ensure an efficient and effective oral communication, leaders should:

a. Keep the message understood by members and vice versa

b. Control over the flow of the communication

Oral communication can be a very effective way of conveying a message as it can spread quickly in an organization. This type of communication is more appropriate when:

a. People are getting discourage: Oral communication provides more opportunities for getting and keeping interest and attention.

b. Emotions are high: Oral communication provides chances to create a climate for understanding.

c. Require feedback: It's easier to get feedback by asking questions.

d. People are too busy or preoccupied to read. The details and issues are complicated, and cannot be well expressed on paper. Oral communication provides better opportunities to gain attention.

e. To convince or persuade: Oral communication provides more flexibility, opportunity for emphasis, chances to listen to and remove resistance, and is more likely to affect people's attitudes.

It is not enough for leaders to have dreams of the future. They must be able to communicate these in ways that encourage us to sign on for the duration and to work hard toward the objective.

A highly effective leadership of organizations relies on thorough knowledge of the ways people organize themselves, how the leaders lead organizations, and the nature of communication among leaders and members of organizations.

In oral communication, the unit of code is the words, and is heavily supported by gestures. Most of the issues and challenges facing leaders and organizations point to the need for a culture of integrity, leadership, adaptability, creativity, engagement, respect, and camaraderie, which relies upon a foundation of effective communication. Most of the issues and challenges facing leaders and organizations point to the need for a culture of integrity, leadership, adaptability, creativity, engagement, respect, and camaraderie, which relies upon a foundation of effective communication. Oral communication skills include:

i. Speaking skill: The speaking style you use has a large impact on the others you are speaking to especially if you want to convince. When speaking, strive to be warm and enthusiastic. Doing this, the others will be responsive and interaction can be formed. Speaking skills have to be learned, practiced and evaluated over a period of time.

    The first rule of thumb to be able to speak effectively is planning what to say. Prepare main ideas to be spoken. Organize your thoughts so they lead to the main idea of the message you are trying to send across.

    Once you have arrived at your main idea, take a short brief and ask others if they are following you or not, to ensure you are both on the right page. Make sure you keep your conversation focused and direct to the point

ii. Telling skill: One of the ways to let others understand your message is by telling a story, reading a quote or telling a joke.

Verbal communication through stories carries power to induce the people to relate to what you are saying or suggesting. A joke usually helps people relax more and is opened to listen to you.

The way you deliver the story can affect the thinking, emotions and behavior of the people. They will able to imagine the idea and will reproduce a response. A story telling with eloquent can give hope to people who are in dire need for encouragement.

The highly effective leaders are fundamentally great storytellers. Creating, fine-tuning, and communicating stories is a fundamental part of the leader's vocation. Leaders achieve their effectiveness chiefly through the stories they relate.

iii. Asking skill: Asking with precise words may allow for answers. It make a difference if you ask a "why" or a "how" question. Questions give you a lot of reasons, understandings and explanations, and lead to your brain thinking for a solution, useful information and a strategy.

By asking questions and wording them specifically, you will invite a positive debate and interaction that will benefit all involved. You become a better listener and entice others to do the same. Unnecessary arguments are reduced when you are able to express yourself with great command of your communication skills. Type of questions includes:

a. Rhetorical - A question to which no answer is expected

b. Direct - A question to a named person can be a useful management device in a class situation

c. Overhead - Question is asked to the whole group, and then a person named to answer

d. Leading - question that suggests the answer

iv. Briefing skill: Let people know why they are doing something. It then becomes more meaningful when they recognize their part in a greater vision. Effective leader has the ability to provide instructional leadership.

v. Sharing skill: To be an effective leader requires strong communication skills and the ability to share. Leaders should focus their mentoring efforts on helping followers. With the responsibility of leadership goes trust.

A highly effective leader must adjust his/her leadership style to fit the situation. The secret is to share the leadership that allowing everyone to join and share in the responsibility without giving up the role as a leader.

Leaders keep people informed, as rational persuasion depends on a firm grasp of up-to-date facts. It is therefore essential for a leader to keep well-informed of developments within the team, and within the organization.

vi. Answering skill: It is a simple communication skill to improve your leadership credibility. People who speak slower and wait two to three seconds to respond are considered much more credible. If you find yourself cutting people off in mid-sentence or running around frenetically in response to pressure, both are warning signals to slow down and pause.

When answering, take your time by paraphrasing the question to be sure you are certain of what it means.

In situations where you do not know the answer to the question, do not make up an answer, instead, say you do not know the answer Remain calm and detached. Allow others to rage while you consider the appropriate response.

Arguing often makes the other party become more defensive and determined to prevail. Let go of your anger. It only clouds the issue and draws you into a quick response.

Whenever possible use kindness as your weapon against evil. Neutralize shouting with soft words. Answer threats with serene confidence. Speak plainly. Don't use foul language or sarcasm. Breathe deeply with long exhalations. Let the anger wash over you. Maintain your presence. Don't exaggerate. Don't lie. Attack the argument and not the person.

Long term relationships are almost always more important than short-term problems. Be an active peacemaker, building bridges of understanding.

vii. Presentation skill: Use simple language - Avoid technical jargon unless you are sure that everyone understands it.

Use your voice effectively, know your subject, know what you want to say- prepare your message carefully, arrange your points logically - Make your explanations as colorful as possible, using examples to illustrate your point, display interest and enthusiasm - Keep your explanation short so you do not risk boring people. Do not swamp them with unnecessary detail, sound convincing and sincere - Use visual aids, where possible, to illustrate your points

Leaders' communication skill is seen by members when they demonstrate it in tone of voice and body language. It's important to spend some time to understand how we come across when we communicate with others. A highly effective leader inspires, energizes, and arouses people to improve organization's performance. They are all effective speakers.

The degree to which leaders embody, communicate, foster, and require such skillfulness will define the degree of success. Be fully present when you are with people. Don't check your e-mail only, but take phone calls when a direct report drops into your desk, in which people need to talk to you. Put yourself on their shoes.

The organization will have in meeting their greatest challenges, and aligning action with the vision and values of the organization.

Simple Communication

Leaders make complex communication as simple as possible. Simplicity is an important element of communication. Simplicity displays a condition which is not complicated; ordinary or common; humble in condition; sincere to the people; free from vanity; not sophisticated. It may also imply a degree of intelligence inadequate to cope with anything complex.

Simplifying the communication not only streamline it, but make it more effective and productive, and leading to greater results.

Simple communication implies the sharing of information with people in a way which is understood and useful to everyone. In a great number of instances, using techniques such as simple communication methods to improve clarity of the exchange and understanding of information will yield positive results for the organization.

We cannot force another to communicate in a manner that works well for us but we can adapt communication methods in order to gain the most from others.

Simple communication is an art form in which many people fail to recognize. Many are unable to clearly articulate a message then insure it has been understood. Simple and clear communication requires:

a. Language: Speak in the same and simple language, foster same perception and avoid bias meaning. Speak slowly and maintain good voice.

b. Active listening: Encourage truly listening to what is being said rather than formulating statements. When the receivers stop listening they will not hear the message being spoken. They should take a quiet moment to listen to what has been said. Many of us talk more than we listen. Ramp-up listening and processing skills so that they know their thoughts and feelings are appreciated and accepted.

c. Confront: Ensure they have heard what you tell and ask them to repeat it in their own words until both parties are on the same page. Using eye contact and gestures may help. Ask each of the other managers in your company to tell you, in their own words. Ensure whether what you thought they understood; whether they were on the same page as you.

You should make sure they have understood correctly, and state their understanding of what they are hearing, ask them to write and summarize if necessary. Don't use a question instead of a command: Tell them what to do. You should directly state what you want people to do.

d. Ask questions and listen to the answers: Encourage them when in doubt, ask! Find out people's preference to communicate; whether they prefer a phone call, an email, or a face-to-face communication. Demonstrate that you respect their preferences by acting on them. Prevent information overload and time pressure that may occur during the communication. Keep everything brief and to the point. Go over the most important facts.

e. Use pragmatic terms, and avoid jargon and slang: Encourage simple terminology whenever possible. Speak it, write it, draw it, and show it. Whatever methods you can use to create a simple understanding, do it. Do not assume everyone has superior knowledge; each of us have strengths and areas of knowledge which other does not.

You may have knowledge they do not, and vice versa. Sometimes it will not be apparent the source of a statement that seemingly lacks credibility when in fact it is based on unstated knowledge

f. Focus on the situation, issue, behavior, not only the persons. We may encounter various levels of competency in communication skills, attitude, and knowledge. Don't pose negative questions: It may invite negative responses. Maintain self-esteem of others

Communication, that is simple, should first eliminate barriers that block the communication, provide simple tools that can be used to improve communication efforts, and involve the elements of communication, i.e. active listening, etc. People who won't act on information they don't understand. People who display clear, simple, easy-to-understand communication are mark of an excellent communicator.

Clear communication is an absolute must to insure the care of people need. Communication is best achieved through simple planning and control; which might help you to do this and specifically at meetings, where conversations need particular care.

Effective communication with organization's members contributes to performance by giving everyone a stake in what the organization is doing. Your ability to communicate will contribute significantly to your professional and personal success.

Leader with high capacity seems to be better at coping with ambiguity and uncertainty. They tend to be open-minded, analytic, non-judgmental, and better at integrative thinking - using scattered bits of information to develop a big picture.

Leadership has as its corner stone, the ability to communicate. When we use the word communicate, we are referring not only to the words one uses to transfer factual information to others, but also to other messages that are sent and received. If the leader communicates effectively, he or she will be sending messages that decrease resistance, and encourage moving through the change more effectively and positively.

8th

ORGANIZATIONAL SKILL

Effective leadership skill includes being certain that the thoughts and attitudes we hold are in alignment with the role we perform. Leaders are organizers. Accomplishing tasks in an organization requires assembling the right people and the right assets at the right time.

Leaders should also have outstanding organizational development skills. At any given moment, able to be grounded about themselves; communicate effectively with others; hold individuals accountable for their actions; facilitate team needs, wants, and performance; and understand how those actions fit into the bigger picture of the organization and what steps need to taken, when, with whom, and how.

Leaders must understand organizational development and the steps needed to fulfill each one. Organizations consist of these components:

a. The structure gives the organization its form and dictates the way it will interact.

b. The followers respond to the structure and the leaders.

   c.   The leaders determine the ultimate effectiveness of the organization as the character and skills that they bring determine the way problems are solved and tasks are accomplished.

The organization's base rests on management's philosophy, values, vision and goals. A leader is to build better relationships by achieving member's objectives, and organization's objectives. He/she must set, communicate, and deploy:

   a.   Organizational values: Leadership is the energetic process of getting people fully and willingly committed to a new and sustainable course of action, to meet commonly agreed objectives whilst having commonly held values. Values of an organization make a substantial difference in organizational performance.

   b.   Performance expectations: The key of success for organizational expectations is member involvement. Leader and followers select and define the essential competencies for success and the related performance expectations.

Effective leaders understand how their work fits into the broader organization and discern the essential context for achieving objectives. They keep up with the pace of change in their environment, actively developing this awareness and seeking opportunities to keep it comprehensive and current. Organizational skills required by a leader include:

   a.   Team building: An effective team building requires a leader with specific skills and attributes which build trust between team members and the team leader. The leader take initiative to making sure each person is doing the part of the whole that they feel they can best contribute to the overall mission.

       When building a team, the leader should consider the basic skills needed by members of the group. He/she should bring knowledge about the organization as a whole - belief systems, climate, desires, values, attitudes and motivations

   b.   Organize meeting: Leaders plan, organize, and conduct productive meetings, i.e. all members should be involved in setting the agenda.

Meetings should be carefully planned so that priority business is acted upon in a timely manner; meetings should start and end with summaries so that all members have a common understanding of what has transpired and what the priorities are; decision-making processes need to be determined; participate and share thoughts they have in the meeting, and achieve desired outcomes, etc.

The skills will help to encourage participation and discourage counterproductive behaviors. The leader makes sure that effective followers tend to be highly participative, and become critical thinkers.

c. Delegation: Effective delegation enables you to direct your focus and energy to other high-leverage activities that only you can do. Effective leaders are those who rely upon their ability to effectively delegate to others.

Delegation empowers people, in which they will take initiative when opportunities are provided, accept responsibility, and be willing to be held accountable for their performance of the assignments delegated to them.

d. Succession: Many fail to recognize that developing others is a major part of every leader's job. They underestimate what will take for a leader to develop the capabilities to take a complex organization into a future fraught with rapid and destabilizing change; that is a succession plan.

The leaders may have fared poorly at selecting and developing organizational leaders. They don't seem to understand what makes a leader or what the job entails. They focus on the wrong people for the wrong reasons.

The greatest growth factor effective leaders have is how quickly they can develop leaders. Linkages must be created, particularly between succession planning and leadership development.

e. Task Allocation: Leadership involves the ability of an individual to influence others to pursue defined goals and objectives. An individual's capability, or competencies, will have significant influence on the effectiveness of that individual's job performance. To be effective in task allocation, a leader must be highly responsive.

f. The effective leaders passionately motivate the team to meet and exceed their objectives. They focus on people, set work standards that are high but obtainable, carefully organize tasks, identify methods to carry out tasks, closely supervise work of the people. In achieving its effectiveness the leaders explain what is to be done, how it is to be done, and when it is to be completed. They make sure allocation of organization resources to meet the objectives.

g. The leaders stress excellence in performance, sets goals that are challenging, and shows confidence in the ability of the people to achieve challenging performance standards.

Effective leaders are generally task-oriented, set high performance goals, and focus on planning, coordinating, and facilitating work. They also give consideration to good interpersonal relationships, allowing subordinates some degree of autonomy in deciding how to conduct their work and at what pace.

A leader must build not only individual commitment but also organizational capability. Organizational capability refers to the processes, practices, and activities that create value for the organization.

The leader needs ability to translate organizational direction into roadmaps, vision into action, and purpose into process. To do so, he/she must demonstrate at least five abilities: to build the organizational infrastructure; to leverage diversity; to deploy team; to design human resource system; and to make change happened.

Team Building

A leader is a team builder. To become a highly effective leader, he/she must develop an effective team. He/she can start by handing off responsibility to the team and letting the team to run with it.

Leaders don't breathe down their necks and nor micromanage, but make themselves available if questions or problems come up. They teach the team to use decision-making system and give them freedom to work through their own decisions. They are ready to alter plans and make new ones. When an emergency hits, team will look to you, as a leader, to be a tower of strength and endurance.

Leaders understand their team's purpose and position within the organization. A team is a group of people coming together to collaborate. This collaboration is to reach a shared goal or task for which they hold themselves mutually accountable. A group of people is not necessarily a team.

A team is a group of people with a high degree of interdependence geared towards the achievement of a common goal or completion of a task; .it is not just a group for administrative convenience. A group, by definition, is a number of individuals having some unifying relationship. To use team building effectively, leaders should:

a. Establish a team goal, such as an opportunity identified by a needs assessment, or responding to a request for funding. The team should be made up of a diverse group of stakeholders, including residents, staff, public officials and private sector individuals.

b. Be ready to justify the criteria for selection, and practice inclusiveness as you assemble the team.

c. Seek members from different technical, socioeconomic, and cultural backgrounds.

d. When the team convenes, begin the meeting with icebreakers to help members become more comfortable.

e. Establish a time frame for identifying goals and making recommendations along with a plan to implement recommendations.

f. Get members to agree on rules the team will follow during meetings. When disagreement occurs, see that ideas, not members, are criticized. Stress the values of openness, trust, and mutual respect.

g. Make decisions by consensus. It will be helpful to have a team member record meeting minutes.

Team members are deeply committed to each other's personal growth and success. That commitment usually transcends the team. A team outperforms a group and outperforms all reasonable expectations given to its individual members. There are several benefits to team building, including:

a. Motivated individuals share in a common interest: A team is a group of people working toward a common goal. Part of any team building process is sharing what has been learned and experienced. Members should share any special interest areas, skills, and areas of expertise.

b. Ownership and responsibility for tasks are shared: To be effective in team building is demonstrate the ability to create a sense of belonging and ownership. The leaders build cultures of ownership where people matter. All members are identified clearly in roles and responsibilities. They must advance organizational involvement and ownership.

c. Problems are solved effectively: Members are directed toward problem solving, task effectiveness, and maximizing the use teamwork. Team member roles are defined to ensure effective ways to solve problems. They work together to be more efficient and effective.

d. Members increase communication: Effective leaders focus on the importance of effective communication skills. It helps team improves their communication effectively, problem-solving.

e. Major areas of concern and needs are identified: Team members should desire to work collaboratively, share thoughts, ideas, and concerns. Each other knows teammates, their opinions, concerns and aspirations for the team.

f. Resources to achieve goals are identified: People are an organizations most valuable resource. Team building is an effort of working together and acts to create a climate that encourages and values the contributions of team members. Their energies are directed toward problem solving, task effectiveness, and maximizing the use of all members' resources to achieve the team's purpose.

Sound team building recognizes that it is not possible to fully separate one's performance from those of others.

Leadership is defined not as what the leader does but rather as a process that engenders and is the result of relationships - relationships that focus on the interactions of both leaders and collaborators instead of focusing on only the competencies of the leaders. The opportunity to work with others provides the chance to not only learn and develop, but also teach and train.

A leader is also able to model and create expectation. They advance delegating, follow-up, motivating and coaching. As a leader, you will only go as far as your team.

No matter your intelligence, your dedication, tenacity and expertise, without a supporting team, you will not succeed. And without leaders in that supporting team, you will fail. Leaders must have the ability to consistently develop and sustain cooperative working relationships, i.e.:

a. Encourage and facilitate cooperation within their team environments and throughout the organization.

b. Be able to build networks and alliances, engage in cross-functional activities and collaborate across boundaries; honor commitments, gain cooperation from others to obtain information and accomplish goals.

c. Able to manage conflicts effectively: Respectfully confront issues and disagreements in a positive and constructive manner to minimize negative impact.

Ensure you look after people and that communications and relationships are good. Select good people and help them to develop. Develop people via training and experience, particularly by agreeing objectives and responsibilities that will interest and stretch them, and always support people while they strive to improve and take on extra tasks. Team building succeeds whenever fulfills:

i. Trust building - Create a sense of trust with team members. Leaders build trust through their actions. Walking-the-talk, role modeling and setting an example describe the consistency of actions critical to building trust among followers. In addition, these leaders trust followers.

The trust of followers must be earned. Trusting them builds credibility and leads to trust of the leader.

ii. Esteem building - Give team members responsibility and freedom to act; recognize their accomplishment, able to identify and understand how they have and can use their strengths.

iii. Pride building is at the core of many high-performing organizations. Pride is a powerful motivator. Building pride is hardly a new idea.

The most effective leaders have always known that the best work is inspired not by economics alone, but also by emotions, and they have engaged employees as allies, creating a sense of accomplishment, camaraderie, and emotional attachment that helps achieve big goals. Pride building strategies include:

1. Personalize the organization: Get involved in the everyday problems of your people to build an emotional bond with your members. Some pride-building leaders will routinely help their people to show their personal commitment to them._

2. Set on pride, not money: It's more important for people to be proud of what they are doing every day than it is for them to be proud of reaching a major goal. That's why it's crucial to celebrate the steps as much as the landings.

   The best pride builders are masters at spotting and recognizing the small achievements that will instill pride in their people. Leaders promote pride among followers, develop a cooperative spirit, and foster the attitude that the followers are members of a winning group or organization.

3. Localize as much as possible: Don't wait for your organization to instill pride. What works in one place might not work in another. And it's often helpful to build emotional commitment.

iv. Image-building - Outstanding leaders as self-conscious about their own image. They recognize the desirability of followers perceiving them as competent, credible, and trustworthy.

v. Performance building - Create conditions that encourage and reinforce high levels of team member performance. A sign of a weak leader is using his/her power of leadership not to get the job done, but simply because they can.

vi. Climate building - The climate is the feel of the organization, the individual and shared perceptions and attitudes of the organization's members. While the culture is the deeply rooted nature of the organization that is a result of long-held formal and informal systems, rules, traditions, and customs; climate is a short-term phenomenon created by the current leadership.

   Climate represents the beliefs about the feel of the organization by its members. This individual perception of the feel of the organization comes from what the people believe about the activities that occur in the organization. Make the environment enjoyable and satisfying.

Leaders recognize that a diversity of experience, knowledge, and cultural backgrounds enhances the quality of the team's work, and are at ease collaborating with individuals with differing viewpoints. It includes build strong teams to meet objectives, capitalizing on individual strengths; promote cooperation between work teams; contribute fully to cross-functional teams.

A leader is an integrator; orchestrate the many activities that take place throughout an organization by providing a view of the future and the ability to obtain it. Success can only be achieved when there is a unity of effort. Integrators have a sixth sense about where problems will occur, and make their presence felt during critical times. They know that their employees do their best when they are left to work within a vision-based framework.

This type of person leads by positive example and endeavors to foster a team environment in which all team members can reach their highest potential, both as team members and as people. They encourage the team to reach team goals as effectively as possible, while also working tirelessly to strengthen the bonds among the various members. They normally form and lead some of the most productive teams.

Organize Meeting

Meeting should not become a social affair, and it is leader's responsibility to keep the group "on task." If you need to speak to only one or two of the meeting's attendees, just go to their cubes and have a conversation. It takes less time, but communicates more information. Meeting will be effective if:

a. Members feel comfortable offering their feedback or ideas; and never publicly criticize or embarrass anyone. The leader should be open to new ideas and encourage people to express themselves.

b. Never fight within the group - Build and foster unity with confidence and allegiance to mutual respect within the group always.

c. Responsibilities are clear - Until responsibilities are shared, the leader can expect to do most of the work.

d. Never waste time, most focused meeting will run into distractions. Start on time, end early.

e. Members know the agenda and ground rules by which the meeting will be run.

In a healthy organisation almost all decisions will be made at the meetings and there will be a sufficient level of discussion to ensure all the members have a good idea of the activity and arguments in the different problems the organisation is involved in.

i. Intra-group meeting: Communication within individual group members. A group leader needs to conduct Intra-group meeting within their respective group members. The purpose of the Intra-group meetings is to enable to gather relevant information, so that they are able to present a clear picture of the issues and offer solutions. This meetings should:

a. Be held as needed: Make sure everyone knows the time and place

b. Agenda should be distributed before preceding the meeting: An agenda gives people time to plan, to think over things that will be discussed, to do assignments and bring necessary information and materials.

c. Minutes of meeting should be documented and distributed to all concerns.

ii. Inter-group meeting: Communication among separate groups. Inter-group meeting is to review problems and solutions that are documented in the intra-group meetings.

Each group leader is required to present issues and the accompanying solutions. This will enable the group leader to follow up actions and decisions, as well as be aware of any issues not previously mentioned. All issues/solutions that are brought for discussion will be recorded and documented. Inter-group meeting will:

a. Carry out of group initiatives: Identify set of actions which coincide with the common objectives and the prerequisites or essential conditions to reach it.

b. Communicate group needs and decisions, actions, and directives

Regular meeting is the best way to ensure that a leader will meet the organization's objectives. Ask people to make the time commitment, and make the meeting as effective as possible. A well-run meeting can get the right people together to make decisions or to discuss some item of common interest.

Delegation

The hallmark of good supervision is effective delegation. A good follower will be able to complete tasks correctly or in a timely manner. Rather than working on improving our delegation skills, sometimes we simply keep hold of more tasks. Being overworked somehow seems less risky than having things done that might not meet our exact requirements.

Effective delegation means giving up a little of what we would like to hold onto while keeping what we might prefer to give up (accountability). Leader delegates authority and responsibility. Do not over control others. It is frustrating for them and time consuming for you.

Delegation is the assignment to others of the authority for particular functions, tasks and decisions. Delegation of responsibility to a person which is not prepared to handle the responsibility may cause frustration.

A leader turns over responsibility to the subordinates. They are allowed greater autonomy because they have both the competence and confidence to accomplish the task on their own. So, delegate your tasks. Involve and utilize the most important resources at hand to your people. But be sure to follow through on their progress. Be generous in praise and recognition. Appreciate all contributions, big and small. Prior to delegating, you need to think some important things, e.g.:

i. The specific of the task or job to be delegated: Effective leaders know what tasks are to be done specifically by them, and what are to be done by others.

ii. The capacity (experience, knowledge and skills) of the individuals as they apply to the delegated task. Decide which person is right for the task. Match skills and personality to the task will maximize productivity. When reviewing potential candidates to take on additional responsibilities, leader should consider level of individual motivation and ambition, skill sets, level of allegiance to the organization, and emotional maturity.

iii. How the delegated person works best - Under what circumstances should he/she shouts for help. Establish a positive work environment where employees are not paralyzed by fear of failure or dismissive of tasks that they think is beneath them. You need to emphasize tools of motivation and communication to nourish enthusiasm.

iv. The current workload of this person: Delegation should challenge, but not overwhelm. If someone can perform a task to at least 70% of your capacity then it is a prime candidate for delegation.

v. Constrains, restriction, i.e. time limit, quality, quantity, importance of task towards organization, possible failures and affect to other things, etc

vi. Resources for this person: If someone is naturally better than you at a task, let them play to their strengths wherever appropriate. Given time and support, staff will come up to speed.

vii. Your expectations or goals for the tasks - Determine the results you want to achieve. Be specific. A more defined goal might be reducing consequences. Details make a delegation works appropriately.

viii. The role you play to ensure the success, through ongoing monitoring, support, coaching, providing of resources, etc. Knowing the results you want is your job, not the job of subordinates to whom you delegate. Motivate them if needed.

Productivity is enhanced when those who have responsibilities feel a sense of freedom to work creatively using their own initiative and imagination. Everyone enjoys the feeling of being depended upon, trusted to do the best possible job, and that the ideas they use in accomplishing their job comes from themselves.

ix. Appropriate mechanisms for controlling the task - Decide what controls and checkpoints you'll put on the person to whom you're delegating; i.e. set checkpoints and report-backs to make sure that things are going smoothly. The most effective is to realize early on that.

x. Define accountability: Don't expect the people to whom you delegate to fail; and readily taking the task back to handle yourself. That's a quick way to undermine their effectiveness; they will never develop in the way you need them to.

A leader must decide what to delegate, how much, when, and to whom. .Even "Super-You" needs help and support. There is no shame in asking for assistance. A leader must help their team members to reach their fullest potential. The purpose of delegation is:

1. Control of your time: Delegation helps you by freeing you up to focus on the matters that really do require your attention. And it helps you develop your people by freeing them up to use their abilities to the greatest extent.

Delegation is a critical decision, mainly because some tasks should be handled only by you but others, which take up your valuable time, can easily be handled by someone else.

Delegating is a way of increasing your time. It allows you the freedom to focus on what you should be accomplishing and to better see the big picture. Only do those tasks that nobody else can do. Determine what it is you will delegate. Look at what you do and ask yourself if this is really where you should be spending your time.

All routine activities and minor decisions should be delegated to others. Also, any tasks that should be performed when you are not there or unavailable are also candidates for delegation. Never keep work simply because you do it better. Delegating certain tasks to others is a way of developing and endorsing those you lead.

Delegating allows people to learn by doing, to take risks and to build confidence. It is one of the best ways to develop that person for further responsibilities and their own leadership responsibilities.

2. Build People: Leaders are builders of people. Leaders bring out the best in people. A leader is only as good as the people he/she leads. Consequently, a leader trains his/her subordinates, encourages them to use their initiative, and gives recognition when it is due.

A leader leaves everyone with whom he/she works - a better qualified person - as a result of skill development, training, experience, and encouragement. Delegation means giving a certain amount of power to make decisions and complete activities to someone else. By sharing this responsibility, you enable individuals to grow and to further develop their knowledge, skills and abilities.

Delegation is to keep high performing members interested and to raise the level of low performers.

Leaders must give those they lead the opportunity to act independently, make honest mistakes, learn, and contribute to the goals and objectives of the organization. When a leader delegates a task, he/she should consider these factors:

a. Information: All that is needed to get started and the resources to find more information and data.

b. Authority: The ability to act on the leader's behalf, which includes the right of one to make decisions, issue directives and allocate resources. This also includes the responsibility and the accountability for implementing and completing the assignment.

i. Accountability: How people are subject to reporting/justifying outcomes and are rewarded or corrected;

ii. Responsibility: The assigned duty to perform a task or activity.

Managers may think of empowerment, as delegating decision making to the lowest level, is possible. But in practice, the empowering bosses delegate responsibility to subordinates without sufficient authority, understanding, resources or supportive guidance to be effective. People who think they are empowered will resist the limitations and guidance that must accompany any responsibility.

Effective empowerment is not: responsibility without authority or resources, authority to "do your own thing" without limits or accountability, power without focus or consequences, or abandonment by the boss.

Delegation is the on-going process by which a leader challenge and interest, increase motivation, and increase opportunities to learn and grow. If this manager continues not to delegate, he may be taking a shortcut to the cemetery because the work will be too big and heavy for him to bear alone. Meanwhile, his subordinates will become bored and lose enthusiasm in their jobs.

Leaders must be ready to hand over their roles. They don't be a monarch. The effective leadership likely means the leaders already have a talented work force in place. Guide the members, but don't implement more parameters than are absolutely necessary.

Succession

Also crucial to sustained organizational improvement is the effective succession of leaders. Succession planning, that is the preparation to replace one leader with another, is one of the most difficult challenges organizations face. It is an ongoing process of systematically identifying, assessing, and developing talent to ensure leadership continuity for all key positions in an organization.

Succession planning does not exist in isolation. It must be interwoven with the organization's strategic objectives and should reflect the way the organization needs to evolve in order to achieve its strategic goals. This means that the kinds of leadership styles, skills, and behaviors you want to develop and promote might be different in the future from those in the existing culture. Organization's approach to succession management influences the perception of the system's effectiveness. It will need:

a. Organizational support: Endorse succession management planning and establish a process and specific steps to implement the program. Senior management/management involved in process of identifying competencies/key requirements for manager and above positions; involving line management in process design, implementation, and execution; Alignment with company strategy, competencies, and values.

b. Identifying candidates: i.e. identifying needs for multiple candidates for each senior management position; using competencies to define readiness; identifying high potentials and high-performing candidates.

Selecting those promising individuals can be the result of evaluating performance appraisals, consulting with other department management staff, and looking closely at productive division heads, creative key staff personnel and those who have shown an aptitude for doing very thorough work and going the extra mile on day-to-day tasks. And always, listening to be aware of those who want to move up, expand their job tasks and grow with the organization.

c. Development process: Expose employees to multiple situations, tasks, projects to build their competencies; coaching and mentoring; establishing on-the-job developmental assignments.

One approach that has worked for many is to identify the rising stars first, then provide a formal management training and development program for each of those employees, followed by coaching, mentoring and making growth opportunities available to them. Concurrently, with their training and development program, it is good to make specific and challenging assignments that are within their grasp and capabilities, yet stretch them in their performance and critical thinking.

Special assignments can include chairing a specific department task force, a short-term committee, or an assignment that does not involve others but that the person must develop solely on his or her own.

An individualized work plan monitored with regularly scheduled weekly coaching and mentoring sessions between director and individual is critical to maximize the person's ability to recognize effective (as well as ineffective) actions, directions, critical thinking process and to see the "big picture" of the task and how it relates to the department or organization as a whole.

d. Other practices:

i. Identify real needs in future: Orientation to the future is critical. Leaders must take care to develop their future successors. Organizations need leaders that can move the company forward

ii.　　Check performance and potential assessment codes for consistency

iii.　　Stakeholder assessment: Assessment approaches with multiple rating sources provide more accurate, reliable, and credible information. The elements of feedback sources consists of superior, peers, subordinates, customers, supplier, corporate interest and one-self.

Organizations faced with executive turnover may simply recruit experienced leaders from other institutions. But attracting talent from the competition is no longer a viable option. Not only is this costly, but a staggering sixty six percent of senior managers hired from the outside usually fail within the first eighteen months. The smart way for succession crisis is to identify and develop the internal talent needed for key executive positions.

Succession management planning may be still debate-able, but it is truly essential to assure a continuity of philosophy, knowledge and direction for the department's or organization long-term success. And succession management planning can be a critical and helpful process to fill those ever-present management vacancies that public works departments are experiencing in today's mobile job setting.

Organizations that don't invest in the development of their members are finding themselves at risk of high turnover rates and lost organizational knowledge and experience. On other hand, succession planning and management development can and do contribute to extraordinary business success.

Some organizations may find it more rewarding to promote a successor from within, while others prefer to get their candidates externally. Although internal promotions are a good motivation for incumbent people to do their best, it is also a good practice to bring in new blood into the organization once in a while.

Task Allocation

The role of the leader is to establish the conditions under which all followers will choose to execute the mission, vision, and values of the organization. Further more leaders review organizational performance. They are ultimately responsible for the group/organization attaining its objectives. Highly effective leadership takes a lot of work and determination.

This involves using task-specific knowledge and experience to guide the group/organization. Leaders must engage in problem solving, delegation, time and resource management, and setting priorities and goals. Leaders must strive for results and provide feedback to ensure effective contributions from all constituents. Effective leaders empower others and model good work ethics.

Leaders need to select the right people for the right jobs, and assign them tasks that fit with their skills and proficiencies. This provides structure. Here is the method to achieve correct role allocation:

a. Break down the broader team goals into specific, individual tasks. List all tasks, and then rank each task in terms of importance;

b. Analyze and list the competencies required to perform each task;

c. List the competencies of each team member

d. Match individuals to task competencies.

Leaders ensure the task is understood, supervised and accomplished

The leader is an individual whose values and character enable them to influence others by providing purpose, direction, and motivation, in order to accomplish the mission and objectives of the organization.

9th

SUPERVISORY SKILL

Leaders need essential leadership skills to survive and thrive, even in the midst of change. Supervision is controlling, directing, evaluating, coordinating, and planning the efforts of subordinates so that the leader can ensure the task is accomplished. Over-supervision stifles initiative, breeds resentment, and lowers morale and motivation. Under-supervision leads to miscommunication, lack of coordination, and the perception by subordinates that the leader does not care.

An organization has the greatest chance of being successful when all of the members work toward achieving its goals. Since leadership involves the exercise of influence by one person over others, the quality of leadership exhibited is a critical determinant of organizational success; in order to influence the actions of members toward the achievement of the goals of the organization. Many people in leadership positions struggle with understanding what makes a great leader.

Supervise means to make sure that orders are understood and followed. Good followers are formed by good leaders. They organize people and processes, ensuring that predetermined goals are accomplished in an efficient and effective manner. Leaders are great at directing, coordinating, and controlling.

Supervision

Highly effective leadership requires a high level of supervision. Supervision, when done correctly, requires a great deal of time, energy, and commitment. A leader is a supervisor. Supervision is keeping a grasp on the situation and ensuring that plans and policies are implemented properly. It includes giving instructions and inspecting the accomplishment of a task. An effective leader is succeeding at supervision.

Forecasting

Many organizations do not do forecasting well; and much more likely to outperform rather than underperform their predictions. Leaders demand honest forecasting.

A leader should be able to calculate or estimate something in advance or predict the future; by examining and analyzing available information; use the information to create a comprehensive plans; and identify those areas that you can reasonably expect to change and will produce a noticeable performance improvement.

Leaders work harder at it. The primary goal of forecasting is to identify the full range of possibilities, not a limited set of illusory certainties. The forecaster's task is to map uncertainty, for in a world where our actions in the present influence the future; uncertainty is opportunity. Forecasting has 5 (five) objectives, i.e.:

a. Determine current perceptions of organization, i.e. identify the people you will have working for you, the organizational structure, and the resources necessary to make it all work.

b. Observe the environment broadly: See things from higher up. By increasing your powers of observation, you will begin to become more aware of what motivates people, how to solve problems more effectively, and how to distinguish between alternatives.

c. Identify the driving force: What you will use to motivate others to perform; i.e. vision, mission, values, and goals

d. Identify differences in perceptions about organization from various viewpoints: Take into consideration different ways of thinking about something. It may help you think about outcomes, identify critical elements, and adjust your actions to fulfill the objectives.

e. Define ideal position: The conditions you have found to be necessary if your business is to be productive; the niche in the marketplace that your business will fill; any opportunities that may exist either currently or in the future for your business; the core competencies or skills required in your business; and the strategies and tactics you will use to pull it all together.

Nearly all organizations still use spreadsheets for some parts of the process. It is possible to produce a reliable forecast using these basic tools, but the survey shows that organizations with the most accurate forecasts are more likely to use more advanced software to do the job. But good technology won't help if the input data is poor or processes are unreliable.

Prediction is possible only in a world in which events are preordained and no amount of action in the present can influence future outcomes. The one we inhabit is quite different-little is certain, nothing is preordained, and what we do in the present affects how events unfold, often in significant, unexpected ways.

Leaders leverage information more effectively. Unreliable forecasts may cost organization finance. To be in an excellent forecasting, you should be focus on

a. Planning: Provide development and implementation of forecasting models, resources planning, measurement tools, analysis and adjustment strategies

b. Systems: The process needs fixing. Apply specific methods to insure that data is gathered and used most profitably; systems which can be developed on purpose and implemented in easy to follow fashion lead all members to perform in a consistent manner resulting in a high degree of predictability

c. Training: Improve the ability of the members to help deliver results that are consistent with organization's desires. Well trained people are successful

Forecasting should not be the preserve of finance. The goal of forecasting is not to predict the future but to tell you what you need to know to take meaningful action in the present.

Planning

Effective leaders begin with the end in mind in all their endeavors. They know where they are going and how they want to get there. They evaluate alternatives, consider their resources and plan constantly and meticulously.

To be effective as a leader, you must develop skills in strategic thinking, which is a process whereby you learn how to make your business vision a reality by developing your abilities in team work, problem solving, and critical thinking. It is also a tool to help you confront change, plan for and make transitions, and envision new possibilities and opportunities.

Without leadership, most strategic plans will end up as dead pieces of paper. Most importantly, when planning occurs without leadership, cynicism increases when members see that the plan is being ignored, or even violated. The outcome of this is that leaders suffer a loss of credibility.

Good plans start with a brainstorming session of all the people involved with the project. This allows everyone to be part of the solution, in addition to gathering the best ideas. One of the primary mechanisms of management is demonstrating leadership qualities which are shown in strategic planning. It includes:

a. Begin the planning: If you want to succeed at something you must plan. Make sure that the followers are familiar with the plan when individual objectives are set. Plan carefully, with your people where appropriate, how you will achieve your aims. You may have to redefine or develop your own new aims and priorities.

b. Initiate action: Most people lack is the courage - the courage to initiate. Initiative means moving outside your comfort zone; seeking out opportunities and being willing to act. A leader must take action - action leads to impact. But actions also possess a separate, equally powerful quality. Actions are unambiguous.

If the leader can highlight a few carefully selected actions, then your followers will no longer have to infer the future. They will simply look to see what actions you take and found our faith and confidence on these.

c. Follow-up: To make meeting follow-up work, you need to develop a culture of accountability. Leader needs to follow-up with the people who participate regularly to ensure action items are under way.

d. Complete the planning: Make final modifications to your plan taking the information you gathered in the previous step into account. A thoughtless leader who never genuinely finishes anything loses the trust of members. The ability to complete things is critical. Nothing's useful unless you actually complete it.

e. Provide feedback: Performance assessment is an important part of your efforts as a leader. If you don't provide feedback, your team members will either get it from someone who does not understand the overall picture. Feedback is the way we make sure we are on track and doing the right thing.

Leader is responsible for planning out the destination of the trip. However, no matter how good a leader is in creating strategy and planning, if the strategies and plans don't get implemented, they are worth less than nothing. The critical link between planning and getting things done is effective leadership.

Leaders manage the planning process so that members feel that they have adequate input into the process; that they are heard, and their values and visions are incorporated into the final plan and its implementation. Spell out your plan of action, asking for everyone's support and showing confidence in a positive outcome.

Assignment

Being a competent leader is about demonstrating firm, fair, and consistent leadership in all aspects of his/her day-to-day living. In assignment; he/she should be able to:

a. Define goals, and continually review it: Plan the actions to achieve it, and provide systems which help the members accomplish it. Roll the tasks down, and select the tasks, which are appropriate for them. Review the progress time to time and try to find ways that simplify things and eliminate redundancy.

b. Recognize the effect of requirement: Identify the actual factors that threats the mission, and find the way to deal with problem/difficult behavior

c. Set the boundaries: Explain the purpose of organization. The competent leader sets clear, unambiguous boundaries. Both the behaviors you want and you don't want. Setting boundaries may include giving the command for shaping a desired behavior. Establishing boundaries is to prevent undesirable behaviors and communicate your control.

    Your boundaries delineate the specific behaviors for which there are specific consequences or ramifications. The most powerful and enduring component of the learning process is whether the consequence of a particular behavior is positive (rewarding) or negative (punishing).

d. Give time. Most people don't achieve anywhere near their creative potential because they never give themselves time to do so. They're so conditioned to quick action that they give up on fresh thinking long before it has a chance to develop into anything.

Sufficient time is the key to making organizational changes that stick. One of the worst aspects of modern working life is the constant pressure to hurry. Give yourself and members some time and space in which to work.

An effective leader is someone who can take full advantage of his/her resources and accomplish whatever their goal may be, molding their own leadership styles and abilities from all of the definitions given.

The ability to be an effective leader depends on the situation at hand. The leader ensures assigned tasks are understood, supervised, and accomplished. Leadership entails getting people to do what a leader wants in an ethical way that brings about fulfillment, respect, and success. He/she define the parameters of the assignment which includes:

a. Create healthy environment for the activity: Proper environment is also important in maintaining high achievements. Leaders remove potential constrains and create an environment that allows creative thinking and activity

b. Show the goal/objective Most people can get excited about a variety of assignments if they know the leader thinks those tasks are important and the importance is clearly described.

c. Provide appropriate time frame: Supervision enables to assess and support performance that respect the time frame, and optimize resources.

Leaders have to give directions. It's part of the job. Give instructions in the ways that work best for your subordinate. Different people process information in different ways. To be most effective, you need to master different ways of presenting instructions so you can choose and use the best way for each subordinate. Use the language that your subordinate likes.

If you use familiar terms when giving instructions, your subordinates are more likely to get the message. If you are familiar with the people who work for you, you should learn about what's important to them and how they communicate. Give your directions in more than one way. Use diagrams and pictures. Demonstrate it. Write important instructions down so your people can carry them away. Check for understanding. Ensure they understand your message.

Leadership is ability to direct others, but more important is to have those people, who are directed, accept it. The strengths of members and the organization are in the strength of the leader.

Controlling

The purpose of this skill is to control the performance of a group so that it will be successful in doing its job and to have fun in the process. Sometimes controlling group performance means you will have to stop behavior that negatively impacts the group, but everyone is happier if the group helps to control itself rather than depend on the leader to do all the controlling.

Once you have worked through the above steps, make sure you brief your team member appropriately. Take time to explain why they are chosen for the job, what's expected from them during the project, the goals you have for the project, all timelines and deadlines and the resources on which they can draw. And agree a schedule for checking-in with progress updates. Make sure that the team member knows that you want to know if any problems occur, and that you are available for any questions or guidance needed as the work progresses.

In delegating effectively, we have to find the sometimes-difficult balance between giving enough space for people to use their abilities to best effect, while still monitoring and supporting closely enough to ensure that the job is done correctly and effectively.

Effective leaders must learn when and how to get out of the way and let others make contributions. The secret of staying in charge is the leader knows that things are controllable. We live in a world obsessed with control: monitoring, measuring, assessing, rating, every kind of controlling. As a leader, your main priority is to get the job done, whatever the job is. Leaders make things happen by:

a. Recognize objectives and have a plan how to achieve them: Objectives reflect the desired outcomes for organization. Leaders set objectives and then drive hard to achieve them.

b. Build a team/person committed to achieving the objectives: Leaders ensure the others commit to the achievement of the objective. The people should have the ability to see what needs to be done and to do it without constant supervision

c. Help the members to give their best efforts: Leaders support members in their efforts to accomplish their personal and organization's goal.

The members should be in your control. Pay attention to small details, the big ones are obvious and get taken care of. The leader's job is to build and sustain high performance by noticing and appreciating when people do things right-especially when they act with courage, integrity, and accountability.

Reinforcing courageous, right-minded action, especially when it turns out to be a mistake, is the only way to encourage people to take risks, and leaders who follow this rule typically build organizations with spirit and pride.

Leaders have far less control over organizations than people believe, but they can be more effective if they understand leadership myths and use them to their institutions' advantage and keep his/her people motivated. Therefore, law of responsibility is:

1. Everyone must accept responsibility for his or her own actions.

2. No one can be held accountable for results that are outside their control.

3. Excellence is shown by controlling what can be controlled and skillfully influencing those areas where influence is possible.

Whenever something goes wrong, we look for who is to blame; who should have been in control and stopped the problem before it developed - but didn't. The route to a better understanding of control begins with recognizing that there are three distinct facts that apply to whatever you are seeking to control:

1. Some things cannot be controlled, whatever you do: the weather, other people's thoughts, the results of most actions, external events.

2. Some things can always be controlled: what you choose to say or do (with very limited exceptions), how you respond to your emotions and moods, what you believe.

3. Many things that cannot be controlled directly, but can be influenced to a varying extent: public opinion, consumer behavior, other people's actions, the effects of your actions.

Contrarily, for people in leadership roles to approach members responsibilities with an attitude of controlling the activities of those they are leading, might be destructive. Control has 3 (three) perspectives, i.e.:

a. People based control: Leaders may deal with high visibility problems. Ignoring minor problems will give leaders many major problems to solve. They will be a problem solver.

b. Cost based control: The aim is to reduce cost. But leaders not only affect financial indicators of performance, they also affect their organization's interpersonal climate and the satisfaction and mental well-being of those they lead.

c. Job based control: A leader that is focused on getting the job done has authority to acquire the resources he/she needs and is willing to pass on responsibility to his/her subordinates with the authority to acquire needed resources. Where get-the-job-done has priority, cost is up front and controllable. Where cost has priority, real cost is uncontrollable, because the project has to deal with a pile of problems that are caused by cost control.

Individuals are most productive when they are doing something they like to do and are doing those things with others that share their enthusiasm for the tasks being performed.

Since leadership is most critical in rapidly changing situations, and since change causes stress, it follows that capable leaders possess a high level of stress tolerance, to keep cool under fire, to keep one's head when, all about, others are losing theirs.

Effective leaders are able to maintain focus under strenuous conditions. The leader also uses charisma, and mind control techniques to persuade people to follow him/her. Charisma or the ability to inspire the admiration of others plays a big role.

Leaders can also make a big difference to individuals when they are abusive or ineffective, or both. As abusive and incompetent management create billions of dollars of lost productivity.

Evaluation

In many organizations, leaders are evaluated solely on results. Evaluation involves collecting and shifting through data, making judgments, whether or not an assessment of worth or merit results. It requires skills, ability, dexterity, sensitivity to stakeholders.

Evaluation is a process of collecting and synthesizing information in order to better understand the merit of an initiative.

Evaluation will serve as feedback to aid in the development and continual improvement. The evaluation plan begins with an introduction that provides background information important to the evaluation such as the goal of the evaluation and those who will be involved in the evaluation process. Effective evaluation includes the following elements:

a. Define and measuring performance dimensions (e.g., define performance with a focus on valued outcomes; outcome measures can be defined in terms of relative frequencies of behavior; incorporate the measurement of contextual performance into the system)

b. Link performance dimensions to meeting internal and external customer requirements

c. Incorporate the measurement of situational constraints into the system

Leaders should have regular performance review and goal setting sessions with each of their followers. Evaluating is part of supervising. It is defined as judging the worth, quality, or significance of people, ideas, or things. It includes looking at the ways people are accomplishing a task. It means getting feedback on how well something is being done and interpreting that feedback.

People need feedback so that they judge their performance. Without it, they will keep performing tasks wrong, or stop performing the steps that makes their work great.

Evaluation is a tool that assists organizations like ours measure our successes, recognize inefficiencies, reorganize when necessary and improve our services.

Evaluating should be done both during and after every activity. Each activity should have a definite goal. The real evaluation happens in hundreds of encounters during everyday work. Do evaluation every day, and use the formal evaluation meeting as an occasion to review and plan with your subordinates.

Evaluations may consist of the administration of tests, data collection, information provided and interview. It will tell us:

a. Effectiveness of the system: Devote your time and energy to making the system deliver good results. Evaluate the system, identify the problems occur, define the needs for improvement; changes in work climate, collaboration, productivity and identify effective practices

b. Achievement and progress: Communicate results; decision-making, leadership pipelines, shared vision, alignment of activities and strategy, and key business indicators. Define further activity that is needed to achieve the objectives

c. Resources maximize resources/funding, evaluate workload; changes in knowledge, skills, values, beliefs, identities, attitudes, behaviors and capacities.

d. Accountability - Clarify the purpose, reflecting willingness to show outcome and fully accept responsibility for the actions and implications. Another point that needs to be covered is, that of the oft time habit that many of us fall into, looking for a blaming when in actuality we need to take on responsibility.

Leaders take the high road and accept responsibility to make changes in such a way to gain that which is needed from the business relationship. Sitting, awaiting the other party to do all the right things, pointing blame and finding all outcomes to be the fault of the other person in the relationship typically leads to conflict. Nothing good comes of it.

One of a leader's responsibilities is to create and utilize a forum for open, constructive communication in which feedback is one important aspect. Feedback, both positive and negative, is helpful to others. Feedback is communicating to a member or group(s) how their behavior has affected us or other people. Effective feedback may:

a. Get attention from the follower: Followership merits attention. Leader will get and hold the attention of followers, especially when he/she give positive feedback

b. Keep the relationship intact, open and healthy

c. Validate the process in future interactions

When you give feedback you are offering valuable information that will be useful to another person making decisions about how to behave.

Feedback is not criticism. Criticism is evaluative; feedback is descriptive. It also, allows us to build and maintain communication with others.

Feedback provides the individual with information that can be used in performing personal evaluation. Providing feedback enhances the effects of goal setting. Performance feedback keeps their behavior directed on the right target and encourages them to work harder to achieve the goal. The purpose of feedback is to change and alter messages so the intention of the original communicator is understood. It includes verbal and nonverbal responses to another person's message. Providing feedback is accomplished by paraphrasing the words of the sender. Restate the sender's feelings or ideas in your own words, rather than repeating their words.

Many organizations are starved for feedback because people don't trust one another and everything is too rigid and hierarchical. Feedback is perceived as useful if it aids in decision-making. Feedback promotes following characteristics:

a. Relate to specific matters: Telling members exactly what they are doing right and wrong. They should know exactly what is expected next. Leaders should identify positives to repeat and specific improvements to be made in future.

b. Focus on behavior rather than on the person: Consider what a person does rather than to what we think or imagine he/she is. Leaders must show that it is OK to make mistakes or to suggest an idea that may not be accepted.

c. Take into account the needs of the ones who are evaluated. Feedback can be destructive when it serves only leader/organization needs

d. Solicit rather than impose: Apply both downward and upward evaluation.

e. Share rather than giving advice: By sharing information, we leave a person free to decide in accordance with goals, needs, etc.

f.   Well-time: Immediate feedback is most useful (depending of course, on the person's readiness to hear it, support available from others, etc.).

g.   It involves the amount of information the receiver can use rather than the amount we would like to give. Overloading on feedback reduces the person's ability to effectively use your comments. When we give more than can be used, we are more often than not satisfying some need of our own rather than helping the other person

h.   Tell what and how to do, not why: The "why" does not contribute to learning or development; it is dangerous to assume that we know why a person says or does something.

i.   Insure clear communication: One way of doing this is to have the receiver try to rephrase the feedback received to see if it corresponds to what the sender has in mind.

j.   Provide appropriate time to get better clarification. Appropriate time may make sure to give effective feedback in the appropriate condition.

Organizations, which are generally built to intent on achieving and maintaining a competitive edge, recognize the importance of effective leadership at all levels in the organization.

Effective leadership involves planning, organizing, controlling, and staffing. Effective leaders plan well, and establish an effective organization, set up an efficient and effective control system, and staff required jobs with the right people. Finally the leader excels at inspiring and motivating subordinates. Evaluating the performance is a form of control because it ties performance feedback to rewards and corrective actions.

Evaluation is an on-going process, taking place informally every day in the organization. Evaluation is formally documented for a given time period. Leaders foster trust and collaboration - and are focused on sustainable superior performance. Best way to improve the organization is by improving yourself; the best way to empower the organization is by empowering yourself.

10th

SURVIVAL SKILL

An effective leader should demonstrate management skills, particularly survival skill. Survival is a process resulting best adapted to the environment; in which people are remaining alive. Being a leader means we make those tough calls, but being a survivor means we have at least anticipated the probable outcomes and prepared in advance to deal with them so as to minimize their negative impact.

In most survival situations, positive mental attitude is essential. Keeping a positive mentality is the most important survival tool one can have. Keeping yourself stress free will help you stay calm and productive. Each type of environment challenges a person with a different range of dangers. Survival skills are skills that may help one to survive in difficult situations. Those skills are:

a. Protect-ability: Leaders are highly vocal and desperately to protect their people and organization. Effective leaders demonstrate ability to control environment in order to protect the interests of the organization. These skills focus on ability to respond to unsafe situations as they occur.

b. Communication: Communication and leadership are inseparable. Effective communication is vital to organization survival and success. Organizational survival and lasting business success depend upon successful managerial and operational response as well as effective communication with external and internal stakeholders.

c. Adaptability: Change is crucial to the survival and growth of an organization. Adaptability defines how well we can deal with change or how resilient we are.

d. Assess-ability: Leaders must have the ability to assess the organization, people, challenge and opportunity. Assessment needs transparency, openness, orderliness, etc. Show the ways to be a truly effective leader and how leadership styles must adapt to the skills and commitment of the people they want to influence, particularly within survival period.

e. Competitiveness: Effective leaders prove highly effective in developing organization competitiveness. The leaders require skill to grow the competitiveness strength of people and organization.

f. Learn-ability: Every one is innate learners, as learning is the cornerstone for survival. Leaders learn new behaviors through observing others, and constantly learn new skills.

g. Judge-ability: People are quick to judge, and mangled, which can cripple their credibility and limit acceptance of their ideas. Really important in a good judge is the ability to listen and consider very thoroughly. Effective leaders judge their success by the success of their followers. The leaders help people come to the point where they judge themselves.

Leadership is about movement, which is taking people, ideas, processes and business from where they are, to where they need to be. Survival leadership is quality of being flexible and adaptable to whatever comes your way.

People learn best by experience and by making their own mistakes. You may face situations that you have not anticipated or learned in the class.

You have to handle these things in real-time without devoting weeks of study to it. Survival leaders know how to go over, around and through any obstacles they face.

A highly effective leader should belief, that knowing who he/she is and what he/she stands for, or where he/she has been and where he/she is now and where he/she is going, is the critical requisite for survival. He/she needs to know what his/her priorities are and therefore what his/her values are.

PROTECTABILITY

Effective leaders identify others' Protect means keep the things safe from danger, attack, or harm. Leaders should be able to protect their organizations against threat. This skill provides them a somewhat comfortable condition to continue their existence; recognize shortcomings and challenges; and establish a more robust and realistic set of solutions.

Survival skills are skills that help one to survive in dangerous situations or in dangerous places. First step towards protecting an organization from risks is to understand the nature of condition you are guarding against. The threat may come from several factors, i.e.:

a. Internal factors - Something within organization that actively contributes the chances of getting failed

i. Finance - Due to uncertainty in future reported cash flows/ uncertainty in earnings

ii. Human resources - Associated with failure to meet the particular nature of each position; fail in succession; sickness, absence, turnover, work related illness and injury, medical and long term disability; or work ethics

iii. Operation - Failure resulting from inadequate processes, people and systems, e.g. Human error, systems failure, fraud or other criminal activity.

b. External factors – Unexpected external situations that affect the organization performance:

1. Market Risk: Refer to the risk that the market value of an investment, collateral protecting a deposit, or securities underlying a repurchase agreement will decline. This type of risk is affected by the length to maturity of a security, the need to liquidate a security before maturity, the extent that collateral exceeds the amount invested, and the frequency at which the amount of collateral is adjusted for changing market values.

2. Price risk: Associated with dramatic price fluctuation of product. Especially product futures market provides a means for all sectors of the product trade to manage or hedge their exposure to the risk of unexpected price fluctuation. By hedging the price of product they must buy and sell, they can avoid the potentially devastating effects of unexpected price fluctuation. It also involves basis risk, a risk that is associated with widening or narrowing the basis between the time a hedge is established and the time it is liquidated. Basis itself is the difference between the specific futures contract for product at a local delivery point. Future price may consider present cash price, cost of storage, insurance and interest charges, and location of delivery.

3. Interest Rate Risk: Sensitivity to a decline in interest rates

4. Customer Risk: Associated with failure to meet the current and changing needs and expectations of customers

5. Currency Risk: Performance relative to currency markets, i.e. spot contracts, forward transactions, window forwards, options, currency swaps, non-deliverable forwards.

6. Energy Risk: Financial risks posed by volatile energy prices (electricity, oil, natural gas, and fuel)

7. Equity Risk: Relate to depreciation because of stock market dynamics causing one to lose money

8. Competitiveness Risk: Affect the competitiveness of the service (in terms of cost or quality)

9. Commodity/Raw Material Risk: Affect the state budgets and company cash flows and makes future revenues less predictable as commodity (raw material) price uncertainty

10. Reinvestment Risk: Uncertainty in the interest rate at which future cash flows may be invested

11. Earnings/Liquidity Risk: Due to uncertainty in future reported earnings/cash flow

12. Social/Community Risk: Relate to the effects of changes in demographic, socio-economic trends, environmental demands, health demands, political change, and associated to public health and environmental quality

13. Environmental Risk: Relate to the environmental consequences of pollution, recycling, landfill requirements, emissions etc. environmental and green supply assurance, commit to conserving energy, water and other resources, reducing waste, phasing out the use of ozone-depleting substances and minimizing the release of greenhouse gases and substances damaging to health and the environment.

14. Employee Risk: Associated with sickness absence, turnover, work related illness and injury, medical and long term disability, employment practice, insurance

15. Political Risk: Associated with failure to deliver either local or central government policy, or meet the local administrations manifesto commitments

16. Model Risk: Risk that models are applied to tasks for which they are inappropriate or are otherwise implemented incorrectly

17. Operational Risk: Loss resulting from inadequate or failed internal processes, people and systems, or from external events,

e.g. Employee errors, systems failures, fire, floods or other losses to physical assets, fraud or other criminal activity.

18. Technological Risk: Associated with the capacity of corporate to deal with the pace/scale of technological change, or its ability to use technology to address changing demands. They may also include the consequences of internal technological failures to deliver its objectives.

19. Legal Risk: Uncertainty due to legal actions or uncertainty in the applicability or interpretation of contracts, laws or regulations

20. Economical Macro Risk: Affect the ability of corporate to meet its financial commitments because of macro level economic changes

21. Contractual Risk: Associated with the failure of contractors to deliver services or products to the agreed cost and specification or failure of corporate to ensure that contracts are properly specified. It must be appropriately managed; achieves value for money by procuring against pre-determined standards not only for the goods, services and works but also for the suppliers that are used; legal, ethical and transparent.

22. Professional Risk: Associated with failure to meet the particular nature of each position.

23. Credit Risk: Refer to the likelihood that a party involved in an investment transaction will not fulfill its obligations. This type of risk is often associated with the issuer of the investment security and is affected by the concentration of deposits or investments in a single instrument or with a single institution. Custodial credit risk is the risk that a government will not be able (a) to recover deposits if the depository financial institution fails or (b) to recover the value of investment or collateral securities that are in the possession of an outside party if the counterparty to the investment or deposit transaction fails.

24. Extension Risk: The risk that a security will lengthen in average life due to slower prepayment speeds. This type of risk is generally associated with mortgage securities.

25. Contraction Risk: The risk that a security will shorten in average life due to faster than expected prepayments. This type of risk is normally associated with mortgage securities.

26. Capital Risk: Refer to the risk that an investor may not recover all or a portion of his or her original capital at the time an investment has been liquidated.

Protect-ability is about your ability to inspire trust, loyalty, commitment, and collegiality among members. Leaders must be aware the need to protect organization's most valuable assets against the threat, which may involve:

i. Defensive mode - Guard against the threat. It an ability to help organization to survive long enough, and to stay productive. When the focus is survival, there is no need to aggressively go after the opponent. Defensive mode prevents predation within the business. It focuses on the following methods:

a. Shielding - Defend or cover up with protecting device

b. Preserving – Keep in unaltered condition; or maintain unchanged

c. Securing – Confine the potential risk, and keep watch

d. Holding out - Sustain the danger

e. Eliminating – Get rid of risk. You can reduce risks but not eliminate them.

f. Evacuating – Take away or stay away

g. Resistance - Actions that oppose motion. Resistance is an extraordinary work for survival.

h. Escaping - Succeed in keeping away from danger.

i. Guarding – Directing the potential harms, keep them under control

j. Evasion – Move in alternate directions; set aside

k. Changing - Make a difference, or become different. , i.e. camouflage

l. Hiding - Make sure people never even know where you're. There is no real openness, the system is closed and every influence coming near is filtered.

m. Baiting and switching - Giving something less expensive than the original one. A bait and switch is a form of fraud in which the fraudster lures in the opponent by substituting.

ii. Offensive mode - Rely on overwhelming direct damage that may lead to predation. It serves to enable new life for future business, which will always prevail in expressing the trait, and actively and offensively create opportunity to benefit the organization, i.e.:

a. Dominating - Display dominance trait which aims "victory," manifested as defeat-related behaviors. Dominants will gain resources.

b. Attacking - Take offensive action and affect harmfully Vulnerability of the offensive action is destabilizing. Offensive mode is generally characterized by attack, or aggressiveness. Attack involves a set of behaviors that enable the aggressive people to reach particular position of the opponent.

Competition and increased failure puts pressure on leaders to both take risks and make good decisions. Effective protection depends on:

a. Type of protection: Prevention against danger, i.e. defensive, offensive or moderate

b. Environment: Situations that potentially attack and harm the organization, i.e. individual – fraud; social - conflict, etc

c. Time: The length of time, a leader and organization can survive, primarily depends on environment and type of protection. Prolonging time for taking action will increase the risk.

d. Man: Efforts of the people. Survival begins by evaluating the risk, capacity of the people, etc.

e. Tools: The means to protect the asset or people against threat. There are choices what kind of tools to be applied and in what combination. The tools, however, are applied in different ways depending on what type of asset is being protected, i.e. anti virus, alarm, etc.

f. Method: A systematic way of protecting organization. Methods of protection are constantly changing. It depends on the character of dangers, internal audit, procedure, etc

Fail to protect organization from threats may lead to violence, exploitation and abuse; which will weaken survival, growth and development. Minimize threats will eliminate you:

a. Operate in and above the fray: Observe what's happening to your initiative

b. Court the uncommitted: The uncommitted but wary are crucial to organization success. Show your intentions are serious, for example, by dismissing individuals who can't make required changes. And practice what you preach.

c. Cook the conflict: Keep the heat high enough to motivate, but low enough to prevent explosions. Raise the temperature to make people confront hidden conflicts and other tough issues. Then lower the heat to reduce destructive turmoil. Slow the pace of change.

d. Place the problem where it belongs: Allow inputs from others, resist resolving conflicts alone - people will blame you for whatever turmoil results. Mobilize others to solve problems.

Asset protection is something you must do before someone is ready to sue you. Leaders should appraise their own strengths and weaknesses, not hesitating to get help in their weak areas when possible. Effective leadership includes the capacity of protection from danger. Dangers within or from outside the organization begin to threaten organization or member's well-being; therefore leaders should act to protect.

Leadership of survival is one's ability to manage risk and the development of resource protection. Leaders should strive to see that the organization is relatively free of aberrations, or disruptions that make organization continuity impossible. Leaders must weigh how much freedom to leave and how much control to exercise. A well-led organization is a generally secure place to grow.

COMMUNICATION FOR SURVIVAL

To be an effective leader, you must have acquired a lot of information to be effective. Things can happen; communication is an important matter of survival. Survival depends on it. If you start communicating in a positive manner, you will have the help on your side when you need them.

If we can understand organizational communication, we will understand the organization itself. Communication defines the transfer of meanings between persons and groups. The purpose of communication may range from completing a task or mission to creating and maintaining satisfying interpersonal relationships.

The survival of an organization depends on individuals and groups who are able to maintain among themselves effective and continuing the relationships. Communication for survival, i.e.:

a. Give signal to other that you need a help to survive: Make sure that somebody knows when really you need it; and tell as much information about your situation to get a back up. Never head into the danger alone. Always have at least two or more methods of communication with your key contacts, so that if one method is disabled, another method can be used. Communication will need to be under principles of trust and honesty, not of ego or pride.

b. Collect information: The ability to collect information in a timely manner will greatly increase your chances of survival in almost every scenario you can think of. There are many different ways to get information. People may have relevant information that the leader does not have. In gaining information, leaders should:

i. Evaluate credibility of information & sources: Leaders must be able to evaluate the credibility and validity of information and its sources.

ii. Recognize inadequate information or evidence: Leaders are able to examine information and evidence and make valid judgments about its adequacy.

c. Provide healthy environment - It is important to establish a positive atmosphere and a sense of sympathetic understanding which helps promoting a spirit of camaraderie.

The survival of an organization depends on individuals and groups who are able to maintain among themselves effective and continuing relationships. Without a doubt, organization's survival depends on communication. It's vital to alert members against danger.

Leadership and communication have been inexorably bound together. Communication skills are the number one requirement for leadership success. Effective communication is not easy, but it is vital to organization survival. Effective communication is also critical to business success.

ADAPTABILITY

Adaptability is emerging as a key leadership requirement. It's a leader's ability to respond effectively to rapidly changing circumstances; which involves the development of novel strategies, adjusting behaviors and strategies to changing requirements, and motivating the team to accept and contribute to the process of adapting.

No one will work for all situations. If the variables change, you must adapt in response to them. It is important that the leader be adaptable in response to different situations. Yesterday's solutions may not necessarily work tomorrow but as a leader, your job is to adapt to the changing times. If you are too rigid in your position, the risk is that you will acquire a reputation for patterned behavior.

The environment in which we live is changing rapidly and in unpredictable ways. Individuals who are creative are able to bring about change and visualize future opportunity. Creative leaders are a critical resource needed to find answers to difficult problems. They are the ones who can navigate the future. They are able to embrace ambiguity and reframe problems as opportunities.

Leaders who are sensitive to how the people around them work best and are flexible in adapting their leadership skills to support the styles and needs of others get the best results. This does not mean that a good leader is someone who is a chameleon, always switching colors to fit the setting. You, as a leader, should be adaptable to:

Change

Change is crucial to the survival and growth of organizations in today's competitive. The status quo requires no leadership. Leadership is required because we want to move somewhere. Leaders know their job is to move people through status quo, to meet the needs of the situations and the people they are leading.

Leadership is about facilitating change within yourself, and your organization. Adaptability is an important skill for leaders to develop in order to respond effectively to this change. Leadership positions people and organizations for change. Change begins with questions. Without a need for change, the concept of leadership is meaningless.

Leadership is the energetic process of getting other people fully and willingly committed to a new and sustainable course of action. A successful change process draws you focus on where are you at the moment; where do you want to take your improvement; how do you best plan to get there – and achieve the results.

An important part of change is alignment with direction; that provides appropriate methods, and fulfills critical roles in moving the effort forward. Do too much and too fast is one of the failure indication of change initiatives.

You should identify the right balance between an aggressive, results-driven approach and the need for sustainable change; and to build your personal ability to work on the right improvement priorities (hint: everything can't be top priority).

Organizations need leaders who can define and guide change while continuing to operate the business; a portfolio of well-scoped and managed initiatives that target the most important needs of the organization and its members; and the ability to execute change efforts promptly and efficiently.

Change relies on strong teamwork and communication; which builds support for process improvement efforts. Determining how best to deploy others who can lead to a strong and flexible change network. Successful change is rarely instant; often, despite a clear vision, need help to "get out of your own way." We get in our own way, when our belief systems are not congruent, which have three components which interact to guide our perceptions and interactions:

    i.   Values, i.e. what we perceive as the ideal state.

   ii.   Beliefs, i.e. the opinions we hold about ourselves, our self worth, abilities and our place in the world

   iii. Assumptions, i.e. the opinions we have about others, what is accepted and rejected and how the world works.

Leaders learn how to develop their own adaptability and to foster it in others, thereby becoming more effective for themselves, the people they lead, and their organizations. Change requires a new attitude and approach. Ones may value the ability to change as a part of their responsibilities. They understand that change will occur, expect it and effortlessly perform during and after the change.

Change is a culture that expects new paradigm and responds it with the understanding, perspectives, tools and techniques to make change seamless and effortless. It is making change a part of business as usual. The result of change is better performance.

The key is to carefully assess organization's needs, priorities and readiness before implement the appropriate solutions, and then working closely with members to achieve the goals with a balanced focus on short-term benefits and long-term change excellence. There are always opposing attitudes against change which demonstrate:

1.   Fight change - People who fight change want to maintain their comfort zone with familiar surroundings. (Status quo) As pressure for change grows, they utilize others to protect their comfort zone. As fighters resist change, their efficiency falls further behind and in time their professional skill has no value to anyone.

2.   Embrace change - People who embrace change thrive on challenges. They are independent thinkers who seek new opportunity, which is found in change. They are leaders of efficiency. The person who depends on proven methods can't understand how blunder's get promoted ahead of those who maintain the status quo.

Leading change requires asking people to confront painful issues and give up habits and beliefs they hold dear. Some people may try to eliminate change's visible agent. Whether they attack him/her personally, undermine his/her authority, or seduce him/her into seeing things their way, their goal is the same: to derail him/her, easing their pain and restoring familiar order. To avoid self-destructing during difficult change, leaders need to:

a. Restrain your desire for control and need for importance. Order for its own sake prevents organizations from handling contentious issues. And an inflated self-image fosters unhealthy dependence on you.

b. Use a safe environment (e.g., a friend's kitchen table) or routine (a daily walk) to repair psychological damage and recalibrate moral compass.

c. Acquire a confidant (not an ally from the organization) who supports them - not necessarily their own initiative.

d. Read attacks as reactions to your professional role, not to you personally. You'll remain calmer and keep people engaged.

A leader must be highly adaptable, to be effective in leading people. Therefore, the flexibility and adaptability are essential. It allows duties are finished more quickly and meet expectations more often. Risks are accurately anticipated, calculated and mitigated. Inspire change to your organization. Usually, change culture involves:

i. Evaluate whether change is necessary: Consider needs to change, expectation against changes, level of changes, advantage for organization, contingency plan if changes are not successful, commitment from the people

ii. Defrost status quo: Plan and manage the implementation stages carefully, rely on the team's commitment to change, which implies:

1. Break the rules: Carefully define and document the desired change.

2. Establish a sense of urgency: Cultivate team spirit throughout the process.

3. Create the guiding coalition: Involvement is creating an environment in which people have an impact on decisions and actions that affect their activities. People are most enabled to contribute to continuous improvement and the ongoing success of their work organization. The improvement process may take steps, i.e. define the problem/opportunity, choose the best people, and correct the problem.

4. Develop a vision and strategy: Vision is the core of leadership and is at the heart of strategy. The leader must embed strategy in the organization: choose excellent team members, pick the right roles, and make the strategic moves.

5. Communicate the change vision: Communicate your efforts to generate interest and enthusiasm. As change is to be implemented, solicit members and feedback, so goals and objectives can be revisited, if necessary.

iii. Introduce new practices:

1. Empower a broad base of people to take action: Leaders take action to change the organization, and show their efforts to adapt to those changes.

2. Generate short term wins: Small changes can lead to a big impact. The organization actively seeks out signs of progress, celebrates the successes, and rewards the people who made the change possible.

    Without short-term wins to renew the organization's energy, most people will fall back in the path of less resistance, which is the good old way of doing things. Most people will soon withdraw their emotional support unless they see visible evidence that the project is producing the desired outcomes.

3. Consolidate gains and producing even more change: Manage stress by maintaining open and constant communication. Be prepared for obstacles and rely on other stakeholders for support.

iv. Ground the changes in the culture: Institutionalize new approaches in the organization culture. A highly effective leader is always looking for improvement and constantly questions the status quo. Change can also create uncertainty and stress within an organization. Change also offers opportunities, if approached thoughtfully and managed effectively.

Dramatic change often creates feelings of uncertainty, self-consciousness, and even fear. Leaders know that even minor change can have a powerful effect. Adaptability is emerging as a key leadership requirement. Adaptability can be developed.

Improvement

Leadership is usually underpinned by good management. In effective leaders employ effective people and surround themselves with people who buy into the vision of the leader. The leader is always looking for improvement and though not a change junkie. The leaders constantly question the status quo, looking for improvement.

One of the most interesting values in organization is continuous improvement. Both individuals and organizations can adopt this value.

Improvement might come in the form of a continuous urge to increase one's knowledge and skills, a desire to improve one's attitudes and temperament, or a desire to do things better or get the best out of things.

An organization can implement the value by continually evaluating and upgrading its procedures, the way it interacts with its customers, the way it treats its members, and many other ways. Any value that is applied can create a positive response from the people.

Improvement is action or process that enhances value. It's more than merely replaces, repairs, or restores to original condition. It implies to better condition, easier of use, and increase the value.

Improvement activities is the strategic aspect of involvement and can include such methods as suggestion systems, manufacturing cells, work teams, continuous improvement meetings, Kaizen (continuous improvement) events, corrective action processes, and periodic discussions.

Improvements should significantly reduce costs, reduce lead times, reduce unnecessary space, enhance workforce empowerment, and eliminate waste. Work quality can be improved by the practice of continuously assessing and adjusting performance using accepted procedures.

Continuous improvement provides activities that bring the things gradually to the desired level, and be constantly reviewed. Since one of the leader's key functions is to lead change, he/she must view resistance as a signal that something is wrong with the process being used to achieve desired change rather than simply passing off the resistance to change as a normal characteristic of human behavior.

Leaders establish a vision for organization improvement and influence others to work.

Innovativeness

Innovation is the lifeblood of an organization. Knowing how to lead and work with creative people requires knowledge and action that often goes against the typical organizational structure. Leaders develop innovation strategy that focuses on boosting the productivity, improving the skill level of members improving the environment for innovation, promoting learning and growth. Leaders must be able to think creatively while taking initiative and calculated risks.

Effective leaders have a vision beyond the immediate work of the group/organization. This involves exploring and integrating diverse perspectives, recognizing unexpected opportunities, and obtaining resources needed to achieve progress.

Developing innovative approaches requires creativity and the willingness to generate and explore ideas that haven't been tried before. This can be difficult for many people to do, particularly if their creative efforts haven't been well nurtured.

Creativity arises from the ability to look at situations from different perspectives or in different contexts. It involves suspending the current notions, assumptions, and beliefs.

Leaders need to understand that everyone has the potential to be creative and think more creatively than they already do. Effective leaders show the greatest skills in survival of difficult circumstances are those who are also the most imaginative and the most creative.

Sometimes imagination or creativity means allowing others to bring forth and suggest and even carry out solutions to the problems or challenges which face us rather than trying always to find the answer ourselves.

Imagination and creativity also involve looking outside the envelope and finding different ways of doing things, even though they have never been done that way before. This means believing in our people and trusting them, but it also means knowing their limitations and holding them accountable.

Innovation is a key to success/survival; therefore greater attention should be paid to innovation as a factor of competitiveness.

Cooperativeness

Cooperativeness means interaction that facilitates the accomplishment of a specific goal through people working together in groups. Set the stage for cooperation from others by:

a. Introducing the idea: Effective cooperation allows every one presents the idea. Others are expressing a willingness to listen other the ideas of others.

b. Continual stimulation by talking about it: Leaders make continual reminder of the positive consequences of working towards common goal.

c. Get others to make an investment by having them participate in the planning.

Collaboration requires effective leadership which encourages cooperativeness. In cooperativeness, people are to balance their attention to the shared goals and cooperative skill building; find a partner, share their ideas with their partner, and probe each other for complete understanding.

Group member should advance willingness and ability to work with others based on the values of self-help, self-responsibility, equality, democracy, equity and solidarity.

Success is measured by how well you forge and form collaborative relationships. You must learn to facilitate, not dominate; influence, not enflame; and disagree without being disagreeable. Recognize that your best ideas for change will be yours alone to carry out if you do not include others. And to bring about real change will require the energy, involvement and shared participation of others.

Beyond cooperation, collaboration involves identifying the needs of all parties involved in the issue, and working toward outcomes that will meet all those identified needs. Cooperative efforts result in striving for mutual benefit so that all group members:

i.   Gain from each other's efforts - one's success benefits other. Each member's efforts are required and indispensable for organization's success

ii. Recognize that members share a common fate; they all sink together. Each member has a unique contribution to make to the joint effort

iii. Recognize no one can do things without other. One's performance is mutually caused by oneself and his/her team members. Cooperativeness skills must be thought to get effective cooperativeness.

Leadership is not just for people at the top. Everyone can learn to lead by discovering the power to make a difference and being prepared when the call to lead comes. A highly effective leader should be able to:

1. Integrate all members to gain consensus for the shared goals

2. Make decision – Define what behaviors to continue or change, and actions that are helpful and not helpful

3. Trust building - Change success needs trust. We need trust does not mean we know how to build trust. Our efforts rely too heavily on our feelings, intuition and perception to tell us what's wrong with others. Fortunately, there is a better way to build trust based relationships. Building trust takes a lot of commitments and efforts

4. Communicate – Leaders communicate to members how well they are achieving their goals and maintaining effective working relationships

5. Manage conflict - Conflict is generally a disagreement regarding interests or ideas. Whether it is within oneself, between two people, or within an organization, it has a negative connotation. Conflict has historically been viewed as undesirable, something to be avoided.

Conflict can be viewed within an organization as negative and not supporting the decisions of management. While conflict can be viewed as negative, it has important implications in increasing the effectiveness of a team's decision-making process.

When disagreement is poorly dealt with, the outcome can be contention, which creates a sense of distance between people, such as feelings of dislike, bitter antagonism, competition, alienation, and disregard. It takes conflict resolution skill, effort and commitment to face the challenge together with the other person involved in the group.

Leadership is an interactive conversation that pulls people toward becoming comfortable with language of personal responsibility and commitment.

Cooperativeness is positively related to effective leadership. A highly effective leader influences others' cooperativeness.

Flexibility

Flexibility is ability to respond appropriately changes in the setting. Adaptability evolves flexibility. In many ways, flexibility is presumed good and inflexibility bad. Flexibility is to cooperate with others and adapt to change. It is ability to adapt to changing situations; to achieve high levels, in which people need to modify behavior and get along with others.

Flexibilities come with provisos adapt different paces, open to personal interactions, actively participate, and provide alternatives; pre-conditions - remove barriers or constraints, and commitments - commit to collaborate and support.

Leaders need to respond effectively to change in the organizational environment, ability to adjust better to change than others, which includes:

a. Cognitive flexibility: The ability to use a variety of thinking strategies and mental frameworks

b. Emotional flexibility: The ability to vary one's approach to dealing with one's own emotions and those of others

c. Dispositional flexibility (or personality- based flexibility): The ability to remain optimistic and at the same time realistic

The leaders should be able to define priorities and manage a portfolio of change efforts, functions that coordinate their efforts, skilled people who can assess opportunities and challenge assumptions, and an environment that accepts uncertainty while avoiding unnecessary risks. They should build the change capability essential to compete and grow in a climate where organization is at risk.

You can also influence organization to be more tolerant of error, and seeing it as a necessary condition for innovation to occur.

Effective leaders search for and discover opportunities, introduce positive change. One aspect of a firm's capability is its flexibility: if the organization invests in know-how in a way that makes it more flexible (in the sense that it can respond more quickly or more effectively to changes in future market conditions), then this affects its profitability, and its prospects for survival.

Adaptability is no longer a nicety or coping mechanism, but a necessary skill for leaders to develop, in order to respond effectively to change. Leaders rarely know what they can do to become more adaptable and foster adaptability in others.

Leaders emphasizes the need to utilize multivariate approaches, check the influence of combinations of traits in specific situations; and use methods to identify trait patterns related to adaptability. Leaders have to learn how to develop their own adaptability and to foster it in others, the people they lead, and the organization.

The adaptability of organizations depends on having widespread leadership that can come from anywhere within an organization, not just from those in top positions of authority. Leadership that is adaptive demonstrates strategies and practices that can help organizations and the people in them break through gridlocks, accomplish deep change and develop the adaptability to thrive in complex, competitive and challenging environments.

In today's business environment change is fast and constant. The key, for a leader to be adaptable, is to embrace change and use it as an opportunity to grow and learn. The more positive experiences that leaders have with change, the more they become comfortable with and skilled at adaptability.

ASSESS-ABILITY

Leaders have capabilities to assess organizational health, and its competitive performance. Assess means estimate the nature, ability or quality of. This is the first and most important step; recognize that you are in a survival situation.

Key to survival is to make sure you stay in control. Assess-ability is ability to evaluate the risks posed to different situations, so that ones can take actions to overcome the problems. It implies:

i.   Recognize how risk factors relate to the situation, whether they have been identified as contributing to the events.

ii. Weigh evidence - Ascertain its relevance, validity, reliability, appropriateness and accuracy.

iii. Recognize and evaluate evidence - Leaders analyze and evaluate evidence effectively, i.e. records, situations, information, incident, etc. They should also evaluate organization's efforts to minimize risk

iv. Develop criteria for evaluation - Examine a situation, and create relevant criteria to use for evaluating some aspect

v. Make decisions - Make appropriate decisions considering relevant implications and consequences

Leaders demonstrate ability to assess their leadership role, to lead or facilitate a group to achieve its goals and the organization achievements. Asses-ability fosters to:

Simplicity

Effective leaders create conditions that enable others to work effectively. Make things simple. Simplify complex situations, as simple as possible, so it can be understood. Highly effective leaders are almost always great simplifier, who can cut through argument, debate and doubt, and offer a solution everybody can understand. The result is clarity of purpose, credibility of leadership, and integrity of organization.

Simple indicates a condition which is not complicated; ordinary or common; humble in condition; composed of only one thing; easy of use; not guileful or deceitful; sincere to the user; free from vanity; not sophisticated. There is no more important personal value than simplicity. Taking the time to simplify anything that is overly complex is a very helpful skill in these rapidly accelerating times.

Simplifying is not only streamlining it, but making it more effective and productive, and leading to greater results. A Creative problem solving is simplicity. Make your messages simple and direct. Don't confuse people with needless complexity. Keep it simple, stupid.

Orderliness

Orderliness is a must for effective organizations. Orderliness evolves to proceed in accordance with some order - being told to do something; determined by rules or a system - units that interact to perform a task; characterized by a neat and methodical arrangement - approach that is used to do something.

Orderliness is adherence to a logically and carefully planned, emphasize observance of a coordinated and orderly set of procedures.

When organizations are not orderly it is hard to be productive. Having an organized plan will help people finish the task in a timely and easy manner. If a leader is consistent in being orderly, then he/she will set a good example and lead others to be orderly also. Orderliness includes

i.   Maintain a tidiness, cleanliness and safety. Create an environment that is pleasant and conducive.

ii. Efficient use of resources and easy to control: Control input and improve throughput to enhance output.

iii. Ensure environments that allow for personal expression. Express ideas and organization in ways that communicate clearly.

iv. Show initiative: See what needs to be done and do it without someone telling you to. Initiative begins with understanding and insight. Measure the gaps between skill deficiency, skill proficiency and actual performance.

v.   Use things for intended purpose: When people have a purpose, they can handle things and utilize it for their own purpose. Will not take responsibility unless delegated by the authority. Develop value engineering to assess importance.

vi. Use good manners – Show care and kindness about others and respect how they feel. Disorganization wastes time, and the resulting confusion causes frustration - which leads to inefficiency and dissatisfaction. Orderliness dispels confusion. Organizing takes time and forethought, but the efficiency earned by orderliness is immeasurable. Evaluate, plan, implement, manage and maintain improved results with lower costs.

Many people fail because of lacks both neatness and orderliness. Effective leaders develop character qualities like orderliness. The leaders have the clarity of their mind and the creativity and orderliness of their thinking. They display effort to improve the orderliness of their organization.

Openness

Openness (i.e. less secrecy) makes to the survival of organizations. Leadership is participation in a shared effort with the intention of influencing others and with openness to be influenced by others. Openness is a state of mind, an attitude toward people, ideas and circumstances. It is the key to our growth as human beings.

People are thought of as being generally open or closed, and so are organizations and societies. A person's degree of openness may fluctuate; you may be more open in some aspects than others. It is not easy to be open because it makes you feel vulnerable and may, in fact, increase your vulnerability.

Openness involves letting things in, especially things you do not want to hear, and letting things out, as in openly speaking your truth. A highly effective leader strives to evolve in the direction of openness; to open their minds to see as many possibilities as they ca; to open their hearts to feel compassion, and empathy; and to open their spirits to the full expression of who they really are.

Openness happens bit by bit, moment by moment, choice by choice. When you model openness as a leader, you begin to influence your organization to develop a climate of openness. Creativity thrives in open climates. Open system is organic; they grow and evolve, whereas closed systems are stifling. They stagnate and wither.

For leaders, it becomes even more critical because without openness, you are closing off your organization and the people you work with - not just yourself - and you are creating a dynamic that is extremely unhealthy. You have to work at openness. As you nurture that in yourself as a leader, you open up your organization to greater possibilities.

Leaders appreciate openness in themselves and others. They try to be open to all aspects of themselves, to their environment, to the divine aspects of other people. Openness should not just be directed to things which fits and confirms compliance; it should also include the allowance of information and influences which might be questioned. An effective leader will:

a. See openness as a fundamental principle of leadership: Seek to create and support open systems. Move from punitive culture to openness to learn from mistakes.

b. Be open to others: Strive to have an open heart and mind, help others to have open hearts and minds; and be open to seeing the divine qualities in themselves and others

c. Foster openness in themselves and others: Use openness to foster their growth and the growth of others, to foster their creativity and the creativity of others, and key to creating infinite potentiality in themselves and others.

Our openness is grounded on our survival. This is part of the survival behavior and protects the individual and organization. An organization must innovate just to survive, let alone thrive. Creativity - the ability to discover connections in our existence - depends upon openness to what is. The ground of creativity is openness.

An effective leader shows how to break out of the box, and become open to all that is. He/she demonstrates how openness alone fuels a leader's ability to be forward thinking and intensely curious, to generate ideas, and to form a vision. Trust is such a key issue in the leader/follower relationship.

Transparency is the openness and forthrightness needed for leadership. Trust levels and commitment to change will be highest when there are no hidden surprises or agendas being forwarded. When leaders and followers both see and know the others' motives and expectations, the relationship is transparent. Effective leaders foster openness and diversity of thought, experience, and culture within the people through interaction with the community.

Predict-ability

Systematic organization is predictable. Put your trust in systems, not in genius. If you want to create a great organization, create thing where your systems unleash the power of your people. A system is a number of inter-connected parts that work together. If you do something to one part of the system, other parts are affected.

Great success comes from creating a system that allows people of average competence to combine to produce results that otherwise could only be achieved by people of great talent or genius.

The most talented individual might be hard-pressed to produce great results in a flawed system. Self-awareness is the foundation for long-term effectiveness as a leader. It measures how he/she responds to problems or challenges, influences others to one's point of view, responds to the pace of the environment, and responds to the rules and procedures set by the organization.

Leaders should be confident of their ability to assess their resources and use it to make strategic decisions. They must be able to locate people within the organization with the knowledge to meet unexpected challenges, such as the rise of competitor.

Humility means, in terms of leadership survival, that we can eventually become wise enough by benefit of our own mistakes and experiences to realize our limitations and honest enough to recognize that the very best of us is but a vessel of clay; and therefore, none of us has all of the right answers all of the time about all of the questions.

COMPETITIVENESS

Effective leaders are committed to increasing railroad efficiency and competitiveness. Many organizations are dealing with low profit margins, and competition is a lot fiercer.

Leaders who tend towards a competitive style take a firm stand, and know what they want. They usually operate from a position of power, drawn from things like position, rank, expertise, or persuasive ability. This style can be useful when there is an emergency and a decision needs to be made fast; when the decision is unpopular; or when defending against someone who is trying to exploit the situation selfishly.

However it can also leave people feeling bruised, unsatisfied and resentful when used in less urgent situations. Competitiveness analysis involves compelling both internal and external factors that affect the organization, i.e.:

a. Collect data: Understanding competitiveness requires objective data and qualitative inputs from stakeholders. When identifying competitive strengths or weaknesses, we have to look for objective evidence

b. Assess future trends: A status quo assessment of competitiveness is useful but lacks predictive power. Remember that organization's sources of competitive advantage today may not necessarily remain competitive in the future. It is important to ensure that the analysis focuses on external trends that drive competitiveness.

    It is also important to identify the fundamental sources of competitiveness that will enable the organization to become and remain dynamic by changing to meet future demands.

c. Assess against the existing vision: Look at the competitive sources of advantage in reference to the organization's existing vision and strategic direction.

Organization which excels period of survival focuses on competitiveness. Competitiveness requires:

Hard work

Hard work is one of the keys to success in life and business. Without it, only few can succeed. Consider why you may not be hard working, and then make a determined effort to change the behavior. Keep up the effort over time. Leaders care of their followers who are not hard working.

Hard work pays off. The greater your capacity for hard work, the more rewards fall within your grasp. Being healthy is hard work. Finding and maintaining a successful relationship is hard work. Getting organized is hard work. Setting goals, making plans to achieve them, and staying on track is hard work. Start your quest to become an effective leader, which includes:

a. Know yourself: Confront yourself with an honest angle. Take time to recognize your specific strengths and capabilities. Use your energies to maximize them. Recognize your weaknesses. Develop a plan to minimize them

b. Know your role: One of your principal responsibilities is the acquisition of accurate information, its correct assessment and the effective decision making that results. Leaders ensure that your staff takes ownership of their role.

c. Know your people: Your followers may come from diverse backgrounds, unfamiliar with "the way it used to be." Discover their needs, interests and goals. Notice hidden capabilities, unused talents.

Hard work means applying your ability with focus and intensity; any activity that you don't want to do; any activity that you find difficult and strenuous. Hard work is an indication that you should stop, stand back and look for alternatives. Not many things are really hard in the sense that they hurt you.

There are many different activities requiring different degrees of effort and compulsion. How much work is to be found in an activity is at least partly caused by the attitude people bring to it. If you are tough, you will recover from setbacks, you will work hard all the time. An effective leader, in the beginning, prepares him/herself to work hard, think hard and seek better leader within the organization.

Endurance

Effective leaders can make their presence felt in any situation. Your endurance exhibits quality or power of withstanding hardship; continuing existence; state of surviving; remaining alive. Endurance measured by the ability to withstand pain, fatigue, stress and hardship. It demonstrates physical vitality, emotional resilience, and mental stamina. Endurance displays, i.e.:

i. Patience: Business requires patience. It contains an emotional element, making the passage of time slow down even more. Patience is a virtue. Giving patience, to reach a definite decision, may make clear the thing that is murky or hidden before. The need for lasting leadership is crucial.

Patience means wait, think, consider alternatives and allowing the true facts show themselves; these are marks of maturity and wisdom. Effective leader must have some patience in his/her development. Effective leaders highly emphasize patience and empathy.

ii. Perseverance: The price of success is hard work, dedication to the job at hand, and the determination that whether we win or lose, we have applied the best of ourselves to the task at hand. Ineffective leaders are too soon to quit. Keep that in mind when lead organizations. Don't keep changing your direction. Your organization will not be able to cope with it. Develop success from failures.

Failure is contagious but success is infectious. Reinforce success; you must reward success. Expect some failures; give the people the latitude to learn. Leaders need mostly to learn to endure our own mistakes and failures.

Leaders accept pain and disappointment. To becoming an effective leader is certainly attainable. It takes hard work. Customers want to work with a leader because a leader team/organization produces results.

Toughness

Being an effective leader today-in an organization is tougher than at any previous time, due in large measure to environment change that occurring faster than ever before-and decision making following suit with equal speed. Toughness means be strong and resilient; able to withstand great strain without tearing or breaking

Toughness decreases as the rate of loading increases. A person may possess satisfactory toughness under static loads (single stress) but may fail under dynamic loads (multiple stresses).

Toughness can be learned. If you are not tough, it just means you need more practice. Just like learning or perfecting a technique or skill, toughness can be learned, refined and honed. Accountability is form of mental toughness. It is the realization of the fact that everyone is personally responsible for their actions. You are ultimately in charge of your life successes and or failures.

Tough means you are willing to stand tall and persevere. Even when your mind and body signal perfectly good reasons for giving up, you go on.

Tough is an ability to make the best from what you are given. Tough means make the decision that replacing self-pity, complaints and dependence with self-reliance, independence and action. You've got to be tough to do the big things in organization, like taking risks, admitting mistakes, and changing bad habits.

Self-reliance and self-confidence will demand your toughness. You must temper toughness with kindness, realizing that many times it will be tough to be kind. Toughness consists of:

Mental Toughness

Mental toughness is a measurement of an individual's vigor or capacity for endurance. Mental toughness means being able to reach personal state of being that allows an individual to perform with his/her greatest potential. It is a state of being where an individual feels most energized, most confident and most strong. It is a state when you have that positive attitude and are enjoying the battle (the competition).

Mental toughness is the attitude that makes a person willing to do what it takes to get the job done. Mental toughness can be acquired through habit and practice, involves using your mind to achieve victory over your environment.

Mental toughness is essentially giving yourself the right messages which allowing you to withstand great strain without breaking. Never lose control of yourself. Mental toughness is having the natural or developed psychological edge that enables you to:

i. Cope that is better than others (e.g., competition, lifestyle, etc): Be more consistent and better than your opponents in remaining determined, focused, confident, resilient, and in control under pressure.

ii. Be more consistent and better than others: Focus your mind not on winning or losing, but on the only thing that you can surely control. Perfect the mindset. No complain. You should turn physical toughness into mental toughness to optimize your potential. Come to practice with a purpose that make easier to stay focus when distracts come. It gives you mental confidence.

Pressure and stress come from within. You put it on yourself. Your interpretation and attitude are important. To reduce it, think positive thoughts. Visualize positive actions. And act as if. Mental toughness is characterized by:

i. Self-Belief: Have an unshakable belief in your ability to achieve competition goals; qualities that make you better than your opponents

ii. Motivation: Have an insatiable desire and internalized motivation to succeed (you really got to want it); ability to bounce back from performance setbacks with increased determination to succeed

iii. Focus: Remain fully focused on the task at hand in the face of competition-specific distractions; able to switch focus on and off as required; not being adversely affected by others performance or your own internal distractions (worry, negative mind chatter)

iv. Handling pressure: Able to regain control following unexpected distractions. Low in mental toughness will feel the effects of stress and strain more severely. They will be less productive and spend more time contending with the physical ailments.

Key component of mental toughness is learning how to condition your mind to think confidently and be able to overcome frustration/self-critical negativity (reframe self-talk into what it is you want to occur). Don't allow frustration to undermine your confidence or focus

Self-control can be acquired by getting tougher mentally. The connection between thoughts and emotions is very real.

Mental toughness may be considered a temperamental dimension in which you are literally assessing the temperament of the individual to predict his or her reaction to the job environment and requirements. Getting tougher mentally means more inside-out learning. Being tough mentally means that you have acquired skills in thinking, believing, and visualization.

Mental toughness means that under the pressure of challenge you can continue to think constructively, non-defensively, positively, and realistically - and do it with calm clarity.

Success in business and in life begins with what you think and how you think, which then directs and guides what you accomplish, short-term and long-term.

In a changing business world, professional skills – and mental discipline - are essential tools for survival. To elevate your overall performance, enhance the basics of your mental discipline which includes mental toughness, acting in a state-of-mental alertness and effective thinking. Think of mental toughness as your strength to develop. Your mindset and mental preparation can be the difference between winning and losing in survival.

Mental toughness is doing whatever is necessary to get the job done including handling the demands of a tough workout, withstanding pain, or touching an opponent out at the end of a race. The real key to excellence in both organization and business is mental toughness. Mental toughness is ability to persevere and deal with obstacles in organization without giving up. An effective leader should not only promote individual mental toughness, but also team toughness.

Emotional Toughness

It describes ability to create positive emotions that enabling you to bring your talents and skills, no matter what negative thing(s) might be affecting you. There are several emotions that can block your potential such as fear, confusion, low energy, fatigue, and helplessness. When you feel these negative emotions you should practice changing your mind set. Therefore emotional toughness is characterized by:

   a. Emotional flexibility: The ability to absorb unexpected emotional turns and remain supple, non-defensive and balanced with the ability to summon a wide range of positive emotions.

b. Emotional responsiveness: The ability to remain emotionally alive engaged and connected under pressure.

c. Emotional strength: The ability to exert and resist great force emotionally under pressure and to sustain a strong fighting spirit under pressure.

d. Emotional resiliency: The ability to take a punch emotionally and bounce back from disappointments and missed opportunities; ready to resume the fight. Most people become entangled in their emotions when faced with negatives, mistakes, and failures. They let the emotions control the thinking. Control your emotions when react to negatives, mistakes, and failures.

The more mental stress experiences overcome successfully the better you are equipped to handle stress. Correct your mistakes and don't protect yourself from mistakes. Analyze your losses and mistakes, learn from it and move on. Don't take losses or criticism personally.

Physical Toughness

A leader with physical toughness demonstrates the ability to conditioning the body to become physically tougher. It is an ability to absorb impact before physically breaking. The body with high strength will have more toughness. The body and mind are intimately connected. Affect one and you affect the other.

A positive (or negative) bodily action translates into a corresponding positive (or negative) feeling and inside your body. In other words, to feel confident people start acting confident on the outside. If you force your body to act alive and positive, it will tell your mind that you are alive and positive.

Thinking positive thoughts will help you get your body in a positive mode. Physical toughening leads to mental and emotional toughening. Toughen one of the three (physical, mental, and emotional) and the other two are made stronger.

Physical toughening is about to develop your ability to handle more physical stress and strain while maintaining composure. Being able to withstand great strain and/or pain on the mat without letting it distract you from your goal is essential characteristic to success in life. Think positively and know that you can perform well despite distraction. Sometimes just having a sense of composure and control of your thoughts is half the battle and can give you extra confidence.

Spiritual Toughness

Spiritual domains can't be measured or perceived. The word spiritual is used not in a religious sense per se but rather to describe ways of thinking; being and doing that are life-sustaining and life-enhancing both for individuals and organizations, themselves and others. Sometimes it takes spiritual toughness and discipline to overcome fear.

Effective leaders know that we have to tap into our inner wisdom to surf the waves of change and emotions that surround us. We have to learn how to be compassionate and wise. Being spiritual doesn't mean being a wimp. On the contrary it requires strength and real toughness - the toughness to be in the pain and see beyond it.

Leaders don't tolerate conditions or processes where people feel the need to compromise their values - to sell their souls for the task at hand; a principle that demands performance, integrity, competence and a non-calloused form of spiritual toughness.

Many leaders are seemingly still not completely convinced competitiveness challenge. They need not feel threatened. It's simply lack a sense of urgency about the situation. They must change. Leaders should be confident of their ability to assess their resources and use it to make strategic decisions. They must be able to locate people within the organization with the knowledge to meet unexpected challenges, such as the rise of competitor.

LEARN-ABILITY

Highly effective leaders must be continuous, lifelong learners. Learning how to survive in an emergency situation is important for leaders. Learning is the engine of all innovation, growth and strategy. Continuous learning helps individuals and organizations maximize their innate capabilities.

Effective leader promotes continuous learning, not only to improve overall performance, but also to involve all members in the ongoing challenge to enhance value. To be successful, leadership must ensure that the organization captures and shares lessons learned.

Learning and growth constitute the essential foundation for organization's success; which can be distinguished from behavioral changes. The purpose of learning is growth, and our minds can continue growing as we continue to live. The more educated, you would become more independent-minded and rational. Learning leadership is fundamentally a self-management task.

Effective leaders recognize that what they know is very little in comparison to what they still need to learn. To be more proficient in pursuing and achieving objectives, you should be open to new ideas, insights, and revelations that can lead to better ways to accomplishing goals. This continuous learning process can be exercised, in particular, through engaging yourself in a constant dialogue.

Leaders need to optimize success by focusing on key issues such as motivation, feedback and mentoring. Learning is process of acquiring modifications in existing knowledge, skills, habits, or tendencies through experience, practice, or exercise. It demonstrates continuous improvement; apply knowledge to provide the best services; individual performance and development; and passion. It demonstrates skills related to the functional area and exhibits commitment to developing personal abilities.

Learning needs humility that means, in terms of leadership survival, we can eventually become wise enough by benefit of our own mistakes and experiences to realize our limitations and honest enough to recognize that the very best of us is but a vessel of clay; and therefore, none of us has all of the right answers all of the time about all of the questions. Learning fosters:

Intuition

Leader often introduces change by announcing it. The response to this approach generally creates rigidity. It is actually the ability to use energy data to make decisions in the immediate moment. 'Intuition allows us to make correct choices'. Intuition is ability to see any event; any object from a viewpoint of the cosmic whole. It's about knowing of something without prior knowledge or the use of reason. All stands revealed the hearts, the motives, causes of all events. Intuition can be said to be a comprehensive grip of the principles of universality.

A person who develops intuition can know anything, without the barriers of time, space and any other obstructions. They are able to sense the invisible. Intuition is true knowledge. Intuition is beyond the logical left brain understanding. Intuition leads us on the right path, leading to enlightenment/freedom. Intuition is freedom, enlightenment.

The intuition is like a second attention; like alertness, constantly monitoring our untoward thoughts, feelings, actions or deeds; which bring us back to focus when our thoughts have gone astray.

Your insight and intuition function with incredible precision. You see the interconnectedness of people and circumstances around you. You often come up with brilliant ideas and insights that enable you to move ahead even more rapidly. Learning to listen to your "gut" (intuition), leaders may use in some way.

Often we think of intuition as a random sense or an idea that came out of the blue. Intuition is, in fact, the result of the brain efficiently processing information, patterns and ideas. By developing your intuition, you can learn from experience and confidently make quick decisions, improving the overall effectiveness of your leadership.

People make effective decisions by listening to their intuition and gut feelings. You must trust your own abilities, instincts and intuitions. A leader who has used his/her intuition achieves success.

Instinct

There's no rule of thumb; let your instincts guide you. It is to mean certain innate, essential drives, urges, or impulses that form the basis of the human soul. We are born with the instinct - for both good and bad. The instinct-for-good is what makes us want to uphold laws by performing deeds of justice, compassion and righteousness.

With regard to your body or surroundings, your instincts are your best early warning system. Listen to the inner voice. Listen to that gut feeling. The instinct-for-bad is what drives us to promote our own well-being and strive for personal achievement and success. Both are necessary for survival. Following reasons may drive people to bad instinct: over-ambitiousness, excessive competitiveness, extreme self interest. To have good instinct we may need to:

i. Commune our thought with nature which can develop insight and intuition

ii. Get our heart in tune with nature and natural rhythms and cycles.

iii. Listen to nature. Each animal symbolizes something; and we can learn something from the nature. Be aware of seeing an unusual animal, insect etc. Today's leader needs to be an information and learning machine. Stay up on best practices, new trends, competitors, and even pop culture. Your adaptability to changing conditions is the key to your survival.

iv. Think through quieting the mind. Look for alert to encourage it

v. Watch it, to make it more trustworthy: Our first instinct is to trust others. Leaders strive to establish trustworthy and long-lasting partnerships.

vi. Give mind good information to work with. When our mind is still we can see more clearly.

The function of instinct is to make you wild and attuned with nature. Your instincts may be off and you may feel foolish. Err on the side of safety and your instincts may save you from danger. Give yourself time or space to consider your options. Our mind could be seen as a glass of muddy water -when we keep thinking, we keep bringing up mud and thus the glass appears dirty.

When our minds are still, even minded, undistracted, alert, mindful, not clinging to anything our thought - then we are open to inner guidance. Increase awareness, concentration, and mindfulness, even mindedness through meditation, breathing, exercises, yoga, and creativity. Think back to a time when you had a hunch about something. That was intuition. It is nothing more than your mind using more than what you are consciously aware of.

Intuition also works as a warning device. Your skill, knowledge and experience determine the potential effectiveness of your intuition.

Intelligence

Intelligence as indicated partly by the ability to conceptualize systems and synthesize massive amounts of information is also characteristic of successful leaders. As a leader, you must know your job and have a solid familiarity with people tasks.

Leaders should practice and support lifelong learning. Such learning promotes personal renewal. On a larger scale, it also promotes organizational renewal. Transforming leaders use and promote the use of critical, creative and reflective thinking which supports the development of cognitive complexity. This provides a basis for multiple frames of reference, situational alternatives or other forms of requisite variety.

Survival is often a question of whether we can outlearn our competition. Your ability to think clearly and react is your most valuable survival skill. Learning to predict your environment is an important survival skill. Effective leaders display ability to learn. Their innate ability to learn from experience is the key to survival, growth and development.

JUDGE-ABILITY

Judgment describes the ability to weigh facts and possible solutions on which to base sound decisions. Leaders should also ensure that you consider other options objectively to avoid justifying your preferred option, hence seeing its benefits more clearly than its downsides. It's a learning process how receptive you are to negative feedback about your preferred option. Most people are less receptive than they think. Good judgment needs:

Expertise

Developing the expertise to become an effective leader may take years. There are three types of positive power that effective leaders use: charismatic power, expert power and referent power. A highly effective leader promotes an image of expertise: Since perceived expertise in many occupations is associated with an education and experience.

A leader should (subtly) make sure that people are aware of his or her formal education, relevant work experience, and significant accomplishments. One common tactic to make this information known is to display diplomas, licenses, awards, and other evidence of expertise in a prominent location. Expert power is essential because as a leader, your team looks to you for direction and guidance.

Team's member needs to believe in your ability to set a worthwhile direction, give sound guidance and co-ordinate a good result. If your team perceives you as a true expert, they will be much more receptive when you try to exercise influence tactics such as rational persuasion and inspirational appeal. And if your team sees you as an expert you will find it much easier to guide them in such a way as to create high motivation:

   i.   If your team members respect your expertise, they'll know that you can show them how to work effectively;

   ii.   If your team members trust your judgment, they'll trust you to guide their good efforts and hard work in such a way that you'll make the most of their hard work

   iii.   If they can see your expertise, team members are more likely to believe that you have the wisdom to direct their efforts towards a goal that is genuinely worthwhile.

An effective leader has expertise in solving challenging problems.

Professionalism

Professional behavior is required to demonstrate a high degree of knowledge and capacity in which one is able to deliver services in accordance with relevant knowledge and skill, and conforming to the standards of a profession. Professionals should honor their responsibility to achieve and maintain the highest level of professional competence; continue their professional development throughout their careers; accomplish to the highest standards of integrity and ethical principles.

Professional acquires and enhances skills and knowledge; enhances your ability to better serve, manages your practice in more effective way; and acquires activities that deal with professional ethics.

Lack of professionalism is what leads to most of the conflicts, delays in decision making and customer (internal & external) dissatisfaction in an organization. An effective leader fosters how to lead others and model professionalism in this highly sensitive world. a leader will be able to lead his/her team in an effective manner if he/she acts professionally.

Decisiveness

Decisiveness is power. Decisiveness describes power to determine the outcome - showing an ability to make decisions quickly; unmistakable - displaying no hesitation; firmness - showing the way to go; criticality - put an end to crucial. It is quality to making risky decisions; which showing the ability to serve others by finalizing difficult and weighty decisions in ways which advance their best interests.

Decisiveness is the ability to recognize key factors and finalize difficult decisions, which need actions include not look back; do what we say; make the right decision and stick to it; look at things from more than one point of view before making up our mind; not give in to others pressure.

A decisive leader is someone who leads without blind impulse but also without waffling. Such a leader is focused, direct, and purposeful; any differing thoughts in that leader's mind are harnessed to make the decision wiser, better, clearer and fuller. He/she is always awake to challenge; eagerly responds to the task; and is provided with complete and accurate information before acting. He/she is able to make good decisions without delay; get all the facts and weight them against each other.

All decisions and actions should be taken in the best interest of the company which is critical for customer (internal & external) satisfaction and for the success of any organization. By acting calmly and quickly, he/she arrives at a sound decision that is clear, firm, and in professional manner. Make a list of the risks involved in making a particular decision, its benefits and potential costs. Make a plan to reduce each risk. Get more information on the pro and contra of various options can help reduce risk if it is available and when time permits. As a leader, he/she may often find himself/herself with the dilemma of making or not making a decision.

An effective leader, who is focused, authentic, courageous and emphatic, must also have the proper timing in making and executing decisions.

He/she must be able to prioritize and move with appropriate speed. An effective leader uses time as his/her ally.

Sensitiveness

Highly effective leaders are empathic, perceptive, sensitive, and insightful. The leaders value the life of their members; he/she will value their partnership with them. Recognize that empathy and finding common ground is the key to his/her survival. The leaders must be sensitive to each follower as an individual.

We make choices every day about doing the right thing. Ethics involves seeing the difference between right and wrong. Ethics are moral rules for the right behavior. Leaders must show sensitiveness to other people's feelings. They are skilled and sensitive leaders.

Courage

Courage is a survival skill for leaders. It means the ability to make tough calls, the ability to acknowledge mistakes, and the ability to accept responsibility for the actions or omissions not only of ourselves but of those in our agency. Courage provides the will to lead. Courage feeds our faith and counters our doubts. Courage keeps us moving forward despite the obstacles we encounter. Knowledge, practice and courage are your weapons against fear. Fears can be rational or irrational, but they are always personal and real. Everyone fears something. To diminish a fear, you must first face it. Associate with confident people. You have seen many who have already done what you fear doing. Now, do what they have done.

Courage grows with action. Fear is learned and must be unlearned. After facing that fear, you will feel exhilarated. Without fear, there can be no courage. Fear provides the opportunity to be brave. The best way to deal with first fears is through a combination of logic and bravery. Courageous is characterized by courage; braveness; valiant.

Courageous means ability to control your fear in a dangerous or difficult situation; and have the courage to stand up for their beliefs. Do the right thing for yourself and others. Have the determination to do the right thing, even when others do not.

An effective leader will take a courageous decision; when other not. The key to courageous is how one responds to what arises on the path, rather than whether individual circumstances are defined as great, good, bad or just plain ugly.

Every situation or circumstance; i.e. success or failure, barrier or doorway; is simply another opportunity for creativity, mastery, and fulfillment of higher potential. The benefits of courageous leadership include the potential for:

i. Increase alignment with your true values, purpose, and higher potential

ii. Greater momentum toward a revitalized vision and renewed sense of the organization's purpose

iii. Higher morale among the organization members

iv. Allow new ideas, and a recalibrating of outdated or stifling processes

v. Promote authentic, dynamic, and effective communication

The challenges facing leaders today are immense, and require great courage to overcome. Standing organization in the face of criticism, yet having the courage to admit when they are wrong, are hallmarks of courageous leaders.

Powerful acts of courage have such a high potential for rocking the status quo, and would demand that we walk our talk about values, mission and purpose.

Courage is what allows you to remain calm while recognizing fear; ability to confront pain, danger, uncertainty or intimidation; able to sustain it in the face of difficulty. Courage may come in making a choice. It comes in knowing what's right and doing what's right.

a. Moral courage means having the inner strength to stand up for what is right and to accept blame when something is your fault. It may not be always a popular action but you carry it out because you know it is right.

b. Physical courage means that you can continue to function effectively when there is physical danger present.

Courage is required to face those dangerous and difficult situations; in the face of pain, danger or even death. You can begin to control fear by practicing self-discipline and calmness. If you fear doing certain things required, force yourself to do them until you can control your reaction. You will never do anything without courage. Do the right thing for yourself and others. Have the determination to do the right thing, even when others do not.

Courage enables one to encounter danger and difficulties with firmness, or without fear, or fainting of heart; valor; boldness; resolution. Leadership is ability that influences, motivates, and enables others to contribute toward the effectiveness and success of the organizations.

Failing to anticipate a problem before it arrives is characterized by gross mismanagement, poor judgment, lack of foresight and even, hidden issues that are impossible to perceive adequately in advance. Good judgment in combination with the right knowledge and skills will give you an advantage in any risky situation.

Skill represents someone's ability. Survival skill is the ability to survive in the uncertainty or dangerous conditions. The most important survival tool is the mind and the attitude it takes.

Effective leaders have ability to develop motivating and satisfying relationships with followers. An important component of this ability is the capacity to understand the individual needs and capabilities of each follower. The leader needs to be able to judge what kind of guidance and support the follower needs to grow and develop in the job. Since each person is different and progresses through different stages, both in life and on the job, the leader must be sensitive to each follower as an individual.

11th

CONFLICT RESOLUTION SKILL

Effective conflict resolution skills have become crucial for today's leaders. Everywhere you turn, the potential for conflict exists. Conflict is neither good nor bad - it just is. We've all seen situations where different people with different goals and needs have come into conflict. And we've all seen the often-intense personal animosity that can result. A conflict arises because of following circumstances:

i.   Individual interests: Conflicts that involve interests; between the wants, desires, and needs of the others. A person's interest is a power; it is his/her attitude plus its strength towards producing effects. Individual interest generated by needs, and its content and direction are partially learned from experience and culture, and partially rational.

ii. Practices or rules: Conflicts of rights, values; concern the correctness or applicability of formal or informal norms. Norms are rules for accepted and expected behavior or what most others do and what most people in that situation consider normal.

iii. Domination: Conflicts as a dominating of one's power against others. Domination conflicts are conflicts about who is on top (and bottom) of the social, economic, and/or political hierarchy. Such conflicts may occur between individual people (i.e. between siblings, co-workers, etc), between groups (i.e. between different racial or ethnic groups), or between nations. These conflicts tend to be very difficult to resolve because no one wants to be on the bottom, and few are willing to share the top.

Some societies do have some form of social hierarchy with some people in stronger, more dominant positions, and other people in weaker, lower positions. Invariably, the people on the bottom want to reverse the relationship, while the people on the top want to maintain it. Unless the top people are willing to share their top position with everyone else, the conflict will most likely continue.

iv. Exclusiveness: Conflict by one excludes the other. Exclusiveness is an attribute of ethnicity. Ethnic community and identity are often associated with conflict. Identities have resulted in intractable conflicts.

For an inter-group (e.g., racial, ethnic, or religious) conflict may occur, when ones have a sense of collective identity about themselves and about their adversary, each side believing the fight is between us and them. Members of groups with identities that place a high priority on being honored and being treated with deference may have difficulty making compromises for or respecting other groups.

v. Diversity: Conflict of different ideas and opinion, different interpretation and perception of the existing organisational values and norms, tasks and competences, and different cultural behaviour and attitudes.

Leaders must understand that the value of diversity is that each individual brings his or her unique experience, skills and commitment to the organization and its mission. The cultural differences that are frequently over-demonstrative cause conflicts.

Conflicts may arise from personal, structural or organisational ambiguity, which so-called 'ethnic or cultural incompatibilities'. In which, when the unsatisfactory situation develops, neither the conflict, nor the actual problems can be solved.

The fact that conflict exists, however, is not necessarily a bad thing; as long as it is resolved effectively, it can lead to growth. In many cases, effective conflict resolution skills can make the difference between positive and negative outcomes. By resolving conflict successfully, you can solve many of the problems that have been brought to the surface. Conflict resolutions purpose to, but not limited to:

a. Increase intra-group understanding: The discussion needed to resolve conflict expands people's awareness of the situation, giving them an insight into how they can achieve their own goals without undermining those of other people. It's a form of aligning with others; i.e. dialogue, conciliation, consolidation, partnership, collaboration, etc.

    Conflict is natural, neutral. So affirm differences, prize each person's uniqueness. Recognize tensions in relationships and contrasts in viewpoint. Work through conflicts of closeness.

    All individuals/organizations preferring the same outcome also coincide in their valuations of other outcomes. Individuals with the same ordering form an interest group and act in a coordinated fashion.

b. Increase inter-group cohesion: Members develop stronger mutual respect and a renewed faith in their ability to work together. Believe that similar interests and values help avoid conflict. Ones may exchange interests: satisfy positive interests of others; i.e.: mediation, merger, association, affiliation, coalition, etc.

Affiliation creates people connections and thus harmony within the organization. It is a very collaborative style which focuses on emotional needs.

c. Improve self-knowledge: Conflict pushes individuals to examine their goals in close detail, helping them understand the things that are most important to them, sharpening their focus, and enhancing their effectiveness; i.e.: moderation, compromise, sacrifice, etc.

Conflict is mutual difference best resolved by cooperation and compromise. If each comes halfway, progress can be made by the democratic process. Conflict is usually disastrous, so yield. Sacrifice your own interests, ignore the issues, put relationships first, and keep peace at any price.

d. Resolve conflict through threats: Pressure and coercion are necessary. Conflict is bad; avoid it. Overlook differences, accept disagreement or get out. Since threats promise a quick and easy victory, people often decide to give them try. The use of threat has a number of serious problems.

Threats do not work if they are not credible. This means that you must be able and willing to carry out the threat if the other side fails to comply with your demands. To do this you must go to the expense of building up your power base, even if you do not plan to use it.

If you do not have it, not only will your current threat be ineffective, your future threats are unlikely to work as well. The use of threats and/or force tends to generate a backlash from the target population.

Even if the threat is not carried out, people do not likely to be threatened and are likely to try to subvert or challenge any changes that are made as a result of threats ; i.e. arbitration, power sharing, (peace) zone, criminal prosecution, acquisition, splitting, dissociation, enclave, separation, demarcation, force, etc.

Unfortunately, threat is not only risky and expensive; but people are likely to try to reverse those actions. Force is a threatening type of social action. It will also influence the conflict.

Avoiding conflict, discouraging it or allowing chronic unhealthy conflict to remain unresolved can be disastrous to organizational health. Effective leaders engage not only in collaboration and but also conflict resolution.

Conflict generally results from poor communications, disruptions in routines, unclear goals or expectations, the quest for power, ego massage, differences in value systems, or hidden agendas. It finds its expression in rude, discourteous and sometimes hostile behavior; selfishness; strident and defensive language; lack of respect; and increased stress.

If conflict is not handled effectively, the results can be damaging. Conflicting goals can quickly turn into personal dislike. Teamwork breaks down. Talent is wasted as people disengage from their work. And it's easy to end up in a vicious downward spiral of negativity and recrimination.

Conflict can reduce productivity, lower morale, create continued problems and conflicts, and cause team members to become frustrated and aggravated with the planning process.

When it is managed appropriately, conflict is actually good, as: Organization might be able to define the purpose and need for any proposed changes or decisions; it may help determine when a current decision or issue needs to be better evaluated, analyzed, or discussed before action is taken; encourage that the team needs to work on cooperation and collaboration, as well as team-building; and improve team communications.

Leaders raise and address team problems, energize people to think and act, and help team members learn to recognize and appreciate differences in each other

Conflict resolution is a way for two or more entities to find a peaceful solution to a disagreement among them. A conflict which is managed with care, can clarify goals, improve communication, and strengthen relationships. Therefore, conflict resolution skills are essential to leaders to help maintain positive momentum of the team.

Conflict is a natural element of high-performing organizations. When conflict is managed well, it can be a highly effective means of identifying and resolving tough organization challenges, often resulting in improved relationships and solutions. A leader is creating harmony and resolving conflicts. The effective leader creates an environment that allows open and constructive exploration of conflict issues.

Dialogue

Leaders find ways to foster productive dialogue. Dialogue describes a conversation in which people "speak openly and listen respectfully and attentively. It requires the breakdown of stereotypes, a willingness to listen and respect others' views, and a willingness to open oneself to new ideas. People in dialogue are to inform and learn rather than to persuade. Most dialogue processes involve people who are engaged in protracted conflict, sitting down together to explore their feelings about each other and their conflict.

Dialogue may not have fixed goal or predetermined agenda. The emphasis is not on resolving disputes, but rather on improving the way in which people with significant differences relate to each other. The broad aim is to promote respectful inquiry, and to stimulate a new sort of conversation that allows important issues to surface freely. While opponents in deep-rooted conflict are unlikely to agree with each other's views, they can come to understand each other's perspectives. Successful dialogue requires, i.e.:

   a. Listening to understand: Hear their words; learn their meaning. Concentrate on direct observation, stick to the facts, dismiss your old thoughts and assumptions, stay in their moment, and defer interpretation. Be still; stay silent inwardly and outwardly.

b. Suspending judgment: Defer your certainty while you explore doubt and new possibilities. Stop, step back, adopt a new point of view, and reflect from this new vantage point. Frame up - adopt a broader reference frame. Allow inquiry to displace certainty. Embrace your ignorance. Be willing to disclose your own doubts. Acknowledge what you don't know and don't understand. Reject polarized thinking. Hold your tongue and defer forming opinions, jumping to conclusions, quick fixes, and assigning blame. Become aware of your inner reaction, but don't react outwardly. Have the discipline to hold the tension within yourself while you silently examine and reflect on it. Identify and examine your assumptions and theirs. Work to understand how this problem works, and how it has arisen. Cope constructively with your fear and anger. Do not attribute motive or intent. Don't yet agree or disagree while you remain curious and reflect. Defer and dismiss conclusions, explore alternative meanings and motives, integrate these new ideas with the whole, and seek congruence.

c. Respecting all: Attribute positive motives and constructive intent to each participant. Appreciate all that is good about them, all that you share in common with them, and all they can contribute. Acknowledge the dignity, legitimacy, worth, and humanity of the person speaking. Allow for differing viewpoints and learn all you can from them. Examine the origins within yourself of any tendency you have to disrespect participants. Resist your temptation to blame. Remain humble and accept that they can teach us and we can learn from them. Attain and appreciate their viewpoint; do not attack, intrude, deny, dismiss, dispute, or discount their comments. Banish violence.

d. Speaking your voice: Contribute your insight to advance the dialogue. Be patient and gather your own clear thoughts before you speak clearly, directly, and authentically. Offer your insights. Share how you feel, what you don't know, and your own doubts and concerns. Speak courageously from your own authentic voice. Avoid sarcasm, barbs, attacks, insults, reification, and condescension. Inquire and ask only genuine questions. Test assumptions. Speak from the first person from your actual experiences. Speak your truth.

Dialogue is an important tool for preventing violent conflict and building peace. It facilitates a shared understanding of complex problems. Dialogue creates a quality of conversation that facilitates the transformation of inter-personal relations. Dialogue excludes attack and defense and avoids derogatory attributions based on assumptions about the motives, meanings, or character of others.

In dialogue, questions are sincere, stimulated by curiosity and interest. In dialogue people speak openly, and listen respectfully and attentively. Derogatory attributions, attacks, and defensiveness have no role in dialogue. Through inquiry and conversation, parties try to integrate multiple perspectives and unfold shared meaning. Dialogue means we sit and talk with each other, especially those with whom we may think we have the greatest differences.

Effective dialogue is a key to helping people or team members solve problems and move forward. Dialogue is the creative thinking together that can emerge when genuine empathetic listening, respect for all participants, safety, peer relationships, suspending judgment, sincere inquiry, courageous speech, and discovering and disclosing assumptions work together to guide our conversations. It is an activity of curiosity, cooperation, creativity, discovery, and learning rather than persuasion, competition, fear, and conflict.

Dialogue is the only symmetrical form of communication. Dialogue emerges from trusting relationship. Nevertheless, the results of dialogue are usually transformative, as people emerge from the process with a much deeper understanding of both their own views and the views of people on the other side.

Mediation

Organization's members need to be more knowledgeable about mediation and conflict resolution strategies, as it can be a highly effective and empowering method of conflict resolution. Mediation is a process in which a third-party neutral assists in resolving a dispute between two or more other parties. Mediation has been used successfully in many different kinds of conflicts.

Conflict if it's handled correctly can be quite constructive. It can signify a need for healthy change and can be the impetus for growth of the organization. It can be an opportunity for the parties involved to directly and truthfully communicate expectations they hold for each other which in the past often times had not been directly expressed.

A leader needs an understanding to non-confrontational methods of conflict resolution that focus upon restoring and building relationships among individuals and groups. In conflict mediation, although some of the same goals appear to exist, the major goal is to resolve the conflict by having the conflicting parties engage in a process whereby each party hears the perception of the other party in clear, uninterrupted, behavioral terms.

The mediator's role is to create a process whereby the conflict is eliminated and the effected parties learn functional conflict resolution skills in addition to solving the present problem at hand. A mediator has no vested interest in the benefit to either party in a conflict. Successful mediation requires a mediator who:

a. Is highly skilled and respected: working collaboratively with both parties with an innovative quality assistance mechanism to ensure high quality mediation.

b. Is authorized to reward cooperation and punish abstinence.

c. Is neutral and impartial: Not connected to the disputing parties in any way and does not stand to benefit by any particular outcome.

    d. Work for settlement and relationship: obtaining a settlement and empowering both parties to act effectively on their own behalf, while recognizing the legitimate interests and needs of the other side. Mediator assists the parties to develop a solution themselves.

Mediation helps involved people become better negotiators. A mediator should work for the benefit of both individuals by creating conflict resolution; i.e. facilitate communication between the parties, assist them in focusing on the real issues of the dispute, and generate options that meet the interests or needs of all relevant parties

The mediator is neither negotiator, which would be attempting to benefit one side in a resolution, nor arbitrator, which is to weight the evidence by both sides and impose a solution. The mediator creates a setting whereby the parties resolve their own conflict with a mutually agreed upon solution.

Martti Ahtisaari, the former president of Finland, winner of the 2008 Nobel Peace Prize, had set the highest standard for conflict resolution and peacemaking from Asia to Africa to Europe. He demonstrated his almost Zen-like patience. It is not merely a sense of calm; he was driven, determined, and direct in expressing his frustrations. But he had an extraordinary sense of the ebb and flow of geopolitical forces, the need to let those forces that couldn't be controlled play themselves out, and the importance of being ready and perfectly positioned when the opportunity for peace arose. (Hans Bool, Lesson From the Nobel Peace Laureate, 2008)

Mediation provides an alternative means of addressing the conflict. Mediation is one of several approaches to conflict resolution that uses a "third party" intermediary to help the disputing parties resolve their conflict. Unlike arbitration, where the third party actually makes the decision about how the conflict should be resolved, mediators only assist the parties in their efforts to formulate a solution of their own.

Thus, mediators bring the parties together (or sometimes shuttle between them), help them describe the problem in terms of negotiable interests and needs rather than non-negotiable positions, and develop a set of ideas for how the interests and needs of both sides can be met simultaneously.

The mediator will then help the parties assess the relative merits of the different options and draft an agreement that works best to satisfy everyone's interests. Mediation also can be a highly efficient conflict or dispute resolution process. Important skill for all effective leaders is to understand others.

Moderation

Everything might be good if it's in moderation. In leading people, there is nothing better than moderation. Since, indeed, moderation means yielding early, yielding early means accumulating power. Moderation is an attitude, state or quality of being moderate. Moderation describes the avoidance of excess or extremes, especially in one's behavior. A moderate is one bears adversity with moderation. We have to believe that our behavior can be changed. To be moderate, ones allow other to take choice.

To achieve moderation, leaders scrupulously avoid extremes and adopt friendly postures. Moderation gives endurance, personal power and unlimited possibilities.

Power Sharing

Power-sharing establishes a more equitable balance of power, makes negotiation an attractive alternative to violence, promotes and expands participation, strengthens confidence in the organization, and encourages a competitive environment. Power-sharing reduces the risk of violent conflict by allowing groups to conduct activities. Power-sharing arrangements help promote legitimacy and a sense of fairness among the groups.

Power-sharing arrangements such as proportionality and resource allocation can help reduce conflict by encouraging formation of broader coalitions.

Negotiation

Leaders should be able resolve conflicts peacefully and equitably. Every desire that demands satisfaction and every need to be met-is at least potentially an occasion for negotiation; whenever people exchange ideas with the intention of changing relationships, whenever they confer for agreement, they are negotiating.

There are numerous situations that need to be dealt with through negotiation. Many people are afraid of conflict because they do not know how to negotiate. In organizational activities, there are many opportunities to use negotiation skills. Indeed, the success of the whole process rides on the ability to negotiate actions and responsibilities among groups or individuals.

The key to finding an agreeable solution is to get the parties to really listen to one another. When that happens, parties who seem to be at odds often discover interests in common for which they can jointly identify solutions.

Good negotiation leads to acceptable solutions that work for both of parties and will strengthen their relationship. Your communication skills automatically improve as you develop good negotiating skills.

Negotiation is an interactive process between two or more parties seeking to find common ground on an issue or issues of mutual interest or dispute where the involved parties seek to make or find a mutually acceptable agreement that will be honored by all the parties concerned.

The primary focus of successful negotiation is to attain additional value in the creation of enhanced agreements during the negotiation process. Successful negotiation requires a mature and responsible approach where people listen to and respect each other. In a successful negotiation, everyone wins. The objective should be agreement, not victory. It needs:

a. Readily available resources: Identify resources that can support the plan you propose. Have relevant facts and materials at hand.

b. Align with the members - No one does a deal solo. A deal requires teamwork, solid team planning, and consistent communication.

c. Avoid resistance and the threat of sabotage: Analyze and understand situation, consider the range of possible opposition and disagreements, and think about response; and aware the opposing views. Some negotiators can be quite intimidating to the point of being rude; others are quite passive and easily manipulated.

d. Team members are to speak with a unified voice: Be prepared to listen carefully to the other parties. Verify that you understand their needs and interests. Negotiation is a real challenge. To negotiate, we need to be able to adapt our behavior and be flexible in our approach.

e. Willingness to implement the deals: Have a deal, in a negotiation, will be very challenging whenever to implement it. It is difficult to make a deal if there is no trust between counterparts. Every single deal, even one-time deals has consequences in the future. The most important element is the authority of your word and the credibility of your actions.

Negotiation may lead to a settlement, but may also simply lead to a pause in the conflict. Negotiation - an attempt to achieve a mutually acceptable solution - is not about winning or losing. It is about reaching a satisfying conclusion for all involved.

The key is that all parties need to gain something of value in order to make compromises worthwhile; to shift the situation to a win-win even if it looks like a win-lose situation. Almost all negotiations have at least some elements of win-win. Successful negotiations often depend on finding the win-win aspects in any situation. Only shift to a win-lose mode if all else fails.

Negotiation will aid you in developing the support you need to follow through on your deals, i.e.:

a. Understand the interests of organization. How the leaders negotiate can greatly impact organization's interest. The leaders should:

  i. Be clear about the limits of what is acceptable, and losses not willing to sustain. Leaders who are assertive are confident and know what they want. They are not afraid to put forward opinions and are willing to listen to the opinions of others. They are not afraid of conflict and will be more than happy to argue their case.

  ii. Define the organization's priorities: Leaders setup and define as many priorities as needed for the organization

  iii. Specify the things to give: The leaders consider things may want to be given to others

b. Communicate and develop relationships. Negotiations take time and are always dynamic. Remember never to unexpectedly surprise your internal allies. Make your intent obvious and ensure you have no hidden agendas. Consistent intent and action on your part enhances your reputation for honesty and integrity. Communication must always be ongoing.

c. Quantify the benefits and costs both to your organization and the opponent. Promote a positive environment

d. Identify criteria: Your internal partners will employ to evaluate the deal. When you discover how your internal partners will evaluate your external deal, you greatly enhance your ability to gain their support for implementing it. You must clarify your alternatives to any agreement. Don't get ensnared into becoming the organization that couldn't say 'No'.

Resources for negotiation come from many corners. To build up and increase our confidence as negotiators; we need to step back and analyze the sources of our personal power and compare them with those of the people with whom we are negotiating, i.e.:

a. Information: Have knowledge that influences the outcome of the negotiation. Planning and research can increase our information power.

b. Situation: Have an effective network and keeping in touch with the moments can increase your situation power.

c. Expertise: Skill which influence the outcome of the negotiation. Improving negotiation skills helps you win better deals. Other areas of expertise could also help the outcome of the negotiation.

A highly effective leader generates higher productivity, lower costs, and more opportunities than ineffective leaders. The leaders create results, attain goal, and realize vision and other objectives more quickly and at a higher level of quality than ineffective leaders. Effective leaders adapt to fit the environment, the vision, and the needs of others.

No matter how you define conflict, the reality is that it's a part of life. What is important is that you recognize and deal with it appropriately. Conflict that requires resolution is neither good nor bad. You can either let conflict or the potential for conflict drag you down or you can use it to lift you to new levels of performance. Understanding what conflict is and why it exists helps shape your response. The important point is to manage the conflict, not to suppress conflict and not to let conflict escalate out of control. Many of us seek to avoid conflict when it arises but there are many times when we should use conflict as a critical aspect of creativity and motivation.

12th

TIME ALLOCATION SKILL

As a leader, your time is more valuable than your money. Time management is important to any leader. Sufficient time is the key to making changes that stick.

One of the worst aspects of modern working life is the constant pressure to hurry. Not only does it create needless stress and tension, it goes a long way to making people seem dumber and more resistant to change than they are. If you want to make some personal - or organizational - changes, and make them stick, slow down and give yourself some time and space in which to work.

The process of developing your time management strategy is to be flexible in your planning. Allow for the unexpected. The only sure thing in your schedule is that the unexpected will happen.

Effective leaders understand these differing points of view on the effective use of time. They know how to leverage the differences in a cross-cultural environment in order to achieve the best balance between speed, risk management, and diligence, maximizing the success of their objectives. The leaders manage time smartly. They allocate time in four categories, i.e.:

TIME FOR ROUTINE TASK

Anybody can drastically improve their effectiveness if they simply take the time to master good habits. Routine things are done the same way every time. Processes have the same steps every time. a procedure or process each time we wanted to accomplish what could be a routine task, providing a service. Leaders ensure staffs performing routine tasks over and over staffs need to understand certain standards or procedures. The leader closely supervises subordinates to make sure they complete the task appropriately.

Once a habit becomes part of your daily routine, the effectiveness just kicks in automatically.

Planning

Planning will help you accomplish tasks in a more effective and efficient. Managing your time is a highly personal skill. Only you know your peak work hours, your attention span, and other needs. To make the most productive use of your time, plan it thoroughly. There are three essential steps to efficient time management. They are:

a. Organizing: Make a list of everything you want or need to do

b. Prioritizing: Consider your list in order of priority, with the intention of doing higher priority tasks first

c. Scheduling: Make a reasonable schedule that you can be sure to stick to.

Effective leaders stick to their reverse time plan and not allow themselves to get caught up. They plan ahead. The leaders should be detail oriented, and highly organized to achieve work effectiveness.

Follow Up

Test and monitor a plan you have decided. Don't just assume the planning will be done. It needs follow up. A task may fail; or even generate things worse. Be sure it's possible to undo it.

A leader does not hesitate to reconstruct mistakes. When you give orders, ask if your instructions have been carried out and what was the result. Otherwise unpleasant tasks you want done will be easily forgotten. Remember what you ask for and confirm it happened. Remember what you offer to do and do it sooner than expected.

Track the exact time you begin and end an activity. Leaders who didn't ask and follow up the tasks were not seen as becoming more effective leaders. The leaders must follow up to check on their progress, their relationship with them almost invariably improves and they become more effective in their dealings with the leaders.

Leaders should not spend their time focusing on events that they can't control; instead, focus on what they can control.

TIME FOR PROBLEM SOLVING

An effective leader must have the capacity and skills to anticipate, identify, solve, prevent, and learn from problems that occur in the work environment. Creative problem- solving skills require positive processes that incorporate strong communication skills, respect for all parties involved, and innovative approaches. When problems are viewed as opportunities, the benefits for both leaders and staff can be highly positive.

Leaders solve problems - followers go to leaders to get their problems solved. Problem solving is simply a method of fighting fires; it does not move the organization forward. An effective leader focuses on team problem-solving strategies of problem definition and solution identification.

A leader has ability to solve problems proactively and gain others' commitment to solutions and decisions. The leaders will make high-quality, effective decisions and learn to recognize how personal bias, tunnel vision, and marginal commitment influence decisions. They provide frequent time-effective opportunities for problem solving.

Problems arise in any group or organization. Leaders display listening and with understanding; and be willing to discuss and solve problems; and be open to ideas. A leader can either react to problems and the resulting change or look ahead and visualize the future with creative problem solving.

Effective leaders anticipate change and learn how to facilitate and manage it. A leader does not have to wait until problems come to him/her. Leaders know to seek solutions before the problems land on the doorstep.

See Pattern

What it does best is see connections, linking information together and remembering the patterns, not the individual bits and pieces of data. One of the most important qualities of a creative problem solver is the ability to see new relationships between seemingly unrelated things.

An effective leader sees patterns and connections where others see only confusion and separateness. To a creative leader, everything is related - and the discovery of that relatedness is what fuels their creative process. In fact, the creative process is very much like a relationship. And like most relationships, it often begins with fascination - that curious state of mind (and heart) that keeps us spellbound, charmed and aroused.

You also need time to reflect and see the links between items or areas of knowledge. It takes time to register the problems fully and understand them well enough to recall them whenever you want. Gather information, investigate the problem and uncover any other hidden effects that the problem may have caused.

Brain Storming

Brainstorming is a great way of generating radical ideas. If the problem does positively need solving, ponder what actions you might do which could resolve the problem. Brainstorm all ideas and write them down.

Brainstorming is a useful and popular tool that you can use to develop highly creative solutions to a problem. It will be needed if an organization needs to:

a. Break out of stale, establish patterns of thinking that may develop new ways of looking at things

b. Develop new opportunities when existing approaches just aren't giving you the results you want

Brainstorming is a lateral thinking process; in which people come up with ideas and thoughts. Leaders are taking enough time out to think and brainstorm to solve the problem of organization and seek opportunities.

TIME FOR DEVELOPMENT

In all the discussion on the subject of personal or organizational development, one subject that occurs far too rarely is time: the necessity of giving yourself and others sufficient time to allow change and development to take place properly.

Time is an essential component in any change involving human beings. Despite all the rush in today's world, and the constant demands for the gratification of desires now, almost any progress people make in their lives takes far, far longer than they usually allow for.

Effective leadership gives appropriate time to develop followers. Leaders recognize the abilities, strengths and weaknesses of their team members, and understand their training, coaching and development needs. They develop ever-growing effectiveness and mutual trust.

Learning

Your brain isn't a bag that you can stuff with knowledge and ideas and expect them to stay there. It allows to escaping rather quickly. By repeating the learning experience, you make whatever you're trying to learn sticky enough to stay put. The learning process has to include a reflection process or we can't learn from experience.

Your first requirement should be plenty of free time to learn, to think, to reflect, and to internalize fresh ideas. Everyone has the experience of thinking. Your brain isn't a bag that you can stuff with knowledge and ideas and expect them to stay there.

Most people's brains are more like boxes full of holes that allow a great portion of whatever is put in to escape rather quickly. New learning is liquid and easily runs out through the holes.

Only by repeating the learning experience you can make whatever you're trying to learn sticky enough to stay. Search internet, ask other people, read books. If necessary, bounce your ideas off other everybody, even if you think they understand less on the subject. Leaders know how to get the data that is out there.

Teaching

An effective leader helps others learn through teaching, training, and coaching. This creates an exciting place to work and learn. Never miss an opportunity to teach your people. Leaders coach by encouraging and developing others who are less experienced.

Members who work for the leader know that they can take risks, learn by making mistakes, and winning in the end. An effective leader can do to improve the effectiveness and retention rates by teaching, which includes:

i.   Training is the acquisition of technology which permits members to perform their present job to standards. It improves their performance on the job the member is presently doing or is being hired to do.

ii. Education is training people to do a different job. Unlike training, which can be fully evaluated immediately upon the learners returning to work, education can only be completely evaluated when the learners move on to their future jobs. It will be used to increase performance in a different job.

iii. Development is training people to acquire new horizons, technologies, or viewpoints. It enables leaders to guide their organizations onto new expectations by being proactive rather than reactive. It enables members to create better products, faster services, and more competitive organizations. It is learning for growth of the individual, but not related to a specific present or future job.

Unlike training and education, which can be completely evaluated, development cannot always be fully evaluated. It will be used to acquire a new viewpoint so that the organization can become more competitive.

Potential learners can actualize their potential to become innovative leaders. Leaders don't just teach, but more than this is inspiring. The leaders devote their time, energy, and talents to improving the quality of teaching and learning.

Empowerment

Manager controls, leader empowers. Empowerment comes as people contribute their full potential in attaining both personal and organizational objectives. Your role as an empowering leader might be considered this:

To create conditions in which all members can contribute their maximum potential capacity to achieve the strategic goals and desired results of the organization in meeting stakeholder needs. Empowerment is not a program; it is a core condition for quality.

Effective leaders believe in a culture that embraces empowerment. The critical conditions for cultivating an empowering environment include:

i.   Develop trustworthiness and trust: an environment where creativity and managed risks are encouraged; and helping people learn from mistakes.

ii. Create a system of win-win agreements as the core process for developing mutually beneficial relationships among members and between the organization and outside stakeholders.

iii. Support and encouraging self-directed work teams.

iv. Align mission and strategy with customer needs and other forces in the dynamic marketplace, and then organizing structure and systems to support the strategy and each other.

v.   Foster personal and organizational self-accountability through consistent and frequent 360 degree feedback.

vi. Adopt an empowering style of leadership and management that nurtures, coaches, mentors, releases, and encourages and supports people in achieving their best.

An effective leader leads more, manages less, empowers, inspires, and energizes their people. The leader is in a position to encourage and empower his/her followers.

TIME FOR INNOVATION

Organizations can spark innovation and create strong ties of loyalty by allowing members to use their creativity and imagination. The innovative-style leader tends to focus on technical matters and often overlooks the needs of people. The result is that there is typically resistance to change.

Leaders' capacities for innovation are a product of their ability to be clear about their motivations for creative responses as well as their ability to open their minds to new ways of seeing and interpreting their own responses and what is happening in their environment.

Leaders must demonstrate the ability to take a long-term view and act as a catalyst for innovative organization changes, i.e. build a shared vision with others; influence others to translate vision into action; determine objectives and set priorities; anticipate issues and opportunities.

Leading innovation is a delicate and challenging process. You need to encourage expansive out-of-the-box thinking to generate new ideas, but also filter through these ideas to decide which to commercialize. Use a balanced loose-tight style of leadership for this purpose.

Loose-tight leadership alternates the creation of space for idea generation and free exploration with a deliberate tightening that selects and tests specific ideas for further investment and development. Looseness usually dominates the early stages of the innovation process; in the later stages, tightening becomes more important to scrutinize the concepts and bring the selected ones to the market.

A balanced approach is essential to loose-tight leadership. Those who remain loose too long generate plenty of ideas but have difficulty commercializing them. Those who lock into the tight mode choke off all but the most obvious ideas, and confine innovation to incremental line extensions of existing products that add little value.

For many of us, this is the tough stuff. Learning communication skills (challenging though that may be) is easy compared to learning how to think in new ways, discover assumptions, work through our competing commitments and address the boundaries we place on our imaginations. And this is essential for developing the capacity for innovation required for effective executive and leadership teamwork.

Leaders can stimulate innovation in the organization, which may need to create a culture of innovation. To be innovative, you should evolve:

Creativity

Leaders demonstrate competencies e.g., critical thinking, and creative thinking. It's not merely about sitting around waiting for inspiration to strike. Most people don't achieve anywhere near their creative potential because they never give themselves time to do so. They're so conditioned to quick action that they give up on fresh thinking long before it has a chance to develop into anything.

Creative thinking is work reflecting, ruminating, "noodling" with odd ideas: tinkering with patterns and unexpected connections. Dreaming or running over odd ideas in your head is the "soil" in which creative ideas grow. You need time to be creative. It's not about sitting around waiting for inspiration to strike.

Creative minds are reflecting, ruminating, "noodling" with odd ideas: thinking with patterns and unexpected connections. Most people don't achieve anywhere near their creative potential because they never give themselves time to do so.

Process, procedure, and rules are important in any organization, but an effective leader knows that creativity is just as important. Sometimes the best way to accomplish a goal is to do something different and leaders know when to encourage and foster that kind of creativity. Creativity means finding ways to get things done, even in the face of obstacles or doubt. To be more creative, a leader should:

i.   Keep an open mind - Sometimes creative thoughts come when you are at your busiest.

ii. Think sideways and upside down - Assume different.

iii. Look to combine one, two or three ideas into one terrific idea

iv. Trust your instincts. If the ideas do not come right away, walk away and begin doing something else - You never know where the next great idea will come from

Leadership is an inherently creative process. Leaders apply their own kinds of action-oriented logic to problems to help them find new wisdom, discover opportunities or see the facts in different ways. Effective leaders naturally achieve creative environments.

Change

Highly effective leaders navigate change. Leaders produce optimal appeal. Change itself also takes time. Action drives change, and change drives progress. An effective leader thinks differently and makes breakthroughs. Climate has a direct impact on bottom-line performance, affecting such things as growth, sales, productivity, efficiency, and customer service. Climate accounts the variance in performance. When climate changes are sustained over time, they essentially shift the organization's culture. Effective leaders have an inspiring vision; foresight and change anticipation is their hallmark.

An ongoing process of development will produce sustainable change. The ability to be an effective leader for change requires a high tolerance.

A leader has to have some ideas about change, about how the future of the organization could be. Constant change has become the measuring stick for leadership effectiveness.

Envision

Spend time for envisioning possible futures can be useful in uncovering options and preparing people for the unexpected. You need to have a clear vision of what lies ahead so you can make a better decision on which route to take. Often just a small shift in perspective changes how you react to a situation or condition and affects the way you approach the intersection. Demonstrate how leaders can learn from failures and then change the process of decision that you employ in the future.

Highly effective leaders know how to use the skills, knowledge, and energy of team members to accomplish the task and mission. The leader must provide a clear and compelling vision to guide the team toward the goal and must model the level of commitment, perseverance, and resilience necessary for mission accomplishment. Visionary opportunity identification is essential to the long-term growth of the organization.

TIME FOR QUIETUDE

Leaders usually have more time to engage in the organization activities. A lot of time and energy is spent on doing and having; a leader needs to give some "free" time to be tranquil, quiet.

Listening

Listen to what your heart is telling you and calling you to do next. Listening to the inner voice is essential. Before you can be truly receptive in this busy world you must first master the quietude. Be quiet; peace; tranquil; calm; and still. Take time to be alone; in place that quiet your body and nurture your soul. Open to the wisdom both beyond and within you to carry sense of stillness.

We believe that quietude is an essential experience, an important value. Quietude and focus will maximize your clarity. Your heart seeks quietude even as the mind avoids it. This is why meditative; contemplative and dream states provide such fertile ground for dialogue with the Universe. Notice your need to speak without saying anything meaningful. Your thoughts, internal speech, are essential to your living experience.

The value of all this noise is helping to confirm your existence. Try paring back the external and internal noise, eliminating what is not essential. If not release yourself from it. As you move more into silence, notice the effects on your heart. You will be more sensitive and caring, have an easier time seeing interconnectedness.

When you practice internal quietude and focus, you will be able to maintain conscious interaction with the others while you are engaged in the noise and activities. Quietude is oriented toward the self. Effective leaders take the time to think through and develop a clear picture of where they want the organization to be in future.

Thinking

Taking time out to think is critical for effective leadership. Leaders are thinking about what would be appropriate for their organizations. Leaders create an environment supportive of imaginative thinking and reflection on problems, causes and future solutions is a strong requirement for innovation to flourish.

Thinking time is also vital, i.e. time to plan, to prioritize, and to choose how best to expend your attention and energy. Doing anything in a rush increases the risks of missing key elements, making needless mistakes, and wasting effort. Make it easier by recalling tasks and list them in some kind of order. But, unfortunately, lists easily become clogged with items if you don't allocate enough time to thinking carefully about what you are doing.

Only an effective leader can think about the future and plan for the future each day.

Reflection

Reflection time cultivates the new ideas and answers that enrich your leadership. Leaders need to step back, take time out, and assess their direction. Clear your mind, stretch and relax, focus on one issue you want to consider, look at the issue from more than one perspective, and continue to mull. Read the signs. Don't ignore them.

It is normal to be apprehensive as you come to these crossroads. Don't let that apprehension freeze you, but let it gird you for the decisions that need to be made and the actions that follow.

Make sure that you take advantage of all the resources you have to make the most informed decision. Leaders encourage themselves having time for reflection.

Uplift

The arrival of a new idea is typically accompanied by a wonderful feeling of uplift and excitement. It's inspiring to have a new idea, to intuit a new way of getting the job done. Highly effective leaders know the importance of heart and recognize people who are contributing to the team effort.

The effective leaders are good at recognizing people who help move the team towards the goal. They recognize their contributions against the achievement of organization. This will maintain enthusiasm and motivation on the way towards a longer-term goal. It is time to stop doubting yourself and find the potentiality inside of you.

We need to understand how we focus our time and energy to be effective. Effective leaders are persons who have the luxury of the time and space needed to develop inner harmony and quietude. Quietude is a necessary consequence of the need for the leaders to resolve complex problems.

TIME TO STOP ACTIVITIES

When you're mental activities happen at a highly increased rate at the moment; it's time to ask yourself: What do I need to stop my activities. Maximize your return on time invested (ROTI). Stop wasting time. See how you really spend your time. Highly effective leaders take the time they need to sharpen their tools.

They stop doing what they're doing. They decide periods of free time where they can choose between several activities. Nothing can stop you but you can stop anything. Time is an ultimate illusion. Stop activities means:

a. Never make a decision: Let someone else make it and then if it turns out to be the wrong one, you can disclaim it, and if it is the right one, you can abide by it.

b. Postpone the deadline: For a week, a day, or even half an hour.

c. Divide and conquer: Break activity in practical and attractive events

d. Every one has price: Find out what the price is

Your spirit operates outside time and space. When there is an emergency where danger is about to approach you faster than you can normally sense, your spirit will compel you to act quickly without pondering. It directs you through your instinct and reflexes. Your spirit can observe things and sense reality beyond your ordinary rate and range of awareness.

Stopping can keep you from going in the wrong direction, expending and wasting an unusual amount of energy heading off in an unproductive direction.

Slowing down

Slow down to make sure you're making the right turns and moving towards your destination. Slow down is not procrastinating. Your time needs to be slowed down to a crawl, so that it can fully perceive everything that is happening no matter how quickly. Slow your time almost to a standstill during the moment of thought. See your perception and action against the moments. This is truly a time manipulation, since your perception seems to manage this trick is that time has been stretched longer or made shorter.

You have to slow time down in your consciousness. It is not time that slows down but you that slows down. See in your mind's eye and memory things slowing down.

Like a picture frame frozen from a movie in motion. It is the way you experience time slowing down or stopping. It would give you time to analyze the situation and the actions of everyone and everything around you. It gives you extra time to determine your actions in a pressure situation. This would be incredibly useful in business, driving your car in traffic, playing games, and life threatening situations.

Postponement

Postpone the meeting, deadline, etc, if possible. Take the long view to see failure and risk. Everything doesn't have to be completed this minute, or today, or even this week. Check in frequently on timelines and deadlines when priorities are conflicting. Identify when you're artificially accelerating a deadline for no good reason.

Cancelation

Never answer every one's every question. Don't spend your whole time answering questions. When you always answer one's every question, you'll forever be answering your member's every question. This will leave you with no time to spend on areas that need your direct attention now. It sounds trite - and it not meant to - but if members are continually asking the same questions because they are having trouble, get rid of them.

If they are decent members asking because they do not know, then teach them. They'll know next time, and you'll both be better for it. Leaders do not postpone unpleasant jobs they are committed to take responsibility. When we make choices to postpone or ignore opportunities, we're constantly on the lookout for highly effective leaders.

Clear Papers

A well-organized workspace is essential for time management. By eliminating clutter, setting up an effective filing system, gathering essential tools, and managing workflow, leaders can easily organize an effective workspace.

Take all the papers on your desk, and around your desk, and put them in your inbox. If they don't fit, just put them in a single pile. Now go through that pile, one document at a time. Don't put any document back on the pile - deal with it immediately, and then move on to the next document, until you've cleared the pile. With each document, your choices are to:

1. Trash: It is merely a pretty piece of paper. Throw it into the dust bin. Always throw away all trash before leaving. If the message you receive is trash (or spam), delete it.

2. Delegate: Task that is not yours to do

3. File immediately: Something that you might use later on

4. Do it immediately: Task that needs to be completed soon

5. Defer it: Task that can't be completed quickly, but it's not high priority. Put the action on your to-do list and the document in an "action" folder.

By listing tasks and setting priorities, you'll be able to execute the next actions needed to accomplish goals. An effective leader must still be flexible, disciplined, and well prepared to confront time wasters.

Organizing an effective workspace, managing workflow, and planning to achieve goals are all strategies that chairpersons can use to reduce stress and be more productive.

Managing workflow makes it easier to plan, and planning makes it possible to strike a balance between what's important and what's urgent. By using time more effectively, you'll actually have more time to be productive.

Hands Free Leave

Free your hands against homework, whenever you leave office. Say 'No' to homework. Don't take work home for the evening or over the weekend unless absolutely necessary.

Workload sprawl can be the result of lazy time management, or a need to have others think you're busy and therefore important. Learn to be efficient during the workweek so that you can reserve your personal time for refueling and personal fulfillment. Quality of leadership is central to the survival and success of organization.

Stop selling, start serving. Give yourself time. Give others time. It's essential, if you truly want to improve your own prospects and advance a more civilized way of living and working.

Managing your time is the key to becoming more effective leader. If you are going to be a leader, you must manage your time efficiently. To do this, you need to determine if you are spending time on urgent or important activities. Effective leaders have ability to manage their time for the purpose of generating more effective work and productivity.

We need to understand how we focus our time and energy to be effective. Consider the effective use of your time. Effective leaders spend their time based on the important and emergency use. Effective time management begins with vision and purpose.

Our productivity is directly proportional to our ability to relax. Only when our minds are clear and our thoughts are organized we achieve effective productivity and unleash our creative potential.

13th

DECISION MAKING SKILL

Leaders must be capable to translate organizational performance review findings into priorities for improvement and opportunities for innovation and reinvention. When decision failures occur, we should not focus on the issues involved, and they to identify the mistaken judgments and flawed assumptions that they made. Leaders do not push further to investigate why they made these errors.

Leaders learn carefully about why decision-making procedures led to mistaken judgments and flawed assumptions, and search for lessons about how to employ a different process when faced with tough choices in the future, i.e.:

a. Determine the composition of the decision-making body; which allows access to expertise; consider implementation needs, and the role of personal confidant, and the effect of differences.

b. Shape the context in which deliberations will take place. Define norms and ground rules will govern the discussions.

c. Determine how communication will take place among the members; and how people may exchange ideas and information, as well as generate and evaluate alternatives.

    d. Determine the extent and manner in which they will control the process and content of the decision. Define roles that the leader will play.

A key skill in becoming a successful leader is the skill of decision making. Good decisions are highly leveraged with low cost/high benefit. A decision-tends to be more effective when the framework for leadership is clear. Quality decision demonstrates the knowledge and skills of effective leadership. The leader encourages group discussion and allows team members in decision making. Effective decision making should consider followings:

    a. Inspire openness and trust: Value diversity

    b. Discourage hidden agendas/surprises: A decision is taken based upon input, as unbiased as possible, from each team member; addresses the team's goal

    c. Encourage participation and collaboration: It would not have been thought of by an individual alone

    d. Encourage innovation and creativity which addresses to a sound solution to the problem

    e. Allow change with purpose

Decisions delegated without adequate strategic context may answer the wrong question, be too risk averse, prioritize the wrong factor, or else simply float back up to the top. The decisions can be made through this method:

    a. Authority without group discussion: Make decision without consulting the group members, but giving an authority to someone

b. Authority with group discussion - The team creates ideas and has discussions, but the designated leader makes the final decision.

c. Expert: Hire/select an expert to make the decision

d. Majority: Based upon 50% + 1 of the people in a group deciding the course of action for the whole group.

e. Consensus: Permit open communication and give chance to influence the decision

f. Unanimous consent: where everyone truly agrees on the course of action to be taken

g. Averaging members' opinions - Separately ask each team member his/her opinion and average the results.

h. Minority - A minority of the team, who constitute less than 50% of the team, make the team's decision

The leaders focus on creating strategy, developing the "decision making system," and making only the critical decisions or resolving exceptions.

Prioritization

Prioritization is the essential skill you need to make the very best use of your own efforts and those of your team. It is particularly important when time is limited and demands are seemingly unlimited. It helps you to allocate your time where it is most-needed and most wisely spent, freeing you and your team up from less important tasks that can be attended to later or quietly dropped. Set your priorities. Focus on those areas you can control and don't waste time worrying about elements beyond your control.

Setting priorities allows you to live life with purposeful intentionality. Effective decision displays priority over the desires of the people.

Never delay a decision that must be made. Make your decision and move on. With good prioritization you can bring chaos to order, massively reduce stress, and move towards a successful conclusion. Without it, you'll flounder around, drowning in competing demands. You can simply prioritize based on:

1. Time constraints: Time constraints are important where other people are depending on you to complete a task, and particularly where this task is on the critical path of important activities. Identify the most important changes to make. Determine the different types of problem, and count the number of cases of each type of problem. By prioritizing the most common type of problem, you can focus your efforts on resolving it.

2. Potential profitability or benefit: Priority that is based on value or profitability is probably the most commonly-used for prioritization. Whether this is based on a subjective guess at value or a sophisticated financial evaluation, it often gives the most efficient results. Compare each item on a list with all other items on the list individually. By deciding in each case which of the two is most important, you can consolidate results to get a prioritized list.

    Leaders evaluate and prioritize opportunities by risk. Prioritize opportunities based on the attractiveness of the outcomes and your ability to take advantage of it. By doing this you can quickly spot the "quick wins" which will give you the greatest rewards in the shortest possible time, and avoid the "hard slogs" which soak up time for little eventual reward.

3. Task pressure: it's a brave (and maybe foolish) person who resists his or her boss's pressure to complete a task, when that pressure is reasonable and legitimate. In prioritizing task because of pressure, you need:

i. Make a list of tasks where you need to take many different factors into consideration.

ii. Plot the value of the task against the effort it will consume.

iii. Think whether tasks are urgent or important. Frequently, urgent tasks actually aren't that important or really important activities just aren't that urgent. This approach helps you cut through this.

iv. Prioritize issues and activities within the group, and give everyone fair input into the prioritization process. This is particularly useful where consensus is important, and where a robust group decision needs to be made.

Setting priorities and managing time effectively is basic to managing individual, team and organization performance.

Highly effective leader takes the time to think, plan and set priorities. They then launch quickly and strongly toward their goals and objectives. They work steadily, smoothly and continuously and seem to go through enormous amounts of work in the same time period that many persons spend socializing, wasting time and working on low value activities.

Thinking clearly and making wise decisions. Careful decision-making requires a sense of right and wrong rooted in character. To make the right decisions consistently, we can't let external influence or peer pressure cause us to do something wrong when our internal conscience is telling us to do what is right. To violate conscience undermines our self-respect and shatters not only our moral authority, but our confidence as leaders. We must also understand how pleasure and pain impact our choices. If we enjoy temporary pleasure with a disregard for its harmful effects on us and other people, we're going to suffer long-term pain.

Leadership demands payback for the near-term to receive lasting benefits. The longer we wait to make positive outcomes, the harder they become. A highly effective leader makes important decisions early then manages those decisions appropriately.

The leaders must give members opportunity to develop quality decision. Never make a decision while in an emotionally charged state or when you're under pressure or under fire. Always check that your decisions and actions are in keeping with your organization's mission statements, values and key business objectives. Ask yourself on a regular basis. Vision and clear goals are keys. Demonstrate how leaders can learn from failures and then change the process of decision that you employ in the future.

14th

CARING SKILL

A highly effective leader is a caring leader – he/she does not only care about his/her people, he/she actively takes care of people. Caring skill evolves to share not only expertise, but acquires more. It means to enhance others with your presence. It means to accept, to make peace, to show how to be, by example. Your job as a leader is to concentrate on what's most important so that it gets taken care of. Then let the rest of the stuff take care of itself.

Caring

Caring costs nothing, it makes you feel good, and it makes those around you feel good because it releases their reservoirs of positive energy. As a result, not only do people feel compelled to care back, but they use some of this newly released energy to care about those around them.

Effective leaders are capable, contributing, and caring. They care. They are compassionate. Care means showing concern for others through words and action. Discover greatest satisfactions that come from kindness to others. People reach out to one another, command the affection and service of others by his/her heartiness and sympathy. Care indicates

a. Close attention – Put intense focus on others; pay more attention. The difference between those who are highly effective is that they pay more attention that the less effective ones.

b. Upkeep - Keep leaders to look after others

c. Assistance - Treatment to those in need

d. Responsibility – Take consequences of action. They belief that leaders are responsible for determining who they are, and how their choices affect their life.

Leadership is essentially about helping people to achieve a better life. Care should consider cultural traditions, personal preferences and values, environment situations, and lifestyles. It may create an integral part of the collaborative team in making decisions, shared responsibility, respect, coordination, and efficiency. Caring skill includes, but not limited to:

Serving

Leaders focus on serving the needs of others, particularly the people on their team. They identify and meet the needs of their team members, because they know that when each member of the team has what he or she needs to succeed, success is much more likely to occur. A leader knows how to identify and fulfill needs, even if they are unusual or different.

Sacrificing

To be a real leader, at times, we need to sacrifice our personal comforts and desires. A leader needs to be able and willing to put the interests of his/her people first.

Developing

Leaders help followers reach their full potential. Effective leadership development hinges on:

a. Focus on the development of leadership, not individual leaders

b. Distribute leadership responsibility throughout an organization

c. Embed leadership development in the context of people's work

Leaders have to develop others as new leaders, looking for individuals who genuinely care about people and organization, and prepare appropriate career development paths for them at all levels.

Educating

The key is to actively involve the members in the learning process by giving them choices as to what they can learn, and by checking constantly to see what they have learned. Find out what they know, put them into a situation where they recognize the need to know then offer them the opportunity to learn. Effective leadership includes teaching and learning, building relationships and influencing people, as opposed to exercising one's power. Educating the people will enable them to:

i. Acquire and sharpen skills and personal attributes: Leaders sharpen skills by learning. They define and sharpen personal leadership attributes; and clarify leadership attributes through feedback and reflection

ii. Have ability to contribute more effectively to organization.

iii. Break through the barriers and reach their goals.

Leaders provide resources in which area of development the followers need to focus on; and help navigate to the appropriate platform based on the required competency. The capable leader is one who can lead others through difficult situations where significant changes are taking place.

Involving

Leadership implies running at the head of the pack, and not driving it from behind. Leadership means involving others. People want to be involved in something important. Give them a whole project or a significant piece of the project to work on.

Leaders encourage working together to achieve common goals, take responsibility for decision-making and problem solving. When you are going to make a change that affects others, get them involved before making the actual change. This increases commitment to make the change work after it is implemented.

Members should be involved in the decision making process right from the start, by contributing their ideas and suggestions. You're a strong believer in team work. Leaders then focus on members' participation. The leaders are also participating in the process with a calm, pleasant, and out-going attitude.

Leaders realize the value of making each local team feel important. They avoid highly centralized project ownership as it makes remote entities feel less valued. These leaders assign local ownership of tasks whenever feasible, promoting a stronger team commitment and often stimulating better information flows between the different entities.

Show Interest

Leaders take a personal interest in people. Show people that you care, and genuine curiosity about their lives. Ask them question about their hobbies, their challenges, their families, their aspirations.

The highly effective leader realizes it is his/her responsibility to provide a highly motivating environment for the followers. When the leader shares some with others, the message is sent that he/she is important.

Everyone wants to feel important. The leaders understand this and find the time to get face to face with the people. It's about telling them something that will make them know you value them and their contributions to the organization.

Trust

As your followers understand that you know them they will feel your trust, then they will come to experience the growth that accompanies that trust and you will find you have developed your most loyal followers.

Trust exists among group members and with the leader. An effective leader builds trust, both with others and among others. The power available to a leader is the trust that derives from faithfully serving.

Coaching

Training and coaching are two different things, although some people use them interchangeably. Training is a structured lesson designed to provide the member with the knowledge and skills to perform a task. Coaching, on the other hand, is a process designed to help the member gain greater competence and to overcome barriers so as to improve job performance.

Training and coaching go hand-in-hand. First you train them with lots of technical support, and then you coach them with motivational pointers. Both training and coaching help to create the conditions that causes someone to learn and develop. People learn by the examples of others, by forming a picture in their minds of what they are trying to learn, by gaining and understanding necessary information, by applying it to their job, or practice.

Real progress towards sustainable development depends on the willingness of people at every level to both give and accept effective leadership. Leader provides explanation of what the job entails and solicits suggestions while still staying in control of the situation; provides a great deal of direction, but he or she also attempts to hear the member's feelings about decisions as well as their ideas and suggestions.

Coaching functions strengthen one's capacity to improve; strive to increase his/her skills; engage in ongoing self-evaluation; involve and participate as part of the learning team. One common guiding action is to teach.

A leader is usually a great teacher. Leaders provide opportunities for their followers to learn and grow. They mentor or coach their followers. As noted above, the relationship is friendly and informal. The leaders treat followers as equals, while providing encouragement for their personal and professional development. They see their role as servant leader and seek to serve their own followers, as well as other stakeholders inside and outside of the college.

Leaders also guide by engaging in moral reasoning and principled judgment, as well as teaching these ideas to their followers. Symbolic actions also provide guidance for others, an indirect but powerful means of teaching.

Leaders are strong advocates of staff development activities, often using them as a reward for accomplishments. Scholarship provides a means of teaching as well. These leaders are scholars in their own right, but also promote scholarship among followers. Train others to do jobs. A leader cannot do them all, nor can others do them if they have not been trained.

Supportive

Effective leaders recognize good ideas and encourage/support the changes in the organization to allow the new ways to be adopted.

Leader involvement and providing supportive conditions are key factors for organization. Effective leaders delegate authority, advance collaborative decision-making, and refrain from being the central problem solver. Leaders are not necessarily resolve differences, but rather encourage and support an environment that builds the potential of the people to lead.

Leader expertise moderates the effects of supportive leader behavior on role ambiguity. The essence of leadership is supportive, not dictatorial. They are relying on praise, two-way communication, and facilitating the work of their members. Leader emphasizes support of the follower rather than control.

Supportive behavior involves concentration on an individual's attitude and feelings. The leader will give praise often, listen well, encourage, and involve others in problem solving and decision-making. Leaders provide recognition and to actively listen and facilitate problem solving and decision making by the members.

Leaders create warm, personal relationships with their team members in order to coax their best efforts. They manage people by exception. When things are going well, leave them alone. When a problem occurs; then help.

Empathy

Treating everyone in the organization with empathy helps leaders earn trust. Leaders who are empathetic create strong bonds. Empathy allows us to create bonds of trust, it gives us insights into what others may be feeling or thinking; it helps us understand how or why others are reacting to situations. Empathy means taking other's feelings into thoughtful consideration and then making intelligent decisions that work those feelings into the response.

Empathy makes resonance possible; lacking empathy, leaders act in ways that create dissonance. Empathy is not about agreeing or disagreeing but is about acknowledging one's belief in tax cuts and trying to understand the reasons for advocating it. A leader uses empathy to share experiences, regardless of whether the feelings are distressing or pleasant.

Empathy emphasizes understanding all of people with no interest in either agreeing or disagreeing. Empathy refers to the ability to perceive and directly experientially feel other's emotions as they feel them, but makes no statement as to how they are viewed. Empathy is the recognition and understanding of the states of mind, beliefs, desires, and emotions of others.

Empathy is about sensing others emotions, understanding their perspectives, and taking active interest in their concerns. Empathy can be achieved by simulating the pretend beliefs, desires, character traits and context of the other and see what emotional feelings this leads to; simulating the emotional feeling directly perceived and then look around for a suitable reason for this to fit. The person using empathy tunes into the entire inner world of the other person.

Empathy during disagreements is not difficult to imagine that the result might be a strengthening of emotional intimacy. Some people are naturally empathetic (people oriented) whilst others need to work on their empathy skills (task oriented). Empathy involves experiencing the feelings of another without losing your own identity. It involves accurate response to another's needs without being infected by them.

Empathy is at the heart of your emotional intelligence. By using empathy effectively you can reduce conflict, increase teamwork and productivity.

Care is an empathy for those who are in need, i.e. viewing other's work situation from their viewpoint; bring your suggestions to the relevant subjects, give help to others; do everything that is supposed to do. It is the opposite of negligence. Care is a type of motherliness or maternal affection types of behavior which include enduring, positive pleasurable contacts with other; watchful attention and awareness of conditions affecting one's activities and emotions; and; tenderness.

Highly effective leadership starts with empathy, the ability to "put oneself in the other person's shoes." Empathy means getting inside the hearts and minds of those you wish to reach. Without empathy, a leader cannot build trust. And without trust, a leader cannot inspire best efforts.

Sympathy

Leaders must be in sympathy with their followers. Moreover, they must understand followers and their problems. Sympathy means agreement in feeling, as between persons or on the part of one person with respect to another. Sympathy is the great lesson which a leader should learn.

Sympathy exists when the feelings or emotions of an individual give rise to similar feelings in another person, creating a state of shared feeling. Sympathy is usually the sharing of unhappiness or suffering, but it can also refer to sharing other emotions as well.

Sympathy is relationship or affinity between people or things in which whatever affects one correspondingly affects the other, i.e. sympathy for the suffering of others

It is generally accepted that in order to evaluate the actions of people, you must first sympathize with them. It's the polite thing to do. Sympathy means any affinities and suggested harmony or concord of feelings or temperament, as well as the capacity of entering into another's feelings. Sympathy must be considered as a sort of substitution, by which we are put in the place of others. In addition to sharing a feeling, sympathy also involves the sharing of a belief.

An effective leader has courage to care, to open his/her heart and react with sympathy. Sympathy involves being less active when listening as compared with empathy.

Tuning in to the other's inner world often readily happens for the listener using sympathy because he/she focuses on aspects with which he/she agrees. Your leadership, your sympathy with and understanding of the group, individually and as a whole, are going to make all the difference in the world to the rest of them.

Sincerity

The key to a leader's impact is sincerity. Sincerity defines quality or condition of being sincere; genuineness, honesty, and freedom from duplicity. It is about earnest and sincere feeling; being open and truthful; not deceitful or hypocritical; naturalness and simplicity; and seriousness.

Sincerity is usually thought of in the context of our words. When you discipline yourself to do what is hard, you gain access to a realm of results that are denied everyone else. The willingness to do what is difficult is like having a key to a special private treasure room. Sincerity can be seen from actions which include:

a. Be on time: Time is an important asset, don't waste it. Punctuality shows that one is reliable, responsible, and professional.

b. Do not make excuses: Winners do not make excuses. Do not make excuses nor let anyone make excuses for you. Take responsibility.

c. Winning attitude: Leaders recognize and attain the winning attitude to overcome difficulties, win people over, and turn problems into opportunities.

d. Gratification: We all want gratification, which is a positive response to the satisfaction of desires, the reward for a job well-done, the fulfilling of one's wishes.

e. Don't complain: We complain when we are not satisfied. Do not point the finger of fault at others. Nearly everyone is doing the best they can with the resources and abilities they have.

f. Answer accordingly: To be sincere means "to be without hypocrisy". Leave no doubt as to which answer you mean. In order to avoid misunderstandings, we need to look at the ways in which answer questions, and also whether or not we are listening to what is not being said. You should be able to adjust your answer accordingly, in order for your answer to make sense.

Sincerity is virtue of speaking truly about one's feelings, thoughts, and desires. Sincere expression carries risks to the speaker, since the ordinary screens used in everyday life are opened to the outside world.

An effective leader brings unique talent and perspective and a sincere commitment to the people and organization. The power of sincere praise to motivate, build loyalty and keep good members.

Forgiveness

Leaders are forgiving mistakes. Forgiveness is hard to do, in which you have to pardon or excuse other who hurts your feeling. Forgiving means we no longer blame others or are angry at those who did us a wrong thing. We are not perfect; we all make mistakes. Leaders must learn to forgive those who have wronged them or the organization.

Forgiveness creates just and fair structures and processes. Because forgiveness places a high value on the inherent worth and well being of people, it leads to the establishment of internal processes and policies which recognize and honor that worth and well being.

When you are ready to forgive, you are ready to begin letting go of resentment, anger, and hurt another person hurts you. In a relationship, to forgive is not to excuse or condone a hurtful behavior.

Fostering forgiveness is one effective mechanism to help the organization heal and bring forth positive energy and resiliency. Just as you would another person, tell yourself that it's okay for all those mistakes, or the should-haves that keep popping up in your mind. Don't dwell on the past and get blocked by events from long ago.

Make every effort to add to your faith, goodness, knowledge, self-control, perseverance; kindness, and love. Before we can persevere at anything, we must have self-control. It is impossible to be an effective individual without self-control. We may have a moment of anger, but we must not become slaves to anger.

Leaders invest considerable time in developing other leaders, are willing to admit mistakes, and share vulnerability in order to serve as effective role models. The leaders who forgive are to give as before. The leader himself/herself competently demonstrates forgiveness to his/her followers. Forgiveness connects the organization's vision and mission with the people who serve in the organization.

Organizational forgiveness is a competency that needs to be developed and exercised by leaders. Leaders can nurture a culture of forgiveness within an organization which can help it heal and recover in times of crisis.

Succession

Leaders care about succession. Organizations build and enhance their leadership capacity internally; they strengthening themselves from within by encouraging leadership from the inside out. Everyone has the capacity for leadership. Relying on a single person to lead the charge reflects a dysfunctional concept of leadership. No one person can do everything.

Succession and leadership development help organizations facilitate organization development and progress to ensure individual and organizational success as well as leadership continuity. This enables an organization to identify and prepare the right people for the right positions at the right time; and help assess leadership continuity, align culture and values with leadership growth, as well as retain and motivate key contributors.

Critical to best practices in succession management and leadership development programs are leadership competencies and stakeholder assessments. The assessments, combined with structured development programs, self-directed learning, and coaching, prepare individuals personally and professionally for future of the organization.

Praise

Leaders offer meaningful rewards and praise. Praise is one of the most effective and immediate ways of rewarding people for their efforts and successes. Praise defines:

a. Expression of respect or admiration - Words that express recognition of achievements. It implies rewards of performance; conclusion of a task for work that is considered well done, and value of accomplishments. Praise should show encouragement and acknowledgement; that inspire with courage and recognize the existence

b. Give worship and thanks - Honoring of a deity. Give honest praise often.

Effective leaders give recognition and praise. Praise indicates positive attitude, and provides recognition and encouragement. It can also increase motivation to excel. Praise is powerful positive reinforcement, a stimulus for learning behaviors.

An effective leader not only influences the goals and strategies of an organization. He/she shows his/her people that he/she cares about them.

Recognition

One of the deepest needs of our human existence is the need to be appreciated. Each and every one of us absolutely loves to be appreciated for who we are and what we do. Leaders may spend a great deal of money and time trying to increase the originality of their followers. But it will make no difference unless they also learn to recognize the valuable ideas among the many novel ones, and then find ways of implementing them.

The most costly element of recognition, however, is not monetary. It is the investment of time, which is something most leaders have far too little of. Yet to ignore the contributions of members' risks far greater costs: loss of enthusiasm, motivation, and commitment. When group member no longer cares, he/she is no longer productive, and that is a cost no leader can afford to bear.

Many people want to be recognized for what they know, instead of what they are, do, have and give with what they know. Ideas and innovation are the most important products of a successful organization, and the true value of a great leader is the ability to encourage and recognize both.

Recognition is important; it builds positive self-esteem. Give genuine recognition and praise. Pay attention to what people are doing and catch them doing the right things. When you give praise, spend a little effort to make your genuine words memorable.

Leaders should understand that in order to establish successful working relationships; they must recognize the assets and potential of others. When people feel valued, they have a greater sense of responsibility; display a higher level of commitment to achieving organizational goals; and are more productive.

Communicate that you care. A leader makes other people feel important and appreciated. The leader excels at creating opportunities to provide rewards, recognition and thanks to the followers. A leader creates a work environment in which people feel important and appreciated. Proper recognition sets up strong patterns of reinforcement that other will emulate; and create a culture of positive reinforcement that eventually will permeate the entire organization.

Show Result

Productive people begin with genuine caring. People usually judge leaders by their results. Effective leaders know that they can't do it alone. The single most important test for whether you're an effective leader or not: look behind you. If you don't have willing followers, it doesn't matter that you're doing everything right. And if you aren't achieving the goals you promised, you won't have willing followers for long.

If organization is going to succeed, a leader needs to convince his/her team to contribute their time and talents to help you reach the goals.

Leaders address values and performance expectations. Result oriented is aimed to achieve maximum outcome base on clear and measurable goals. People will work with more enthusiasm if they know clearly the expectation; get involved in establishing the expectation; are allowed to achieve it in their own way; and obtain a feedback mechanism. It evolves time, money and capacity.

A leader's ability to move others effectively is also the result of their capacities to move people. He/she possesses the ability to organize skills and talents of others to an observable result. To get successful result, you need to describe:

a. Vision - A common goal leads to a common vision that enables everyone to challenge the rules and create a better future

b. Tasks which include all work, activities, and services performed

c. Responsibility to be accomplished by the tasks performed

d. Method, which maximize efficiency and productivity. People need flexibility to accomplish both at work and in their personal lives

Key to success and achievement is insuring that the activities people are engaged leads to a constructive, useful purpose. Those who value real results from actions they take make far greater use of their time, leading to higher levels of success and achievement.

Leaders live and die by results. Results, of course, come in many forms and are measured and evaluated in many ways. Effective leadership is about bringing the best out of people; bring about exceptional results.

Leaders should be able to show people and organization achieves outstanding results.

Leaders achieve not just average results but more results faster continually. You are never more effective as a leader as when you are helping others be better than they are - even better than thought they could be. If people know that in working with you, they will improve their job performance, boost their career, and enrich their lives. People don't care how much you know, until they know how much you care.

Gratitude

If you show that you care about them, you inspire people to work harder, reach higher, and achieve more; get them to support you and go above and beyond in everything they do. Gratitude is feeling of emotional indebtedness towards another person; often accompanied by a desire to thank them; or to reciprocate for a favor they have done for you.

Take it to heart, for there's no such thing as an effective leader with a bad attitude. Gratitude is an easy and remarkably powerful step in building the type of community that is essential for successful teams. Look at your team members and say thank you.

Leaders reward good behavior. Although a certificate, letter, or a thank you may seem small and insignificant, they can be powerful motivators. The reward should be specific and prompt. Do not say something general, such as for doing a good job, rather cite the specific action that made you believe it was indeed a good job.

Pay is one of the tangible ways you can reward people for doing good stuff. It's another form of praise in visible, tangible form. Don't limit your thinking about pay to just money, though. Pay people with time off, recognition, choice assignments, small gifts, and special bonuses to encourage the behavior you want.

Gratitude is an easy and remarkably powerful step in building the type of community that is essential for successful teams.

Caring energizes everyone around you. When you open up and really care about people, you make them feel really good about themselves. This releases the reservoir of positive energy that resides in all of us. Caring means showing sincere interest in and genuine concern for others. It includes consideration, compassion, empathy, sympathy, and nurturing.

Caring does not mean tolerating or ignoring shoddy performance, violations of company policies, bad attitudes, or dishonesty. What it does mean is seeing humans as the most important resource in an organization - and the resource with the most overall potential. Leaders who are caring will likely be rewarded with cooperative and supportive behavior in return.

Careless person can't become a successful leader. Leadership calls for respect. Followers will not respect a leader who does not grade high on all of the factors of a pleasing personality. Effective leaders care about other people. Leaders who are caring will likely be rewarded with cooperative and supportive.

15th

ENFORCEMENT SKILL

Enforcement is an act of enforcing, which may need force to get the things done correctly. It describes the range of procedures and actions employed to ensure that organizations or persons, potentially failing to comply with laws or regulations can be brought or returned into compliance and/or punished through action.

Leader has to recognize that some violations against value and ethical behavior so severely threaten the well-being of people and the organization that these violations should carry with them harsh consequences, i.e. sanction. The clearest way to show what the rule of law is to recall what has happened when there is no rule of law. Enforcement should foster rewards and punishment in balance. Enforcement functions to:

a. Protect organization's values against violation or abuse, i.e. fraud, indiscipline, etc

b. Promote ethical behaviors, i.e. comply to the rules, laws, norms, mechanism, procedures, etc

Managers were expected to be the boss, evaluator, or judge. Leaders come with vision and integrity and a range of other traits which are associated with being paragon of virtue. Leadership involves the following:

a. Assuming responsibility for showing the way, or setting the direction

b. Speaking out about what can be done to achieve the organization's mission more effectively and efficiently

c. Adhering to the core beliefs that depict what is appropriate and inappropriate behavior in how the members approach their work, how they manage internally and how they relate to the community.

In today's rapidly changing world the authoritarian leadership that valued compliance, conformity and command control hierarchies will not be able to keep up with the pace of change. Leader must become a partner, facilitator, cheerleader, supporter, and coach in order to be successful.

In enforcement process, leader's task is to accomplish the organizational mission by means of the greatest resource, people. They must be able to successfully use a variety of leadership styles depending on the task, mission, and individual.

Ethical Behavior

The key driver of a leader's effectiveness is doing the right behaviors. Leaders ensure the organization environment is free from disruptive, hostile, or violent behavior. Therefore, it should not be tolerated. The stature of any organization depends on how successfully it enforces ethical standards.

Organization's codes embody not just codifications of right and wrong but also the calling's ideals, aspirations, and sense of trusteeship; includes detailed enforcement procedures, which clearly expresses the organization's vision of philanthropy promoted through responsible fundraising. Leaders have to challenge un-ethical behavior, which includes:

a. Abuse power: Large differentials in the relative power of leaders and followers can also contribute towards abuse.

b. Hoard privileges: Leaders that hoard power are also likely to hoard wealth and status as well

c. Encourage deceit: Patterns of deception, whether they take the form of outright lies or hiding or distorting information, destroy the trust that binds leaders and followers together

d. Act inconsistently: Diverse followers, varying levels of relationships and elements of situations make consistency an ethical burden of leadership. Shadows arise when leaders appear to act arbitrarily and unfairly.

e. Misplace or betray loyalties: Leaders cast shadows when they violate the loyalty of followers and the community.

f. Fail to assume responsibilities: Leaders act irresponsibly when they fail to make reasonable efforts to prevent follower's misdeeds; ignore or deny ethical problems; don't shoulder responsibility for the consequences of their directives; deny their duties to their followers; and hold followers to higher standards than themselves.

Leaders provide effective system for managing ethical behavior within the organization. They show a plan for consistently enforcing the expectations through the consequences. Everyone should be accountable for his/her behavior. Ethics enforcement includes handling and preventing un-ethical behavior.

Prevention begins by educating members about ethical fundraising. Members have vital interest in understanding the enforcement process, which protects the standing of organization and its members. Enforcement emphasizes ethical behavior over punishment.' It will be reflected in the leader's commitment to prevention, ease of access to ethics advice, and opportunities for remediation.

Punishment

Enforcement is an organization's requirement to impose a kind of behavior, i.e. act with ethics. It implies obedience of the people against rule/law. Punishment is not the primary goal of enforcement. Punishment is the mirror image of praise. It's a negative consequence that follows negative behavior.

Punishment is the tool you use to get people to stop stuff. If you figure out what's most important for people to quit doing in your organization, rig up some kind of negative consequence for them if they do it.

If you zap people too much with negative consequences, they don't just quit doing the stuff that you don't want them to do. They quit doing pretty much everything. That's why rule by fear and controlled ferocity cultures have a devil of a time getting people to take initiative. They've been zapped so often they're just not willing to risk it. The problem is that lots of organizations forget about it. They maintain reward and promotion systems that reward behavior.

Violent behavior is a form of serious misconduct that undermines the mission of the organization and threatens the integrity of community as a whole.

Enforcement needs power. Leadership and power are inextricably intertwined. Power describes one's ability to get the outcomes he/she wants. Leadership models that are oriented toward power and control continue to be problematic for the organization.

Power-oriented leadership laden with posturing, protectionism, cynicism, and adversarial-ism may contribute to a low-trust ministry environment in which leadership effectiveness is marginalized. Realize that power comes from all locations and positions, not only from those higher in a hierarchy.

There is also power (and risk) in having a clear purpose, enough information, and a good relationship with others. These forms of power enable you to be a force for change, beyond playing by the organizational rules. If you have the desire and willpower, you can become an effective leader.

Almost anyone can use power, but it takes skill to use leadership. Leadership power is much more than the use of force; it is matter of influencing others to truly want to achieve a goal. Power forces others to achieve a goal. Power refers to a capacity that a person has to influence the behavior of another, so that he or she acts in accordance with his/her wishes. This power is a capacity or potential as it implies a potential that need not be actualized to be effective. That is, a power may exist, but does not have to be used to be effective.

A person has the potential for influencing 5 (five) points of power over another:

a. Coercive power - Power that is based on fear. A person with coercive power can make things difficult for people.

b. Reward power - Compliance achieved based on the ability to distribute rewards that others view as valuable. Able to give special benefits or rewards to people.

c. Legitimate power - The power a person receives as a result of his or her position in the formal hierarchy of an organization. The person has the right to expect you to comply with legitimate requests.

d. Expert power - Influence based on special skills or knowledge. This person earns respect by experience and knowledge.

e. Referent power - Influence based on possession by an individual or desirable resources or personal traits. You like the person and enjoy doing things for him or her.

The power comes with leadership responsibilities, but power like any other tool or resource can be used, misused, or even abused. The misuse of power is a major mistake which has potential to damage operations and objectives of organization.

Although your position as a manager, supervisor, leader, etc. gives you the authority to accomplish certain tasks and objectives in the organization, this power does not make you a leader; it simply makes you the boss. Leadership differs in that it makes the followers *want* to achieve high goals, rather than simply bossing people around.

Leadership is not just a matter of position; it is communication, creation, vision, innovation, value, confidence, participation, and intellectual curiosity. Leaders must be able to communicate, discuss, and ask for inputs from everybody in the team and organization. He or she must be able to articulate a vision and involve people willingly in the operations. Leaders provide a predictability and transparency that gives credibility to organization and its members.

Commanding

Commanding is the authority vested in an individual appointed to a position in the chain of command. Command carries with it special powers of responsibility and accountability which are associated with the position.

Persons who display leadership skills are considered the most valuable asset of an organization. These persons should have to receive greater recognition and get more high-profile assignments; because they know how to maximize their individual performance while simultaneously influencing others to do their best. This requires an ability to positively encourage others to strive for higher levels of commitment and performance.

Leadership is an important element of conflict. The leader soothes fears and gives clear directions by his or her powerful stance, commanding and expecting full compliance (agreement is not needed). They need emotional self-control for success and can seem cold and distant. This approach is best in times of crisis when you need unquestioned rapid action and with problem members who do not respond to other methods. Commanding is making sense when:

a. Efficiency is created by repetitive action. There has to be a better way. Doing the same task a couple of times can take up a substantial amount of time. Commanding can be an essential way to reduce number of repetitive task that you may spend doing more productive work.

b. Adapt to situation that resists change. Making a change requires a kind of leap of faith; therefore a leader needs to decide to move in the direction of the unknown on the promise that something will be better for the organization.

c. Magnitude of problems creates a combative environment. Change may have created a combative environment where everything is a fight and folks come out with both barrels blazing to solve every issue. Leader should bring environment that fosters trust, creativity, and collaboration - all of which are necessary for long-term survival of an organization. Leader should tell members to sit together for a brainstorming session to share opinion or best ideas, or coordinative meeting to find a good, productive argument or debate

In commanding your followers; you should avoid being hard-boiled and sarcastic. Your duty is to produce a well drilled organization. It is necessary to have the people working for you.

Leaders demonstrate patience and expertise; and through these the followers have in you to do your part as leader. Leadership is process of influencing others to accomplish the mission by providing purpose, direction, and motivation.

Effective leadership transforms human potential into effective performance. In a tough situation you may not ask, but command them, as it's required for enforcement. Make it clear, brief, and to the point. Extinguish the use of the person's name in relation to any commands. If it is a life and death emergency; you must get the dog's attention by any means possible.

Every time you expect people to comply with your command, first ensure that you have set up the environment for success.

The leadership approach needs to move away from command and compliance. Sometimes it is appropriate to move to involvement which gains the commitment of those being led. This gains the enthusiasm and commitment of people.

Conducting

Leaders are doing the right things consistently well. Conduct is defined as a mode of personal behavior. Only individuals can behave. The conduct of an organization is a reflection of the conduct of the individuals making up the organization. To shape the conduct of the individuals who follow us, we must be able to hold them accountable for their behavior. But first, we must be held accountable ourselves.

Accountability is a willingness to explain your actions. If our actions are indefensible, we'll be stripped of the real authority to exercise moral leadership. We must submit our behavior to the scrutiny of trusted advisors before dictating the conduct of those we lead. As leaders, we set the tone for the conduct of the individuals in our organization. People do what people see. Conduct is learned through observation; teach what we know, but we reproduce who we are.

Directing

Leaders set directions and seek future opportunities for organization. Directive behavior involves concentration on how do to a task. A leader with a directive style will tell and show people what to do and will provide feedback frequently.

Leaders who have a direction orientation decide what needs to be done and communicate this to subordinates. This leader engages in one-way communication; spells out the employee's role and tells the employee what to do, where to do it, when to do it and how to do it; and closely supervises performance. Three words can be used to define directive behavior: structure, control, and supervise. The leader tells the people what, how, when, and where to do various tasks.

The degree to which a leader may be directive depends upon a number of factors, i.e. uncertainty in the situation, little time is available, a short-term increase in productivity is needed, or they exercise a high degree of positional or organizational power.

Leaders have an overall sense of strategic direction for the organization and recognize the importance of their organization having strategic direction

Guiding

As a leader, you have to get your people to trust you and be sold on your vision. People want a strong vision of where they are going. Leader has to provide goals, direction, training, support, feedback, and recognition - to develop followers' skills, motivation, and confidence to excel. The result is an organization, where people feel more empowered, engaged and open to new challenges.

Mentoring is extremely important because it's one of the best ways to break down the barriers between the leaders and the followers, the hierarchical structure that cripples many organizations.

Influencing

Leadership is the process of influencing others to accomplish the mission by providing purpose, direction, and motivation. Leading means the manner and approach of providing direction, implementing plans, and motivating people; influencing people in reaching a goal. Influencing is usually seen as something you do to someone.

Leadership is influencing people to get things done to a standard and quality above their norm; and doing it willingly. Influence marks an individual or group to do what the leader wants done. Influencing emphasizes 2-way communication. Influencing strategies includes:

a. Show enthusiasm for an idea: Enthusiasm is a form of persuasiveness that causes others to become interest and willing to accept what the leader is attempting to accomplish. Enthusiasm shown by a leader generates enthusiasm in followers. Genuine enthusiasm is an important trait of a good leader.

b. Dialogue: Leader is to be committed to providing high quality professional development in dialogue facilitation; and believes that the key to personal and organizational vitality lies in hosting and convening conversations that matter. Dialogue forms the foundation for shared mission, vision, values, and goals. It is the catalyst for meaningful and long-lasting change.

c. Build a coalition with key supporters: A coalition is an alliance of separate organizations formed to execute a particular purpose. Coalition brings together a wider range of skills, ideas, experiences and connections. The coalition may require that you compromise with other coalition members.

d. Foster peer pressure: Peer influence leads members participate in productive endeavors. Peer pressure motivates ones who strive for excellence as individuals and members of a group. Motivation is encouraged through positive competition, recognition, loyalty, teamwork, organizational pride, and the setting of personal goals.

Leadership is an art. Bad leadership is usually due more to clumsiness than to ill will. Leaving aside the natural bullies - most of whom, except in circumstances where bullying has been imposed as the norm, have neither the intelligence nor the perceptivity to earn positions of real authority - people who fail as leaders usually do so simply because they are ill at ease in positions of leadership. Use active voice to tell what to do. Instructions tend to be more like a series of commands.

A good leader makes instructions clear. When you give instructions, you let the members contribute whatever they can. It may not be as good as what you would have done, also might be better than your idea. Successful instruction may also consider:

a. Develop a good working relationship: Relationships can only work for the organization if they also work for the people doing the relating. Leader should be focus on practical interactional and communication skills that improve interpersonal relationship; able to influence the quality of relationships between others

b. Communicate impact - Identify and address member cues that reflect willingness to take action and those that indicate resistance. It will enable to questioning and creating new concepts and ideas.

c. Offer help - Allow to submit requests, whenever members are unable to resolve a problem. Effective leader ensures the followers to achieve their goals by providing support, be a role model and offering educational programs

d. Actively follow-up on requests - Leaders who discussed organization improvement priorities with their followers, and then regularly followed up with these followers, showed striking improvement. Leaders who did not have ongoing dialogue with colleagues showed improvement that barely exceeded random chance.

e. Make it easy - We work at making things easy, and that's hard work. But it's worth doing. Members are not stubborn, they want to make things easy, they just don't know how to do it

f. Give support - The benefit of a support is that your members won't be down; on other hand when you really need support, someone will be there. Therefore be available for them. If you're not sure what to say or do, just ask. Be supportive, but not smothering Sometimes you can give support, and other times you'll need to receive it. Don't expect yourself to always be served.

When you tell a member, what you want done, instead of giving an order, you give them the freedom to come up with their best way of getting that task done. It may not always be the best way, and you may have to do some monitoring and guiding, but there is also the chance that they will come up with something better than what you planned. When you give instructions instead of orders there is a tendency to be less clear about the expected outcome.

Instructing

Leaders provide adequate instructions. Time is lost if things are not done correctly. Instructing means you explain how to do something. Giving good instructions, whether written or spoken, requires a certain kind of mindset.

In many cases a leader instructs members to complete an assignment before the day is over, because it must meet a deadline. To achieve the purpose, leader should ensure these points, i.e.

a. Get their attention – Leader should address that the instruction is not a request but it's an order.

b. Be specific - Make sure that your instructions are as clear and comprehensible as possible. Be more efficient and not complicate the things.

c. Tell briefly - Think about how much you're going to explain at a time. Make it short and clear.

d. Talk slowly – It will allow more time for your people to process and comprehend your instructions. Control the speed of your speech - slow down slightly if necessary.

e. Use active voice to tell what to do - Instructions tend to be more like a series of commands.

A good leader makes instructions clear. When you give instructions, you let the members contribute whatever they can. It may not be as good as what you would have done, also might be better than your idea. Successful instruction may also consider:

a. Develop a good working relationship. Relationships can only work for the organization if they also work for the people doing the relating. Leader should be focus on practical interactional and communication skills that improve interpersonal relationship; able to influence the quality of relationships between others

b. Communicate impact - Identify and address member cues that reflect willingness to take action and those that indicate resistance. It will enable to questioning and creating new concepts and ideas.

c. Offer help - Allow to submit requests, whenever members are unable to resolve a problem Good leader ensures the followers to achieve their goals by providing support, be a role model and offering educational programs

d. Actively follow-up on requests - Leaders who discussed organization improvement priorities with their followers, and then regularly followed up with these followers, showed striking improvement. Leaders who did not have ongoing dialogue with colleagues showed improvement that barely exceeded random chance.

e. Make it easy - We work at making things easy, and that's hard work. But it's worth doing. Members are not stubborn, they want to make things easy, they just don't know how to do it

f. Give support - The benefit of a support is that your members won't be down; on other hand when you really need support, someone will be there. Therefore be available for them. If you're not sure what to say or do, just ask. Be supportive, but not smothering Sometimes you can give support, and other times you'll need to receive it. Don't expect yourself to always be served.

When you tell a member, what you want done, instead of giving an order, you give them the freedom to come up with their best way of getting that task done. It may not always be the best way, and you may have to do some monitoring and guiding, but there is also the chance that they will come up with something better than what you planned. When you give instructions instead of orders there is a tendency to be less clear about the expected outcome.

Counseling

A highly effective leader is able to lead him/herself, effectively communicate with others, solve problems, and persuade others to own their problems. The leader must be able to counsel members in order to help them. Listening is the most important key to counseling. Be careful not to give advice, instead use questions to help the individual arrive at their own solution to the problem. Feel free to give factual information, but cautious about giving advice.

A person grows if he/she is able to think problems through for himself/herself. Leadership means understanding that people are more important than things.

You need to be able to lead yourself, effectively communicate with others, solve problems, and persuade others to own their problems. Counseling has a powerful, long-term impact on people and the effectiveness of the organization.

Counseling is talking with a person in a way that helps him or her solve a problem. It involves thinking, implementing, knowing human nature, timing, sincerity, compassion, and kindness. Leaders should demonstrate the qualities of an effective counselor (respect, self-awareness, credibility, and empathy) and employ the skills of good communication.

Ruling

Leadership is the ability of an individual to set rules for others and lead from the front. It is an attitude that influences the environment around us. Rule encompasses:

a. Responsibility: When you take complete responsibility and accept ownership, without making excuses or blaming others, you experience a sense of control that leads to the personal power that is the foundation of charisma. Develop a sense of responsibility among your followers.

b. Accountability: Accountability is a concept in ethics that involves either the expectation or assumption of account-giving behavior; willingness to stand up and be counted; as part of a process; reflecting personal choice and willingness to contribute to an expressed or implied outcome. Similar to responsibility, i.e., a position of power due to recognizing one's causative activity; accountability implies:

i. The willingness to acknowledge responsibility to others, and the willingness to fully accept responsibility for one's actions and their implications

ii. Practice in a sound and sustainable manner, maintain accountability for their practices and are held accountable for any deficiencies in their activities

iii. Apply the positive dynamics of focused feedback to help themselves and others move away from excuse making and blame shifting

iv. Develop a clear understanding of how ownership and accountability drive organizational results

v. Best practices that create a culture of accountability. Accountability is being answerable or responsible for something. All successful people are moving toward more empowerment, enlightenment - and creating a culture of accountability.

With accountability comes a measure of discipline. Accountability is the opposite of permissiveness. Holding people accountable is really about the distribution of power and choice.

When people have more choice, they are more responsible. When they become more responsible, they can have more freedom. Accountable means decisions and actions are clear, reasonable and open to examination; committed; accountability results, and quality; serve and protect the long-term interests of all; challenge; taking on big challenges and seeing them through; continuous improvement.

People who live successfully do not shift the responsibility for their circumstances to other people. They accept accountability of their actions, consequences, and experiences.

Responsible individuals are life-long learners, seeking to increase their skills. They welcome change, and they change with the times. They communicate with others clearly and live with a spirit of cooperation. Leadership is the ability of an individual to set rules for others and lead from the front. It is an attitude that influences the environment around us.

To be a highly effective leader, you may need the whole set of leadership skills.

16th

VALUE LEADERSHIP

A highly effective leader is creating value through leadership. Leaders must have a rock-solid value system which is congruent with their followers values. Leadership in value means respect and share common value and beliefs, and promote ethical behavior. Principles of value leadership include:

a. Human relationships: Hire people who share organization values and treat members with respect; create an environment in which people who fit with their cultures create superior value

b. Teamwork: Encourage people from different functions to work together for organization ends; solve problems more quickly and develop more profitable solutions to business problems

c. Experiment frugally: Encourage people to develop new products and processes without spending too much money; experiment frugally which can tap members for ideas that lead to new products and streamlined operations

d. Commitments: Say what you'll do and do what you say; build trust between company and employees, customers, and communities

e.   Humility: Defeat the arrogance that often comes from success; encourage doing what allowed people to become successful in the first place.

f.   Winning attitude: (in business) Sustain market, leadership create superior value for customers. Interaction among the skills is often the most difficult aspect of the strategy for competitors to understand and replicate.

g.   Community: (in business) Contribute corporate time and money to people or organizations outside the company's core circle of operations. As whenever companies let employees pick the recipients of corporate charity, they feel better about the company because the company is giving them a chance to feel the joy of giving.

When companies enrich their local communities, they can overcome community resistance to change. When companies solve a big societal problem, they exercise a unique power to enhancing their global reputations.

The leaders value the highest standard of personal and professional ethics based upon honesty, integrity, and trust. Leader's skill in enforcement emphasizes well-functioning of the organization's values by:

a.   Communicate organization's values, i.e. rules, laws, etc

b.   Provide enforcement resources, i.e. assistance, enforcement staffs, finance, etc

c.   Set methods for producing compliance, i.e. set guidelines, make rulings - avoid the appearance of impropriety, show recognition – rewards system, etc

d.   Promote understanding and support for enforcement of organization values, i.e. campaign program, training and coaching, etc

e. Challenge violation against the enforcement: Set enforcement actions, i.e. investigation - investigate ethics queries and complaints, punishment - impose sanctions

Leaders provide an atmosphere where people see the value in positive manner. Followers are treated with dignity and respect and learn to be accountable for their actions. Leaders provide opportunities for growth and, on other hand, members live organization's values on their daily life. One of the best ways to understand leadership is to connect it to value-creation, which includes:

Leading

Who you are as a leader determines what you do in leading. Leadership means leading others, and involving them, not driving and coercing them, then how much more is it true in matters where self-sacrifice is not the issue.

The world today is running at such a fast-pace that those who cannot cope will surely be left behind. And the best way for people to cope is to strive to possess the most important ability that is to lead. Leadership means going ahead or showing the way. To lead is to help a group define and achieve a common purpose

Affirmation

Poor leadership habits spawn poor leaders; or they create enough discomfort that the leader figures out how to do it right. Affirmation means telling that something is true. This skill implies a conviction based on evidence, experience, or faith.

Leadership is the art of getting someone else to do something you want done because he wants to do it. An affirmation is used when a person cannot take an oath because of some convictions. Developing a positive mindset is one of the most powerful and positive attitude.

Affirmations are believed to be a very powerful means of reprogramming the mind. They appear to be most effective when repeated in a quiet and restful state of mind and body, and when the desired outcome is vividly experienced in one's mind and resulting emotions are felt.

The absence of affirmation leads to wrong ingredients, stimulating the people in an obsessive and shortsighted direction with disastrous results.

Encouragement

Leader encourages people to think, to innovate, and to be creative. A simple thing like an attentive nod can boost people's confidence. Encouragement implies to inspire with hope, courage, or confidence. It strives to give support and stimulation. As leader of an organization, you may need to encourage:

a. Values: Allow the group to establish values and thereby take ownership. The value will have to support the organization's objectives.

b. Creativity: Ask people to come up with new ideas and ways to do things. Give them credit and recognition for the idea. Encourage them to develop their plan of action and give you a detailed explanation.

c. Individuals to compete against themselves to achieve more. Let it be a personal challenge to become better as an individual-not competing with others but self.

The heart of leadership is the passion for the cause. It defines our purpose. To encourage members, you must get to know them, find out their strengths, help them overcome their fears and the obstacles that hold them back, praise their achievements and support them through bad times.

It's important to encourage the hearts of your followers as they carry out the vision; show appreciation for individual excellence - recognition of those who went above and beyond the call of duty; and set an example for others to follow.

When leaders and their organizations grow in influence, they face increasing opportunities, some of which tempt them to abandon their heart. Leaders are challenged to remain true to their guiding passion when surrounded by distractions. Encourage people, particularly the quiet ones.

Trust

The way trust is developed is a good indicator of a highly effective leader. Leader builds trust, both with others and among others.

A leader who can be counted on to fulfill commitments fosters strong trust. Trust, you will find among the most effective leaders Trust your people, you will earn trust also from them.

Transformation

Effective leadership is the most valuable commodity yet few really know how to attain it. People can come to expect transformational change stemming from the leader. Therefore, an effective leader should:

a. Create a shared vision - A vision is descriptive picture of a potential future of the organization. The vision is an articulation of a collection of ideas shared by the leader and followers.

By synthesizing the ideas and elevating them in a way that touches on the needs and dreams of followers, the leader begins to elevate the vision to a moral level (doing the right thing).

That vision may have originated with the person at the head of the organization, but often is an articulation of a collection of ideas shared by the leader and numerous other members.

b. Communicate the vision - The vision is first developed through dialogue. To keep the dream alive, it must be repeatedly articulated in many forms. Communicating the vision is a key to instilling shared meaning and purpose.

   Communication regarding the vision is used to excite, inspire, motivate and unify both followers and leaders. The communication is a two-way sharing that facilitates the process of elevating the moral purpose of the shared vision, building relationships, and shaping the culture of the organization.

c. Build relationships - Building relationships reflects the interactive, mutual and shared nature of transforming-leader behaviors. A web of high-quality relationships makes it possible to communicate, to affect the shared vision and to shape the culture that supports the vision.

   Shared values are important to the nature of the relationships and facilitate achievement of the vision.

d. Develop a supporting organizational culture - Organizational culture is the shared values and beliefs of the organization. Shaping culture contributes to building relationships and internalizing commitment to the shared vision. Leaders must be clear about their own values and ensure that their behavior consistently reflects those values.

e. Guide the implementation - Leaders conduct themselves and even communicate through their actions. These actions help build relationships and shape organizational culture. However, transforming leaders also guide implementation of the shared vision, rather than relying exclusively on the actions of empowered followers

f. Exhibit character - Leaders should be principle-centered, believing in and demonstrating honesty, integrity, trust and other qualities. They are particularly noted as being ethical, perhaps even noble. These leaders are guided by principles of justice, equity, dignity and respect for every individual.

An important role of the transforming leader is the ability to clearly articulate the shared vision, values, and beliefs of the college - repeatedly - in exciting and enthusiastic ways. The skilled leader inspires followers, provides encouragement and enhances motivation. Followers are mobilized to action.

Leadership for transformation means being willing to take risks by questioning existing ways of working, and considering how tasks might be done differently. To become a transformational leader requires a mind shift to a different way of being

Simplicity

There are two principal kinds of simplicity. One is easily produced: take a quick, superficial view, based on some scrappy sound-bite, and ignore anything that might add complexity. The other kind of simplicity is tough, demanding, and may take years to achieve. That comes from long and careful thought, thorough research, and a profound understanding of all the elements involved.

Most of the problems we have and talk about today sound very complicated, but they aren't. They're simple. And complications actually hide solutions. When you're trying to solve a problem, always bring it back to the simplest formulation.

Simplicity is the leader. Simple indicates a condition which is not complicated; ordinary or common; humble in condition; composed of only one thing; easy of use; not guileful or deceitful; sincere to the user; free from vanity; not sophisticated. It may also imply a degree of intelligence inadequate to cope with anything complex or involving mental effort. Taking the time to simplify anything that is overly complex is a very helpful skill in these rapidly accelerating times.

Simplifying a work not only streamline it, but make it more effective and productive, and leading to greater results when compared to its former complex arrangement.

Everything can be kept simple (not gradually and painstakingly made clearer and simpler to grasp) by ignoring the complex bits and skimming over anything challenging to the mind. It's about being able to boil things down to their essence and thereby bring complex issues down to a simple problem statement.

Imagination

The imaginative leader has a clear view of future needs and opportunities. He/she also understands the current problems and needs of the organization and finds ways to include people in the vision.

Leaders are ones who can navigate the future. Make timely and appropriate changes in your thinking, plans, and methods; show creativity by thinking of new and better goals, ideas, and solutions to problems. They are persons who can translate thought into action and execution

Leaders keep things light and have fun rather than being too serious; because it may block productivity. Imaginative leader is one who has the organizational and personal skills to carry out new ideas and to arouse the interest and enthusiasm of the people.

Focus

Leaders set goals and focus the energy of their subordinates. If there are no goals, the mental and physical energy of the followers will be unfocused, applied to the wrong things or, perhaps, not applied at all. If there are too many goals the focus will be diffused. A leader analyzes his/her operation and selects those few goals which are critical to the achievement of key objectives.

A leader promotes the important goals until they become a "way of life" in the organization. No one can give great emphasis to all things all of the time. Leaders concentrate on the most important.

Effective leaders stay focused on the outcomes they wish to create, and don't get too married to the methods used to achieve them. They provide this 'outcomes focus' for their organization by emphasizing the mission, vision, values and strategic goals of their organization and at the same time building the capacity of their organizations to achieve them.

The capacity building emphasizes the need to be flexible, creative and innovative and avoid becoming fossilized through the adoption of bureaucratic structures, policies and processes. Focus emphasizes:

a. Always accentuate the mission, vision, values and goals of the group. Focus on results, not on activities or personalities.

b. Evaluate time to time the results he wish to achieve

c. Build the group's capacity

Never ignore a concern of one of your people. While it may seem trivial to you, to the other person it is a problem that will continue to destroy their thought.

Leaders are focused on the bigger picture. But leadership is not only about the big picture. Unfortunately, too often, we focus only on the events and the behaviors and we fail to see the larger structures, so our efforts to develop more effective leadership often fail.

Inspiration

Leader inspires people to have the confidence to take risk, energizes people, and can help them develop their skills in creative technique. Inspirational leaders would more than likely be able to do just that inspire their subordinates and others around them. They also would be skilled at intellectually stimulating others regardless of the other people intellectual capabilities. They probably have a high degree of empathy for others and their belongings.

Effective leaders create an inspiring culture within their organization. They supply a shared vision and inspire people to achieve more than they may ever have dreamed possible. They are able to articulate a shared vision in a way that inspires others to act. The leaders are people-oriented leaders that bring this strength to ministries that need a more relational orientation.

Inspiring means display confidence in all that you do. By showing endurance in mental, physical, and spiritual stamina, you will inspire others to reach for new heights. The leader inspires in his/her followers, because he/she believes it also for him/herself. They inspire high levels of commitment, articulate a compelling vision of the future, motivate constituents to vigorously pursue common goals, and stimulate superior performance in others.

One of the differentiating factors between management and leadership is the ability or even necessity to inspire. A leader is one who can instill passion and direction to an individual or group of individuals. The inspirational leader, on the other hand, discusses change, holds meetings, and explains why change is needed. This creates a more open, trusting organizational culture.

People respond more willingly and positively, and give more of their true potential, when you give them a meaningful, inspiring future to move towards. Providing inspiration and leading the envisioning process are integral parts of leadership. Leadership also has elements of strategic thinking and planning for making the vision a reality, empowering others to contribute, orienting people to the task, evaluating progress, and supporting and monitoring accountability.

Leadership can and should be transformative - proposing and helping others develop new ways of doing and being - but it also must demonstrate a day-to-day commitment to the strategies and tasks necessary for change to happen.

Leaders keep their eyes on the mountain top, but they plan adequate provisions and carry their share. Leaders inspire their followers to go beyond whatever is minimally required to get a job done. That inspiration isn't based on coercion, but a dedication to the leader's goals and vision. Therefore, the followers are willing to make sacrifices for the organization's objectives.

To inspire, you must both create resonance and move people with a compelling vision. You must embody what you ask of others, and be able to articulate a shared vision in a way that inspires others to act. You must offer a sense of common purpose beyond the day-to-day tasks, and make work exciting. Inspiration evolves:

a. Enable: Leaders understand their roles are enabling members to discover, develop, and effectively use their capacities; i.e. encouraging personal growth; helping them gain knowledge; aiding in skill development; assisting them in working with others; and providing appropriate settings.

b. Empower: Effective empowerment provides the space to get the task completed, the space to innovate, and the feedback mechanism to both improve results and to motivate the organization. The empowerment must also bring rewards to all parties, and sanctions or challenges for improvement. To empower others, you have to trust and be willing to take a risk.

Leaders spend a considerable amount of time finding opportunities to help those around them succeed and to help the people catch a glimpse of their potential. Empowerment can be done through following actions:

i. Coach - Develop members through a focus on strengths and the future

ii. Provide measurement parameter that able to show progress against the goals, which also encourages dialog and continuous improvement.

   iii. Give feedback - Provide members with open, direct, and immediate feedback on their actual performance as compared to the expected performance and they tend to correct their own deficiencies. If you want to empower people, honor their ideas. Give them room to challenge the status quo. Give them room to move - and, by extension; move mountains.

   People feel good when they're encouraged to originate and develop ideas. It gives their work meaning, makes it their own, and intrinsically motivates.

  c. Energize: The leadership role demands the skills of energizing the organization to act. The more energy the team generates, the more energy the leader has.

A leader inspires others to follow by setting an example. He/she sets the direction and strives to influence people to follow that direction. He/she will demonstrates as a role model to whom adopts a persona that embodies his/her mission and vision, and is worthy of imitation. Getting people to accomplish something is much easier if they have the inspiration to do so.

Inspire means to breathe life into. And in order to perform that, we have to have some life ourselves. Three main actions will aid you in accomplishing this:

  a. Be passionate: In organizations where there is a leader with great enthusiasm about a task, a trickle-down effect will occur. As a leader, you must be committed to the work you are doing.

  b. Involve the members in the decision making process: People who are involved in the decision making process participate much more enthusiastically than those who just carry out their boss's order. Help them contribute and tell them you value their opinions. Listen to them and incorporate their ideas when it makes sense to so.

  c. Know what your organization is about. The fundamental truth is that organization is not made up of people. The organization itself is people. Every decision you make is a people issue. Your organization may make a product or sell a service, but it is still people.

A leader's primary responsibility is to develop people and enable them to reach their full potential. Your people may come from diverse backgrounds, but they all have goals they want to accomplish. Create a "people environment" where they truly can be all they can be.

An effective leader inspires others to have confidence in themselves. Leaders are positive and enthusiastic. They give hope and inspire others to make things happen. The inspirational leader, on the other hand, discusses change, holds meetings, and explains why change is needed. This creates a more open, trusting organizational culture.

Leadership implies using every opportunity in order to inspire and attain excellence. Leadership energizes people and inspires them to overcome obstacles to change.

Influence

Leadership is the process of influencing others to accomplish the mission by providing purpose, direction, and motivation. Leading means the manner and approach of providing direction, implementing plans, and motivating people; influencing people in reaching a goal. Influencing is usually seen as something you do to someone.

Leadership is influencing people to get things done to a standard and quality above their norm; and doing it willingly. Influence marks an individual or group to do what the leader wants done. Influencing emphasizes 2-way communication. Influencing strategies includes:

e. Show enthusiasm for an idea: Enthusiasm is a form of persuasiveness that causes others to become interest and willing to accept what the leader is attempting to accomplish. Enthusiasm shown by a leader generates enthusiasm in followers. Genuine enthusiasm is an important trait of a good leader.

f. Dialogue: Leader is to be committed to providing high quality development in dialogue facilitation; and believes that the key to personal and organizational vitality lies in hosting and convening conversations that matter. Dialogue form the foundation for shared mission, vision, values, and goals. It is the catalyst for meaningful and long-lasting change.

g. Build a coalition with key supporters: A coalition is an alliance of separate organizations formed to execute a particular purpose. Coalition brings together a wider range of skills, ideas, experiences and connections. The coalition may require that you compromise with other coalition members.

h. Foster peer pressure: Peer influence leads members participate in productive endeavors. Peer pressure motivates ones who strive for excellence as individuals and members of a group.

Motivation is encouraged through positive competition, recognition, loyalty, teamwork, organizational pride, and the setting of personal goals.

Leadership is an art. Bad leadership is usually due more to clumsiness than to ill will. People, who fail as leaders, are ill at ease in positions of leadership.

Motivation

You'll never know how good you are as a leader unless you are motivating others. Motivation comes from within each individual but you can become the source, and when you are able to affect their thinking, you can help them improve their lives.

A person's motivation is a combination of desire and energy directed at achieving a goal. Influencing someone's motivation means getting them to want to do what you know must be done.

A leader is a person who can effectively manage both the strategic and the human side of business, who inspire cooperation and creativity in reaching shared goals.

Motivation seem to be clear communication of vision and goals, ongoing support and coaching, appreciation, modeling effective behaviors, and reinforcement for positive action - all excellent skills most leaders aspire to have. You have to motivate the people in your organization to work toward the common goal. However, the only really effective way is to lead them.

Leadership is how you get your team fired up and willing to follow your plan. Leadership can be learned like any other skill. Leadership can be improved with practice. It needs self motivation. Motivation is a force or impulse that encourages and pushes you to take action. It can arise from external factors or internally driven.

We are inspired by possibility or necessity. We either do what we should do, must do or think we can do. External motivation can come from rewards, hearing a moving speech or encouragement from others.

Motivating begins with introspection, begins with self-examination, begin from the inside out. Internally driven motives are more effective to push you. They are the voices you hear or the images that pop up in your mind and from your gut feeling.

Your behavior and personality are shaped by your beliefs and they affect your motivation and performance. Motivation is often described as getting others to do something because they want to do it; people respond with increased effort and enthusiasm for the task at hand and intrinsically strive for success.

Motivation is a force to help people to achieve goals, desires, or ideas in life and work. It has a direct relation to the thought processes that are elicited under various internal and external conditions. In the work place, leaders have most effect in the shaping the motivation of people in the performance and improvement of products and services.

Humans are motivated by many different needs. You have to examine your needs to empower you to take actions to the realization of your goals. When you feel confident, in control and directed your energy increases and you are motivated to make plans and take actions.

The best motivation is self-motivation. Self-motivation is a driving force within you that activates your actions without being directed by others. It is a fire from within. Becoming self-motivated gives you the power to decide. You make your own choices and hold yourself responsible to the results from your activities or inactivity.

Your motivation starts to sprout from your internal desires for gains and to avoid loss. When you become aware that you have unmet needs in any area of your organizations, you look for the solutions. Other people cannot motivate you. You can use external triggers to aid in your motivation. Things outside you may be a stimulus.

Motivation is the force that pushes you along the path. Goals give you the passion and the energy to intensify your actions. Accomplishing your goals gives you the feeling of self-fulfillment and personal satisfaction. Your emotions affect your motivation. They stir you to take actions.

Motivation is a force or impulse that encourages and pushes you to take action. It can arise from external factors or internally driven. We are inspired by possibility or necessity. External motivation can come from a rewards hearing a moving speech or encouragement from others. Motivating begins with introspection, begins with self-examination, begin from the inside out. Internally driven motives are more effective to push you.

Leaders carefully select the best methods that stimulate and nurture the motivation levels of their teams and individual team members.

Thoughtfulness

A leader is a kind of person who mastered lateral thinking skills and can create a climate for creativity and to transform your organization into innovation. Thinking is about

a. Passionately care about and being involved with a cause

b. See the problem in order to explore it.

The essence of leadership is clarity of thought leads to simplicity, which leads to focus and powerful communication. As leader, you need to share experiences and foster the learning and development of others.

Thought leader is person who is recognized among their peers and mentors for innovate ideas and demonstrates the confidence to promote or share those ideas as actionable distilled insights. He/she actively promotes and discussed ideas that are relevant to their peer-base. His/her statements are often assumed to have the experience and knowledge behind them to support what they are saying. Becoming a thought leader by embracing the exchange of information can help to propel your organization.

Thought leaders are being recruited to work within huge organizations. Thought Leaders have a lot in common, having a public outlet for their thoughts, having something valuable to say.

Sense of Exemplar

Leaders, as exemplars, invest more meaning in things they do than when others do the same things. So, effective leaders need to act in ways they want their followers to emulate.

To lead is to be in the front of your followers leading the way. A leader leads by example Leadership is not magic. It is not a gift that some people have and others don't. It is not standing back and telling others what to do. It is not belittling or demeaning others who don't do what you tell them to do. You will lose valuable influence if you do not give example to the standards that you recommend, like wearing a complete uniform, etc. Members need a model to follow, their leaders may be the only good example they know.

Leading by example means set the example you want others to follow, including continuous learning.

A leader should be a good role model for his/her members. They must not only hear what they are expected to do, but also see. Leadership will be easily getting acceptance by example rather than by any other means. True actions speak louder than words. Your team members imitate what you do and say. You are the role model for them. Therefore, you must be clear about how you want your team to perform, in which consistently you perform in the same manner by yourself.

Leader is a role model that others imitate; exemplifies the assessment criteria and sets the standards for becoming a member of an organization. Leader-image-building sets the stage for effective role-modeling because followers identify with the values of role models whom they perceived in positive terms.

When you develop your character by setting high standards and then disciplining yourself to live consistent with the highest principles you know, you become the kind of person who is admired and respected everywhere. You become the kind of leader who radiates charisma to others.

Leaders know what they value. The leadership values are, but not limited to:

- Ability
- Acceptance
- Acknowledgement
- Activity
- Achievement
- Accomplishment
- Accountability
- Action
- Accuracy
- Advance
- Adventure
- Advantage
- Agreement
- All for One & One for All
- Alertness
- Ambition
- Appearance
- Appreciation
- Appropriation
- Approach
- Approval
- Art
- Attentiveness
- Attractiveness
- Audit
- Aura
- Authority
- Autonomy
- Availability
- Award
- Awareness
- Balance
- Beauty
- Belonging

- Benefit
- Boldness
- Bottom
- Boundary
- Brand
- Braveness
- Brotherhood
- Calmness
- Capability
- Capacity
- Career
- Caring
- Cautiousness
- Celebration
- Certificate
- Certification
- Challenge
- Championship
- Character
- Cheerfulness
- Cleanliness
- Competitiveness
- Creation
- Credibility
- Championship
- Chance
- Change
- Charisma
- Charity
- Chastity
- Children
- Choice
- Citizenship
- Clarity
- Collaboration
- Colorfulness
- Commitment

- Communication
- Community
- Compassion
- Competence
- Competency
- Competition
- Completeness
- Compliance
- Concern for Others
- Confidentiality
- Conscientious
- Consistency
- Consistence
- Contentment
- Content Over Form
- Contribution
- Concept
- Conclusion
- Conformity
- Content
- Continuity
- Control
- Cooperation
- Cooperativeness
- Coordination
- Courage
- Culture
- Customs
- Creativity
- Criteria
- Crystallization
- Decision
- Decisiveness
- Dedication
- Definition
- Degree
- Democracy

- Desire
- Detail
- Determination
- Development
- Difference
- Dignity
- Diversity
- Dignity
- Diligence
- Discernment
- Discipline
- Discovery
- Discretion
- Distance
- Donation
- Dream
- Dynamic
- Economical
- Efficiency
- Effectiveness
- Eligibility
- Empathy
- Empowerment
- Encouragement
- Endurance
- Enlighten
- Enthusiasm
- Enjoyment
- Evolution
- Environment
- Equality
- Excellence
- Excitement
- Existence
- Expectation
- Experience
- Expertise
- Fairness
- Faith
- Fame
- Family
- Family Feeling
- Famousness
- Fearlessness
- Fertility
- Figure
- Flair
- Flexibility
- Forecast
- Forgiveness
- Form
- Foundation
- Frank
- Freedom
- Friends
- Friendliness
- Friendship
- Fruitfulness
- Fulfillment
- Fun
- Function
- Fundamental
- Future
- Generosity
- Gentleness
- Global
- Globalization
- Glory
- Goal
- Good will
- Goodness
- Governance
- Gracefulness
- Gratification

- Gratis
- Gratitude
- Gratefulness
- Greatness
- Growth
- Guaranty
- Happiness
- Hard work
- Harmony
- Health
- Heart
- Help
- Heritage
- Hero
- History
- Holiness
- Holistic
- Home
- Honesty
- Honor
- Hope
- Hospitality
- Humanity
- Humility
- Idealism
- Idol
- Image
- Impartiality
- Impression
- Improvement
- Inclusiveness
- Income
- In-covenant
- Independence
- Individuality
- Influence
- Information
- Initiative
- Inner peace
- Innovation
- Innovativeness
- Input
- Inspection
- Inspiration
- Integrity
- Intellectuality
- Intelligence
- Intention
- In the moment
- Involvement
- Job
- Joy
- Justice
- Justification
- Kindness
- Knowledge
- Label
- Laughter
- Law
- Leadership
- Learning
- Legality
- Lesson
- Level
- Life
- Listening
- Literacy
- Luck
- Love
- Loyalty
- Luxury
- Magic
- Management
- Marriage

- Market
- Maturity
- Meaning
- Media
- Mediation
- Meekness
- Meeting
- Memory
- Merit
- Mindfulness
- Mission
- Moderation
- Modern
- Money
- Morality
- Motivation
- Mystic
- Myth
- Name
- Neatness
- News
- Negotiation
- Neighborhood
- Network
- Nature
- Neutrality
- Nobleness
- Nurture
- Obedience
- Objectives
- Objectiveness
- Objectivity
- Openness
- Opportunity
- Orderliness
- Organization
- Originality
- Other
- Outcome
- Ownership
- Paradigm
- Partnership
- Passion
- Patience
- Patriotism
- Peace
- People
- Perception
- Perfection
- Performance
- Perseverance
- Persistency
- Personality
- Persuasiveness
- Philosophy
- Picture
- Planning
- Pleasure
- Popularity
- Population
- Position
- Power
- Profit
- Practicality
- Practice
- Prediction
- Predictability
- Preference
- Preservation
- Principle
- Priority
- Privacy
- Privilege
- Prize

- Productivity
- Professional
- Progress
- Progressiveness
- Promotion
- Properness
- Prospect
- Prosperity
- Protection
- Punctuality
- Purpose
- Qualification
- Quality
- Quantity
- Question
- Quietude
- Record
- Recognition
- Reconciliation
- Relationship
- Registration
- Regularity
- Relaxation
- Relevance
- Reliability
- Reliance
- Religiosity
- Report
- Representative
- Reputation
- Resourcefulness
- Respectfulness
- Responsibility
- Responsiveness
- Result
- Reverence
- Reverential

- Reward
- Rights
- Role
- Romance
- Rule
- Sacrifice
- Safety
- Satisfaction
- Save
- Secularism
- Security
- Selection
- Self-esteem
- Sensitiveness
- Sense
- Serenity
- Sensuality
- Seriousness
- Service
- Sexuality
- Share
- Signature
- Simplicity
- Sincerity
- Situation
- Size
- Skill
- Society
- Solution
- Soul
- Soundness
- Space
- Specialization
- Speed
- Spirit
- Spirituality
- Sportiveness

- Stability
- Standard
- Star
- Statement
- Statistic
- Status
- Stewardship
- Strength
- Structure
- Success
- Suggestion
- Supervision
- Support
- Survey
- Survival
- Sympathy
- System
- Systemization
- Target
- Teamwork
- Technology
- Thoroughness
- Thriftiness
- Thought
- Tidiness
- Time
- Timeliness
- Togetherness
- Tolerance
- Top
- Toughness
- Tradition
- Tranquility
- Trust
- Trustworthiness
- Truth
- Truthfulness
- Universe
- Union
- Unity
- Understanding
- Uniformity
- Up to date
- Utilization
- Validity
- Value
- Variety
- Verification
- Victory
- View
- Virginity
- Virtue
- Vision
- Vocation
- Vote
- Warranty
- Wealth
- Welfare
- Willingness
- Wisdom
- Witness
- Work

Effective leadership is the foundation for creating value within an organization. The leader must first recognize people's value. Leaders and followers have congruent value systems. Leader values are the guiding principles that determine leader behavior, which, in turn, motivates and inspires follower behavior.

REFERENCE

1. Clark, D. R., Art Of Leadership, Big Dog And Little Dog's Bowl Of Biscuits, USA, 2004

2. Trevor Gay, Leadership And Management – Chalk And Cheese, Rattle-The-Cage.Com, USA, 2004

3. Major Jeffrey C. Benton, Promoting Leadership In The Air Force's Management Environment, Air University Review, USA, 1982

4. Kevin Grauman, Leadership - Top 10 Attributes For Greatness, American City Business Journals Inc., USA, May 6, 2005

5. David Straker, Leadership Vs. Management, Changingminds. Org, Syque, UK, 2002 – 2008

6. Mitchell Alegre, What Leaders Do, Transforming Leadership , USA, April 25, 2008

7. Gemmy Allen, Leading, Supervision, Mountain View College, Dallas – USA, 1998

8. Vadim Kotelnikov, Leadership Versus Management, 1000ventures.Com, USA, 2008

9. Bill Gaw, Traits Of Strong Leadership, Milo Media, WI – USA, 2008

10.John Maeda, Leader Vs Manager, Toughts On Simplicity, Cambridge, Massachusetts USA, 2008

11. Murray Johannsen, Leadership And Motivation: Three Cognitive Theories Leaders Must Know, Legacee Management Systems Inc., USA, 1996-2008

12. Stephen Moulton, Leadership By Expectations (LBE), Action Insight, Inc., Colorado - USA, 2008

13. Leslie L. Kossoff, From Manager To Leader, About.Com, A Part Of The New York Times Company, USA, 2008

14. Jef Allbright, Leadership, Jef Allbright's Blog, USA, 2003

15. Mlcooper, How To Be A Leader, Not A Boss, Ehow, Inc., WA - USA1999-2008

16. A. J. Schuler, Psy. D., How To Be A Better Boss: Business Leadership Tips, Schuler Solutions, Inc., Virginia – USA, 2003

17. Lewis P. Orans, Learning About Leadership, Pine Tree Camp, USA, 2008

18. F. John Reh, The Toxic Boss Syndrome, About.Com, A Part Of The New York Times Company, USA, 2008

19. Dr. Larry Richard And Susan Raridon Lambreth, What Does It Take To Develop Effective Law Firm Leaders?, American Bar Association, USA, 2003 - 2008

20. Manfred Davidmann, Style Of Management And Leadership, Solhaam.Org, USA, 2008

21. Mitch Mccrimmon, Ph.D, Leaders Or Managers? How Do Leaders Differ From Managers?, Self Renewal Group, UK, 1996-2008

22. Haygroup, What Makes Great Leaders: Rethinking The Route To Effective Leadership, Hay Acquisition Company I, Inc., PA – USA, 2008

23. Answers.Com, Effectiveness, Answers Corporation, Israel, 2008

24. Wikimedia, Management Effectiveness, The Wikimedia Foundation Inc., USA, 2008

25. Holly Culhane, SPHR & Associates, No One "Best" Leadership Style, The Ken Blanchard Companies, USA, 2005

26. Sandra Larson, What Makes For An Effective Leader?, Authenticity Consulting, LLC. MN – USA, 1997-2008

27. A. J. Schuler, Psy. D, How To Be A Better Boss: Business Leadership Tips, Schuler Solutions, Inc., USA, 2003

28. Jack Stevenson, Leadership, Iscribe.Org, USA, 2002

29. Wally Bock, Leadership: Can Anyone Learn To Be A Great Leader?, Three Star Leadership Enterprises, NC – USA, 2008

30. Bill Gaw, Traits Of Strong Leadership, Milo Media, WI – USA, 2008

31. Bizhan Nasseh, Leadership And Motivation, Bizhan Nasseh, IN – USA, 1996

32. Ken Keis, Are You A Transforming Leader?, Workplace Performance Technologies (Pty) Ltd, South Africa, 2008

33. D. Kevin Berchelmann, 5 Irrefutable, Non-Negotiable Laws Of Leadership You Must Know Now, Nielsen Business Media, Inc., USA, August 27, 2007

34. Jim Martin, Surviving At The Top Of The Heap, Unisys, USA, 2008

35. Gwyn Myers, Ph. D & Associates, Types Of Communication, My Own Business, Inc, CA – USA, 2003-2007

36. Matthew Peschong, Four Types Of Business Communication , Smartads , Canada, 2002-2008

37. Barbara Taylor , Improving Verbal Skills, The Institute For Management Excellence, USA, August, 1997

38. Falikowski, INTERPERSONAL COMMUNICATION AND PERSONALITY TYPE, Mastering Human Relations 3rd Edition, Pearson Education Canada, Ontario - Canada, 2008

39. Jamie Walters, Organizational Communication, Ivy Sea, CA – USA, 2008

40. Kendra Van Wagner, Types Of Nonverbal Communication, About.Com, A Part Of The New York Times Company, USA, 2008

41. Fatimah Musa, How To Improve Verbal Communication, About-Personal-Growth.Com, Malaysia, 2005 – 2008

42. The American Heritage® Dictionary Of The English Language, Fourth Edition., Definition Of Expression, Houghton Mifflin Company, USA, 2000

43. Ryan P. Allis, Non-Verbal Communication, Zeromillion.Com, USA, 2002-2008

44. Jim Clemmer, Inspiring And Energizing With Strong Verbal Communications, The Clemmer Group, NO – USA, 1996-2006

45. Rose B. Coggins, Developing Good Written Communication Skills And The Word Processing Student, Yale-New Haven Teachers Institute, 2008

46. Chaplain (LTC) James W. Daniels, Jr., The Art And Craft Of Supervision: A Facet Of Leadership, The Army Chaplaincy, USA, Winter 1998

47. John F. Morrow And Joan Pastor, Eight Habits Of Highly Effective Audit Committees, American Institute Of Certified Public Accountants, Inc., New York – USA, 2004

48. Lt Col Sharon M. Latour, USAF And Lt Col Vicki J. Rastdynamic Followership: The Prerequisite For Effective Leadership, Air & Space Power Journal, USA, 2003

49. Steve L. Wintner, The Art Of Effective Delegation, The American Institute of Architects,, 2007

50. Charles Orlando, Leadership Development Practices Of Top-Performing Organizations, Ninth House, Inc., USA, 2008

51. Sam Phillips, Fostering Excellence: Behind Every Great Employee Is A Great Coach, Society Of Actuaries, USA, 2008

52. Joni Daniels, CEO Skills, Www.SQ.4mg.Com, USA, 2002

53. Alan Chapman, Leadership Development Tips, www.businessballs.com, England, 2008

54. C. Dean Pielstick, The Transforming Leader - Why Leaders Can Lead, Northern Arizona University, 2007

55. Nan Henderson, M.S.W., The Resiliency Route To Authentic Self-Esteem And Life Success, Resiliency In Action Inc., CA – USA, 2008

56. Daniel Goleman, Working With Emotional Intelligence, University of Hawaii, USA, 2002

57. Shannon T Kalvar, 10 Things You Can Do To Organize And Lead Effective Meetings, CNET Networks, Inc., A CBS Company., CA – USA, May 17, 2006

58. Professor S.P. Kothari & Associates, Forecasting with confidence, KPMG International, USA, 2007

59. Jane Doeleadership Forecast™ Coaching Report, Hogan Assessment Systems, Inc., USA, 2005

60. Peter Horn, Leadership: Six Rules For Effective Forecasting, Peter Horn & Co, Switzerland, 2007

61. Paul R. Bernthal & Associates, Leadership Forecast 2005–2006: Best Practices For Tomorrow's Global Leaders, Development Dimensions International, Inc., USA, 2008

62. Robert Bacal, Leadership - How Planning Transforms Into Doing, Bacal & Associates, USA, 2007 – 2008

63. Cary W. Adams, Leadership Qualities And Leadership Skills Can Be Developed With Leadership Training, Adams Six Sigma, USA, 1999

64. Michael Mckinney, The Courage To Initiate, Leadershipnow, USA, 1998-2007

65. Susan M. Heathfield, Meeting Management Success Tips, About.Com, A Part Of The New York Times Company, USA, 2008

66. Jeff Wuorio, 8 Tips For Becoming A True Leader, Microsoft Corporation, USA, 2008

67. Moc Klinkam, The Leadership Practice, Northwest K9, USA, 2004

68. Luther Waters, Jr., Control - The Leadership Oxymoron, Ohio State University Extension - Leadership Center, USA, 2008

69. Wally Bock, How To Give Better Instructions, Wally Bock, NC –USA, 2006

70. Bruna Martinuzzi, Leadership Skills: Become An Exceptional Leader, Mind Tools Ltd, USA, 1995-2008

71. Jeffrey Pfeffer And Robert I. Sutton, The Half-Truths Of Leadership, Harvard Business School Press, USA, 2008

72. TheFreeDictionary, Survival, Farlex, Inc., Pennsylvania - USA, 2008

73. Terry Mangan, Executive Survival Skills, The National Executive Institute Associates Leadership Bulletin , USA, February 1995

74. Stephen, Collaborative Intelligence Speaking Topics, Zenergypd Inc., Canada, 2007

75. Herrera, Acquiring The Habits Of Highly Successful Students, Life, Money & Development, Venezuela, 2008

76. John R. Vaughn & Associates, Applied Leadership For Effective Coalitions, National Council On Disability, USA, February 14, 2001

77. Tom Ticknor & Associates, Process for Becoming an Effective Communicator, Quality Assurance Institute, USA, 2007

78. Leadership Development Team of the CRCNA, Leadership: A Working Definition, Christian Reformed Church, USA, May 2004

79. Team Coordination Training Student Guide, EFFECTIVE LEADERSHIP, Coast Guard Headquarters, USA, August 1998

80. DICTIONARY.COM™, Defensive, Dictionary.com, LLC,USA, 2008

81. Laura R. Thatcher, Derivation of Offensive Selection From Natural Selection as It Relates to Sexual Strategies, Rochester Institute of Technology, USA, June 2004

82. D. Caroline Blanchard, Mark Hebert, and Robert J. Blanchard, Continuity vs. Political Correctness: Animal Models and Human

Aggression, The Harry Frank Guggenheim Foundation, USA, 2007-2008

83. Green, Brian; Foelber, Robert, Space Weapons, The Key to Assured Survival, The Heritage Foundation, USA, February 2, 1984

84. Hye Yeong Kwon, Rebecca Winer and Tom Schueler, 8 Tools of Watershed Protection, Environmental Protection Agency, USA, September 12th, 2008

85. Ronald A. Heifetz and Marty Linsky, A Survival Guide for Leaders, The McGraw-Hill Companies Inc., USA, 2000-2008

86. Dennis McCallum, Areas of Leadership Responsibility, Xenos Christian Fellowship, USA, 2008

87. Dr. David Chappell & Amy Burya, The Assessment Project, Ohio University, USA, 1997

88. John Smith, Four Levels of Communication Disruption: Alternative Communication Routes in the Case of an Emergency, Remnant Saints, MT – USA, 2001

89. R.J. Rummel, Understanding Conflict And War, University of Hawai'I, USA, 2008

90. Kristen Allodi, Jerry Greene, Ed Gries, & Mick Rakauskas, Norms in Conflict - Crackdown on Prom Wear, Social Psychology/Miami University, Ohio, USA,. March, 1999

91. Guy Burgess and Heidi Burgess, Domination Conflicts, Conflict Research Consortium, University of Colorado, USA, 1998

92. Udogu, E Ike, Perspectives on Contemporary Ethnic Conflict, Journal of Third World Studies, CNET Networks, Inc., a CBS Company, USA, Spring 2007

93. Louis Kriesberg, "Us" versus "Them", The Beyond Intractability Project, CO – USA, July 2003

94. Anne Myer Byler, Styles of Conflict Management, Mennonite Conciliation Service, 2000

95. Joan Esteban & Debraj Ray, Conflict and Distribution, Department of Economics, Boston Universit, USA, April 27, 1999

96. Leland R. Beaumont, Dialogue: Thinking Together, EmotionalCompetency.com, USA, 2005-2008

97. Development Assistance Committee, Dialogue, OECD, USA, 2005

98. Tri Junarso, Comprehensive Approach To Corporate Governance, iUniverse Inc., USA, 2006

99. Tri Junarso, 7th Principle of Success, Trafford Publishing, Canada, 2007

100. Nicole Dean, "7 Habits" Outlined, Showmomthemoney™, USA, 2004-2007

101. Lothar Katz, Effective International Project Leadership, Leadership Cro ssroads, Dallas – USA, 2004

102. Dr. Paul E Adams, Common Sense Leadership, Adams-Hall Publishing, USA, 2004

103. Marshall, Why We Don't Do What We Say, Marshall Goldsmith Blog, CA – USA, May 20th, 2008

104. Trent Hamm, Review: The 7 Habits Of Highly Effective People, The Simple Dollar, USA, May 27, 2007

105. Jeffrey L. Sedqwick & Associates, Essential Skills For Leaders: Creative Problem Solving, Office Of Justice Programs, USA, 2008

106. Linda Silverman, Ph.D., Effective Techniques for Teaching Highly Gifted Visual-Spatial Learners, Gifted Development Center: a service of The Institute for the Study of Advanced Development, USA, 1997 – 2008

107. Richard W. Riley & Associates, What is Effective Leadership for Today's Schools?, Perspectives On Education Policy Research of U.S. Department of Education, June 1999

108. Dr. Rick Johnson, Effective Leaders Are Driven by a Model, Leadership Gurus International, UK, 2007

109. Michael K. Magill, MD, Becoming an Effective Physician Leader, the American Academy of Family Physicians, USA, 1999

110. Bill Thomas, 5 Awesome Actions of Highly Creative Leaders!, Quick Solutions, Australia, 2002

111. Franklin Covey, How Highly Effective Leaders Navigate Change, Deliver Results, and Create the Future, Franklin Covey Co., USA, 1998

112. J.T. Taylor, M.A., Five Levels of Decision Making, Team Building, USA, 1993 – 2007

113. John S. Cowings, Strategic Leadership and Decision Making, Maxwell-Gunter AFB, USA, 2008

114. Lynley Sides, Management Decision Making in Early Stage Companies, the Sides & Associates, USA, 2003

115. Travis Wright Develop A Sense of Urgency, Cultivate Greatness - Leadership Training, Personal Development, & Life Hacks, October 1, 2007

116. Dr. John C. Maxwell, Leaving a Legitimate Leadership Legacy, INJOY, Inc., USA, 2006

117. Robert L. Webb, Elements of Visionary Leadership, Motivation Tool Chest, USA, 2003

118. Rosemary Rein, How Do Successful Leaders Spell Survival, EzineArticles.com, USA, 2008

119. Wally Bock, The Five Ps of Leadership, Digital Age International, Inc., USA, 2003

120. Harry Paul and Ross Reck, Put Yourself and Your Team On the Road to Real Results, Self Improvement Inc., USA, 2006

121. Tejvan Pettinger, Do You Have the Characteristics of an Effective Leader?, PickTheBrain, USA, September 19th, 2007

122. Stephen L. Spanoudis, Great Leaders, Stephen L. Spanoudis, Usa, 1994 – 2007

123. Barbara Kellerman, "Attention Must Be Paid", The President And Fellows Of Harvard College, USA, 2007

124. Richard M. Ayres, So You Want To Be A Leader?, The National Executive Institute Associates Leadership Bulletin, USA, April 1994

125. Michele Erina Doyle And Mark K. Smith, Shared Leadership, Infed.Org, Uk, July 02, 2008

126. John D. Wessels, Ph.D., Enforcing Positive And Productive Behavior, Ten Sigma, USA, 2003

127. Howard Young, Rediscovering Servant Leadership, Enrichment Journal, USA, 2008

128. F. Hawkins, Toward A Theory Of Military Leadership, The Military Conflict Institute, USA, 2008

129. J. Donald Walters, The Art Of Supportive Leadership, Ananda Yoga Portland, USA, 2008

130. Daegan Smith, How To Lead People, The Good Manager, USA, 2005

131. Joseph S. Nye Jr., Soft Power & Leadership, Center For Public Leadership - The President and Fellows of Harvard College, USA, 2008

132. F. John Reh, The Best Leader I Ever Knew: Leadership Lessons, About.com, a part of The New York Times Company, USA, 2008

133. Meir Liraz, How to Lead Your Employees to Top Performance (Tips), BizMove.com., USA, 1998-1999

134. Jonas Clark, Encouragement: The Christian Leadership Connection, Jonas Clark Ministries, USA, 2004-2008

135. Rodger Constandse, 10 Qualities of Highly Effective Leaders, Effexis Software, LLC, USA, 2007

136. C. Dean Pielstick, The Transforming Leader - Why Leaders Can Lead, Nothern Arizona University, USA, 2007

137. Michael McKinney, Simplicity: Focused and On Track, LeadershipNow, USA, 2007

138. Hal Halladay, Leaders Empower, LeaderNotes – Know More Media, USA, 2006

139. Ben White and Sharon Otterman, House panel faults Lehman's leadership, the International Herald Tribune, USA, October 6, 2008

140. Richard Stengel, Mandela: His 8 lesons of Leadership, The Practice of Leadership, South Africa, 2008

141. Hans Bool, Lesson From the Nobel Peace Laureate, EzineArticles.com, WI – USA, 2008,

142. Aditya Vikram Birla, Transformational Leadership, Aditya Birla Management Corporation Pvt. Ltd, India, 2008

143. Shane Schick , Bill Gates Needs To Brush Up On His People Skills, ITWorld Canada, Canada, December 14th, 2007